Every blessing
(Timothy Horner O.S.B.

Timothy Horner OSB

. . .

LEARNING ALL THE TIME

A MEMOIR

1920 - 2010

SAINT LOUIS

ABBEY PRESS

2012

LEARNING ALL THE TIME

A Memoir

1920 - 2010

Learning All The Time, A Memoir 1920-2010
Copyright ©2012 Saint Louis Abbey Press, All Rights Reserved

Published by:
Monograph Publishing, LLC
1 Putt Lane
Eureka, Missouri 63025
info@mathisjones.com

Library of Congress Number:
Cataloging in publication date: On file

ISBN # 978-0-9853093-2-9:

Printed in the United States of America by Signature Printing, www.sbpbooks.com

Cover Design by: William E. Mathis
Book Design by Ellie Jones and William E. Mathis
Monograph, LLC
Copyright ©2012 Monograph Publishing, LLC, All Rights Reserved

CONTENTS

	Foreword	6
1	Birth	8
2	Early Childhood	10
3	We Move to the Country	13
4	Boarding School	26
5	Ampleforth	30
6	Christ Church	50
7	Cry 'Havoc'	56
8	Phoney War	59
9	Service in England	65
10	Bound for the East	74
11	We Train for the Jungle	77
12	Action in the Jungle and Beyond	84
13	We Occupy Thailand	100
14	The End of my Service in the Army	105
15	Becoming a Monk	112
16	Back to Ampleforth	116
17	A Change of Continent	133
18	We Cross the Atlantic	138
19	Arrival in Saint Louis	142
20	Our Preparations	145
21	Monastic Life, USA	161
22	The Drive to the West Coast	167
23	School Opens	170
24	Thoughts on Education	176
25	Non-Scholastic Activities	182
26	The School Develops	190
27	Acclimation (Acclimatization)	197
28	The Rough and the Smooth	200
29	We Start to Make Ourselves Known	206
30	Expansion	215
31	Sabbatical	221
32	I Retire from Headmaster	238
33	Monastic Adjustments	248
34	Outside Activities	251
35	A Workshop in Japan	262
36	Pastor of Saint Anselm Parish	267
37	Back to the Monastery	282
38	The Old Silk Road	287
39	Quietly Active	291
40	Epilogue	298

Glad to be in England, I start learning.

FOREWORD

This is a memoir, not an autobiography, remembering how I acted, and how I reacted to what happened to me, more than describing my feelings and character, though no doubt I shall, like the characters in Shakespeare's plays, by my actions and reactions unwittingly reveal much about my feelings and character.

When I was in high school in England, the school library had a section devoted to biography. Some of the books were about people who stood out from the crowd, whose lives I wanted to read simply for that reason. These had titles such as *The Life of the Duke of Wellington*. Others had titles such as *The Life and Times of Eugene Field*, whose life would be of interest to a limited readership, but whose times might have a far wider appeal. This memoir is of the second kind.

When I was born in 1920, the British Broadcasting Company (now Corporation) did not exist, London still had many horse-drawn vehicles, only main roads were of tarmac, telephones were primitive, seldom used, and had no trans-Atlantic capability, cars were unusual, and aeroplanes, as they were called, were rare enough to cause excitement. Cameras were large and very unwieldy; 18-wheelers, bulldozers, jets, televisions, space travel, computers, wikipedia, cell-phones, facebook, texting, blogging, twitter, GPS, etc. were far in the future. Younger people today are sometimes surprised that there was life before those conveniences, and are often interested in what it was like.

Electricity was replacing candles, oil lamps, and natural gas as a source of light, and to some extent of heat, but wood- and natural gas-fires and coal furnaces were still very common, and most cooking was done over coal. Central heating, hoovers (vacuum cleaners), labor-saving devices for the kitchen and elsewhere, were coming in. Outdoors, grass was still cut by scythes or by hand-propelled lawnmowers; earth was moved, and trenches dug, by hand. So, in my lifetime, much has changed, and much of what I grew up with has been superseded and now is news again.

In the same period, there have been over two hundred wars, but counts vary, and only one, World War II, directly affected me. The cliché about long periods of boredom punctuated by moments of sheer terror applies not only to war but, analogously, to everyday life, and especially to religious life, both of which tend to have long periods of routine activities punctuated by events of greater news-value, even if not of greater importance.

There is a problem here for the writer: one cannot, without boring the reader, go on and on about the routine, even though the routine does go on and on, so one turns to the events. But that makes it look as if one's life were a continuous series of events, which it is not. I hope the reader who wishes to get a valid impression of the life described here will make the necessary adjustments.

I learnt to spell in England, but have spelt many more words in USA, where I have spent nearly two-thirds of my life. I have tried to use US spelling, but sometimes for events in UK I have used UK spelling. When different words are used for the same thing, I have mostly used both words. If the action is in UK I have put the UK word first: boot (trunk); if in US, the US word: trunk (boot). When I came from India to England, I had to become *acclimatized* to English ways and weather; when I came to the United States, I had to become *acclimated* to American language, ways, and weather.

I have taken the title from a fragment of Solon who, in the early sixth century BC, led the Athenians towards democracy. It is a pentameter, and part of a fragmentary poem, in which he seems to be seeking a happy death at the age of 80:

γηράσκω δ' αἰεὶ πολλὰ διδασκόμενος
(I grow old, learning much all the time).

In the nursery, in school, in college I was learning directly; but I went on learning in the army, in the monastery, and in the parish, though much of that was both learning the job and doing it at the same time. Even in retirement I learnt about writing a book, besides much else. Learning has always been, and still is, a large part of my life.

Finally I thank my friend of long standing, the late Barbara Nauer, for applying to my text the wealth of her experience of teaching English and writing books. She has read the whole memoir and reduced the faults; all remaining inaccuracies or inelegances are my own.

One

BIRTH

I was born on 24 August, 1920 at Quetta in Baluchistan, just in time for tea. This was long before the partition of India, so Baluchistan, or 'place of the Baluchi people', was in the North-West Frontier Provinces of India. It is now part of Pakistan. Quetta, being a hill-station, is cooler than the plains, and during the summer anyone who could do so moved there, or to some similar hill-station. The Indian Army's Staff College was also there. More recently it has been in the news because of the war in Afghanistan. I was christened John Michael Stuart Horner soon after my birth. When I later asked where the 'Stuart' came from, I was told that King Charles I had once held court at the family home at Mells in Somerset, and, in return for all the expense entailed, we had been permitted to add Stuart to our forenames.

I have been asked with surprising frequency why I was born in Quetta. The pert answer is 'because my parents were there'. Why they were there is a question that does deserve a serious answer. In 1920, the British Empire was still a force in the world, and the British Raj was similarly a force in India. This meant that young Britons were needed for a variety of administrative and other posts in India and around the world. My father was born in 1889. He served in World War I, was in the Persian Gulf when it ended, and decided to join the Indian Political Service. At least, I think that was the service he joined. He used to tell me that the Political Service was greatly superior to the Indian Civil Service (or was it the other way round?) and I used to get into trouble for not remembering which.

My mother's father was in the Indian Civil Service. She, a beautiful young red-head, came out from England to join her parents, and since beautiful young women of any color hair were rare, it was not too long before she and my father were married. He was twenty-nine and she eighteen; he was a member of the Church of England and she a Roman Catholic. He was educated at Westminster and Christ Church, Oxford, where he first read Mathematics and then switched to Law; she received a very good education from Belgian nuns, who moved to

Essex at the outbreak of World War I. A year after their marriage, I was born. About 1929, my father returned to England and was, after the necessary studies and eating of dinners, called to the Bar. He retired from being a successful barrister (trial lawyer) in 1977 at the age of 87. In World War II, he joined the Home Guard (National Guard), was in command of the company protecting the House of Commons, and ended as a full colonel.

When my parents were in India, the English there lived in some style: servants, ayahs (nannies), the Club, horses, polo and tent-pegging, tennis and swimming. I remember Mother, on her return to England, going to play tennis. Having served, which she did with a dashing underhand service, and having completed the rally, she turned and waited for the ball-boy to supply her with another ball; but in England there were ball-boys only at Wimbledon. But life in India was also adventurous. Mother once went for her bath only to find a cobra coming up the drainpipe. Daddy shot it with his shotgun. She always liked Kipling's Indian stories for the cobras, secretary-birds, mongooses and such in them.

I lived in India for only eighteen months, and then, in 1922, was brought back to England to live with my paternal grandmother while my parents were in India. Maybe if I had had brothers and sisters, I would have stayed in India, but there were none. I am not conscious of any memories of India, and when I returned there in World War II, there was nothing that seemed familiar. I am told that the person I was saddest to leave was my Indian ayah, and also that I nearly died during the voyage through the Red Sea. The ship had fans, and a large awning to provide some shade on deck, but it must have been a hard time for my mother. It also meant that I arrived in England with the tag of 'delicate child', a noisome albatross for a boy.

My parents then returned to India. In the days of the British Empire, it was common for young couples to find themselves in distant parts of the world keeping the Empire going. When they had children, they had a hard choice, largely, but not only, concerned with education. There were English schools in, say, India, but usually not so good as those in England. There was often a bad climate and the danger of strange diseases, and perhaps other dangers. Should they keep their children with them, or should they send them back to England and not see them for several years?

Two

EARLY CHILDHOOD

y paternal grandfather had just died, and I may have been intended to be a therapy for his widow, my grandmother. I do not know how successful that was for her, but it turned out wonderfully well for me. Perhaps I would have been brought back to England anyway, but the decision must have been precipitated by the death of my grandfather.

I never knew him. Educated at Eton and Balliol, he took over the John Birch Company, a family business on his wife's side. It was a diversified business in London in the City: import/export especially with China, engineering, acoustics etc. It took some part in building Africa's Cape-to-Cairo railway. He gave my grandmother some handsome Chinese furniture of mahogany inlaid with ivory, and a beautiful ivory mah-jong set. He had a very high opinion of the honesty and courtesy of the Chinese.

One of his favorite stories was of a *nouveau riche*, who announced to his fellow guests at a dinner-party that he had just bought a new coach-and-four. He took it out for a trial spin, rounded a corner and found in his path a great tree fallen across the road. 'So I whipped up my horses and we sailed over it in grand style.' The family doctor was also at the table and said, 'That's odd: I was out the other day in my pony and trap and the very same thing happened to me. I rounded a corner and found in my path a great tree fallen across the road. So I said to my pony, "Gee up, lass" and we popped under it like a weasel.' I think I would have liked my grandfather very much.

My grandmother, who was born in 1860, was something of a victorian *grande dame*. Without being imperious, she was ever fully in charge. She expected family and guests to conform to the rules of the house, especially the times of meals. Even her second husband grew quite anxious if he was out in the car and in danger of being late back.

During her first marriage, when she was living in the suburbs of London, she was an active hostess, but the guests tended to be musical and literary rather than in London Society. She took comparatively little interest in the family tree and Little Jack Horner. He was a historical figure, the steward of the Abbot of Glastonbury. He helped Henry VIII with the dissolution of Glastonbury Abbey. He is my grandfather thirteen times removed. He bought Mells Manor in Somerset – we hold the receipt – and did not, as the nursery rhyme suggests, steal it. Or my grandmother may have lacked interest because Katharine Asquith, née Horner, to whom Mells Manor House had passed after the deaths of two potential male Horner heirs, had become a Catholic and had built a chapel in the garden, where Mass was celebrated. Katharine married Raymond Asquith, son of the Prime Minister, and Asquiths now live there.

I can remember only one childhood visit to Mells. That was when my great-aunt Frances, the wife of Sir John Horner, my grandfather's oldest brother, was holding a garden-party-cum-village-fête. She certainly was a *grande dame*. She was also drawn and painted by some of the Pre-Raphaelites. Only after World War II did I visit Mells again.

My grandmother lived, with her daughter, Olivia, in a tall house, now turned into flats (apartments) in Surbiton, about twelve miles southwest of the centre of London. It was then nearly rural. The unpaved side-street that ran on one side of the house led straight down to the River Thames. I used to run ahead of my nanny to cross the road at the end of the street and climb the bank on the far side of the road to see if there was anything exciting on the river. She used to shout, 'Look both ways, Michael, there might be a car coming.' Today that road is a major four-lane highway, and no nanny would dream of letting her charge run towards it. I do not remember our having a car in Surbiton, nor do I remember carriages arriving at the house. We certainly had bicycles, but my only memory is of walking and taxis.

It was a handsome house. The top floor was an attic; then there was the nursery floor, then bedrooms, then the drawing-room and dining-room, and kitchen, pantry, larder and so on. I imagine there was a cellar. The roof was of slate, and after a severe storm, the occasional slate tile was blown off, and we would find it next morning in pieces on the lawn or vertically embedded in it. It would have sliced a head in two. In the kitchen were a cook, a parlor-maid and a scullery-maid. One of them was from Glasgow, and for a while I talked with a Glaswegian accent, for which I was firmly rebuked. The line in *My Fair Lady* about 'making some other Englishman despise him' was more true then than now, and speaking the King's English with a proper accent was *de rigueur*. Our family attached much importance to pronunciation. The rooms have left no impression on my memory except that the chairs in the drawing-room all had antimacassars, little cloths on the chairs to prevent macassar hair oil, or later Brylcreem, made popular by Rudy Valentino, from staining the fabric of the chair.

I remember more of the garden. There was a magnificent plane tree on the right, a fair stretch of lawn, and then a bed of peonies with dahlias and other flowers, and more flower-beds. There was a walled vegetable garden beyond that. One hot summer's day I was allowed, aged three or four, to shed my clothes and run on the lawn while my aunt Olivia played the hose on me. I was almost literally ecstatic and jumping out of my skin, but spoiled it all by making such a fuss about stopping, – even when they had me inside, I sat down half way up the back stairs and refused to go on – that it never occurred again. I suppose I learnt some kind of lesson from that: a least I still remember it. I also remember going to a morning school, playing, and building sandcastles in a sandpit and learning from large alphabet blocks how to spell. My first word was, of course, C-A-T.

There was also a strange figure, who appeared at twilight on a bicycle, carrying a long, thin pole in his hand. He zigzagged down the street, and after each zig or zag that part of the street became illuminated. He was the lamp-lighter and was lighting the gaslights. To me it seemed magical. The streets whose lamps he lit were not paved, which was odd, since those in the country, when we moved there, were being surfaced, with the help of a steam-roller, with what we called tarmacadam.

There were three of us living in this large house: my grandmother (hereafter 'Granny'), her daughter, Olivia, who was also my favorite aunt, and I. They both used to sing to me, and I joined in, from such books as *The Baby's Opera* and *The Baby's Bouquet*, to which names I never objected. They read to me, a common practice before wireless and TV, from A.A.Milne, to whom I did object, from *The Wind in the Willows, Uncle Remus*, and from tales by Sir Walter Scott. I lived here until I was five.

Three

WE MOVE TO THE COUNTRY

But Olivia was soon to be married and her three brothers had dispersed long ago, so it was time to move. The house chosen was an old Elizabethan farmhouse, Bridge Hall, with four acres of ground and a little brook at the bottom. It was in Sussex, a little over forty miles south of London, and ten miles north of Brighton. We moved in 1925 when I was five. The farm still existed, but the farmer lived in another house on the farm. Bridge Hall was a mile and a half north of Burgess Hill, and was on what had been the main, two-lane road from London to Brighton. When we first went there, a stage-coach still carried passengers from London to Brighton. As there was a dangerous junction just south of our driveway, we heard the coachman's hunting horn every time the coach ran. We never went either to London or to Brighton by that means, but we did sometimes go out to watch, and sometimes even waited for the coach. It was bright and shiny, and the coachman and postilion wore a smart livery, so sight and sound were both worth waiting for. It stopped running soon after our arrival.

There was what I remembered as a longish driveway leading up from the road to the house, but when I visited as an adult, it had shrunk to thirty yards. The house itself was of two storeys with a basement. There was a hall with a rack of walking sticks and umbrellas and, under the staircase, an early upright telephone with mouthpiece and a detachable receiver, which you held to your ear. On the left of the hall was the dining room, used for all meals except tea, and, beyond that, a greenhouse with a vine. Behind the dining-room was the kitchen, inhabited by Cook and Gertrude. Gertrude had 'followers', of most of whom Granny disapproved. In the kitchen was a large coal-burning range. Beyond it were the scullery, larder and coal-hole. At the end of the hall was the butler's pantry with all the silver and crockery but never a butler. On the right of the hall was the drawing-room with a fine open fireplace with inglenooks and massive fire-dogs. We burnt wood and peat, which produced a fine pile of ashes, used as fertilizer in the garden.

13

Behind that was the long room, the far end of which was my playroom, with my toys and books.

I remember only too well the fact, but not the cause, of my last tears of sheer rage as I was sitting at the table at my end of the long room. On another occasion I found a box of kitchen matches on the table. I struck one and was so startled when it lit that I nearly dropped it into the box. For a number of years Granny used paper spills instead of, or as well as, matches. These spills were pieces of paper folded lengthwise like a concertina and then dog-eared at the top. Being longer, and lasting longer, than a match, they made lighting a fire easier and safer. We used them well into the 1930s.

In the middle part of the long room we had tea in the afternoon, and the near end of the room, which, like the drawing-room, had an open fireplace, was sometimes used for entertaining. The six or seven bedrooms were upstairs on at least three slightly different levels, so presumably parts had been added to the house at various times. The most notable feature of the bedrooms was the doors, which were under six feet in height and had the original hard, oak frames. As most of the men in the family were over six feet, their visits to me when I had the normal round of childhood diseases, usually started with their banging their forehead on the lintel. All the doorframes, beams in the ceilings, half-timbering and so on, were of oak and had been there from the beginning. The main beams were fifteen to twenty feet long and ten to twelve inches square, and so hard that when we wanted electricity installed, the electricians were unable to drill adequate holes into the beams, but simply blunted their hand tools. The half-timbering was structural, not appliqué. There must have been more bedrooms somewhere as Cook, Gertrude, and my nanny, Polly Hector, all lived in.

In front of the house was a grass tennis-court and beyond that a 'wilderness', in the midst of which was erected a swing, on which I spent many hours. Between the swing and the tennis-court was a hammock, which Doctor Goodman, of whom more later, had brought back from South America. It must have been tough because it stood up to years of rough handling. The wilderness ran down to the stream, which either was or flowed into the River Adur. It was notable for the presence of Reggie, the swan. We never saw a mate, but Reggie kept appearing for as long as we were there, invaded our territory when bored, had five fights with our fox terrier, Chip, and won three. Granny was afraid that he might attack me, but our gardener, Ball (Mr. Ball to me), assured her that I was safe in the wilderness as 'Reggie always keeps to the paths'.

On our side of the stream there was a very small flood plain, where grew tufts of grass and other vegetation. That was also where we made our bonfires. In the summer the grass around the bonfire was very dry and if there happened to be a branch sticking out from the bonfire, it could easily set the surrounding grass on fire. The temptation was great and I succumbed. It was a lovely blaze, which we had some difficulty in extinguishing. I was never quite accused, but there was an atmosphere of suspicion, and that was my last act of arson.

As you came up from the stream, to the west of the wilderness there was a summer-house at the far end of a long bed of roses, which loved the Sussex clay and had exotic names like Madame Edouard Herriot. At the other end of the rose-bed was a goldfish pond and a bank of ivy and periwinkles. Next was the orchard and the beehives, then a vegetable garden. Behind the house was a long bed of asparagus and a wonderful bird-proof cage, about thirty feet square and off limits to me, with many kinds of fruit bushes: gooseberries, red and black currants, strawberries, raspberries, loganberries and what we called American blackberries, which were larger but less sweet than the wild blackberries in the fields around us. There was also a grape-vine in the greenhouse. There were several bee-hives, tended by Ball; Granny alleged that he had learnt bee-keeping by reading the fourth book of Vergil's *Georgics* (in translation). He certainly produced honey from the bees, and I remember him bringing back swarms with the din of a mallet and bucket, as the *Georgics* (iv.64) prescribe. He was helped by Dival, who had a club-foot but managed a scythe with great skill.

Granny had a green thumb, but did not pass it on to me. I was allotted a plot of clay, which seemed to me enormous, especially when I started to dig it. It never really engaged my enthusiasm, but I was once given a large lily bulb, with instructions on how to plant it and water it, and how long to wait. The wait was to be to three weeks. I waited an eternity of ten days and could bear it no more, so I dug up the bulb to see how it was getting on. It had started to sprout, so I replaced it in its hole. Despite this, in about three weeks it appeared above ground, and in due course produced a really beautiful flower. But gardening was not my forte. Nonetheless I did pick up a fair amount of gardening lore, and could bothrecognize, pronounce and spell an eschscholtzia when I saw one.

There was a house on the other side of the road from us. The son of the family owned a Bugatti and perhaps had girl friends. Granny considered him rather 'fast' and there was no social contact. Farther up the road towards London was another family, who lived in a house called Abbotsford, named in honor of Sir Walter Scott. With them we did have occasional contact, but most of our friends lived in the other direction, in Burgess Hill.

I do not remember any great amount of entertaining at my level, but fairly often we had grown-ups to tea. For me, at least, tea was a strict ritual: scones (rhymed firmly with 'dons'; Those who rhymed them with 'drones' were scorned) or bread and butter first, and nothing else was allowed me until I had eaten that; then, bread, butter and jam, or perhaps sandwiches of cucumber, tomato, or mustard and cress (grown by me), then sponge roll or cake. Perhaps once a month we started with muffins or, more rarely, crumpets.

The grown-ups ate lunch and dinner in the dining-room, but I had them with my nanny on a large table in my play area, until I was judged fit company for the adults. The most interesting meal was breakfast, which we all had together, and which consisted of porridge or cereal, a cooked course which might be bacon and eggs, or sausage, or kedgeree, or a kipper, followed by toast, butter, marmalade and fruit, with coffee and hot milk in large, wide cups. The sausages were really of pork; their like has not been seen since World War II. There was in fact a Catholic joke, current during that war, that it was permissible to eat sausages on Friday as there was no meat in them. Kedgeree was a mixture of rice and fish; the kippers had been herrings, and were good if you could avoid the bones. This fine meal at 8.30 a.m., supplemented by 'elevenses' consisting of a glass of milk and a cookie or two, had to take me through to lunch at 1.30 p.m. Tea was at 4.30 p.m. and dinner at 7.30 p.m., though it was some time before I was allowed to stay up for that.

Our daily activities were various. At the start of the next academic year after our arrival in Burgess Hill, I began going to a rather avant-garde school called the P.N.E.U (Parents' National Educational Union). It was a girls' school, but took in boys for the first two years. We were taught the usual subjects, started French and had one or two classes a week in Musical Appreciation and Eurhythmics. The former taught us to recognize the sounds of the various instruments in an orchestra; the latter was a mixture of physical training and dance. When the teacher arrived for French class we all stood and intoned '*Bon Jour, Mademoiselle, commen tallez vous?*' I knew it was a greeting, but no details, so, later, I looked unsuccessfully in a French dictionary for *taller*. During the mid-morning break of fifteen minutes, we played tip and run, a version of cricket designed to enable as many people as possible to bat. Another boy and I devised a means of beating the system and stayed batting for the whole break. We were proud of our achievement, but it brought us only rebuke.

School ended soon after lunch, and someone would come to meet me and we would walk home. It was about a mile and a half, so I had at least three miles exercise a day. If the weather was unusually bad, I was driven to school, and sometimes Polly met me with a stroller with a seat, probably when I was recovering from a cold or other debility. On the way to or from school, we crossed the village common. Every now and then there was a game of stoolball in progress. The game has some similarities to cricket, but the wicket, the bat and the method of bowling are quite different. Neither Polly nor I understood the game, but it may have sparked in me what later became a great love of cricket. On Sundays I went to Mass at the Catholic church in Burgess Hill. Mrs. Hood was a Catholic, who lived a little farther out of town than we did. I walked from our house to a fork in the road, down which she came in a rather grand car, and picked me up for the ride to church. Rightly, no one worried about any possible dangers in that.

Outside the school terms, the most common routine was to go shopping with Granny in the morning and for a walk in the afternoon, but there were many variations. The regulars in the shops, whether buying or selling, all knew one another, so shopping was the occasion for interchange of news as well as of acquiring eggs, coffee, shoes, whatever. The grocer showed me how to use two wooden paddles with grooves in them to make pats of butter with an interesting pattern on them. I was fascinated by the haberdashery, which from each sales counter had a system of overhead wires, on which ran little containers which the sales clerk would fill with the bill and the cash and pull the trigger to shoot it over to the cashier. In due course the cashier shot it back with a receipt and the change.

On one occasion Granny left me in the backseat of the car while she went into a shop. While she was away, the car started to roll slowly down the hill. With, as I thought, great presence of mind, I reached over, took hold of the steering wheel and guided the car to the other side of the street, where I stopped it with the hand-brake. I then sat back thinking, 'What a good boy am I!' Granny, however, was convinced that I had leant over, released the handbrake and put myself in jeopardy. That was the first time that I reflected that grown-ups really were not omniscient after all. It also made me unduly sensitive to being disbelieved.

The High Street must have left a special mark on me. The PNEU school was on the High Street; the steering incident occurred on the High Street; and so did another incident, which I can remember in surprising detail. Granny and I were driving up the hilly end of the High Street just before the railway station when I noticed on the far bank of the railway embankment a billboard reading, DON'T BE MISLED: CAMP COFFEE IS BEST. The sign had a golden bugle on it, and some of the lettering was in red. Pronouncing it to myself as MIZZLED, I asked Granny what 'to mizzle' meant. She unraveled the problem for me. I have often wondered why I should remember that sign, and only that sign, with such clarity.

It was usually Polly and I and our dog, Chip, who went for walks, but if there were house guests, they might come too. There were fields with cows, a bull, cowslips and buttercups; there were woods and streams with anemones, crocuses, primroses, violets, daisies, and other flowers. At the right time of year, we used to go for a picnic to the Balcombe woods to see the carpet of bluebells, and also to admire the Balcombe viaduct. That ended when they were enclosed and an officious gamekeeper drove us out. I was much influenced by Arabella B. Buckley's nature book, *Eyes and No Eyes*. I was determined that no one should label me 'no eyes' and developed quite sharp eyes, especially for variations of color. When we did jigsaw puzzles, and others relied on shape, I relied much more on color. This sharpness of eye got me into trouble later on, but made those walks much more enjoyable. .

As Chip grew older, he started towards the end of a walk to limp. One of our guests, who had a rather uncritical sympathy for animals, picked him up and carried him home. After that, whenever she was there, Chip's limp started sooner and sooner, until one day a lorry passed by and Chip leapt out of her arms and went like a greyhound after it. That cured her. But Chip was indeed growing older, and one day he limped out into the garden, crept under a bush and there died. Is it too anthropomorphic to think of that as a sense of dignity and propriety, possibly coming from long domesticity? I never saw the body; whether that was good or not I do not know. Granny went to look for him, and I remember very vividly waiting for her to return and seeing her in the twilight walking slowly up the garden path back towards the house to tell me what by then I already knew from her sombre gait. We never had another dog, but Teddy, a marmalade cat, survived for many a year, growing crosser and crosser. The safest approach to him was from the back and from above; you could then keep both his forefeet on the ground and so prevent him from scratching. What was ornery about him was that I would be petting and he purring, when without warning he would scratch.

Sometimes it was not a walk but a drive. Granny had a four-door Morris Cowley with a hood that covered the passengers, not the engine, and had to be raised or lowered by hand. It folded back and was stowed behind the back seat. The side-windows were sheets of talc with short prongs that fitted into holes in the tops of the doors. The top of the talc must have fitted somehow into the hood. The car had no heating and no cooling, so it was necessary to take rugs, unless it was high summer. Cooling was seldom needed. It had a stick shift with three forward gears and a reverse, a starting handle (crank) and also a self-starter. There was a running board outside and a dashboard inside with a choke and a lever to advance or retard the spark. There was a hand-blown horn with a large rubber bulb, which the driver squeezed. One Christmas, we installed the very latest thing, a Klaxon electric horn. The car would seat four comfortably and five uncomfortably, and had a top speed of a little over forty miles an hour. In it Granny, in my eyes, cut quite a figure driving around the countryside, at least until a cousin came to stay. He had an MG, which, to my admiration, would do 50 mph in second gear. We had several favorite excursions for picnics on the South Downs, a range of smooth, bare hills between us and the sea, but there was always the danger of overheating the engine on the climb. One popular destination was a clump of wild raspberry bushes; another was the clump of trees planted in the shape of a V to celebrate Queen Victoria's Golden Jubilee. We sometimes visited the artists' colony at Ditchling to watch them weaving and to buy their products. On the Downs, as the soil was chalk, there were scabious in abundance, many smaller flowers and countless chalk-blue butterflies. The Downs, besides being beautiful, were a good weather forecast: when they were especially clear, it was sure to rain.

When the D'Oyly Carte company was in Brighton, playing Gilbert and Sullivan's *Mikado*, we made one of our periodical excursions there. On another such excursion we were stopped in Brighton by the police, who asked to see Granny's licence. The car had recently been stolen, and then was found in Stoke Newington, a northern suburb of London, and returned to us. The Brighton police had been informed of the theft but not of the car's return, and an alert young Bobby had remembered the number on the car's licence plate (RO 1777) and spotted it on the street. As Granny looked so little like a thief and I, at that age, so little like a thief's accomplice, we had little difficulty in persuading him to let us drive on. We were startled, but soon recognized that it was a credit to the police. His remembering the number also shows the scarcity of cars even in a city the size of Brighton. Occasionally we went as far as Worthing, or to Box Hill, which was almost too steep a climb for us. In one place we had to turn and go up backwards, as reverse gear had the lowest reduction.

There were other activities indoors and outdoors around Bridge Hall. I had the usual toys, tin soldiers, and games, and I played with them but without spending endless hours on them. The indoor activity on which I spent more time than on any other was reading. Having no brothers or sisters, I was seldom interrupted. I can remember Andrew Lang's Golden (and other) Fairy Books, a wonderful book of animal stories, Kipling's Jungle Books, Just so Stories, Kim, and others, books by Ernest Thomson Seton, a little of Fenimore Cooper, Rider Haggard, Agatha Christie, and much else. I was quite happy to re-read favorite books, and still am, but back then I had time to do so.

We had a wireless set. To get sound, we had to manoeuvre its 'cat's whisker' to tickle its crystal in the right place. The BBC had been founded in 1922, and was three or four years old when I started to listen. It may well have been the only station on the air. I listened mainly to the Children's Hour, of which I remember nothing except their very distinctive and slightly patronizing signing off, 'Good night, children, Good night', with a strong accent on 'good'. I had firm preferences among the speakers and readers, but those were very much the days of 'grown-ups know best', and long before feed-back and evaluation were common currency, so no one thought to ask the children what they thought of their Hour.

I heard any amount of classical music, of which Granny and Olivia were both very fond, and which both of them played (piano and violin), but which was never used just as a background to other activities. Granny tried to get me playing piano-duets with her, but the only one who enjoyed the results was our dog, Chip. As soon as we started he used to come and jump up on a stool behind the small, upright piano and lean his ear against the back of it. He must have liked the vibes.

I also remember hearing one of the earliest running commentaries on a sport. The Radio Times had published a diagram of a soccer field divided into squares. Arsenal was playing soccer. One man was describing the play, 'He's running down the wing', and a second supplied punctuation in a low, lugubrious voice, 'Square three;' 'He has beaten one man,' 'Square one', and so on. It was not Jack Buck, but it was very new and exciting at the time, and did help us to visualize the scene.

The wireless was in the drawing room, and that was where two other activities took place: reading aloud and mah-jong. I loved them both. Most of our reading, after the nursery, was adventure stories: *Treasure Island*, some Buchan, and several volumes of Scott. Scott I especially enjoyed, and so was given *The Talisman* to read on my own. It was only then that I found out how clever Granny had been in omitting the interminable descriptions, which, when I read the book myself, I found boring. I later found rather the same with Dickens. At the age of ten, I was given *Oliver Twist* as a holiday task for the summer. I hated it, and still find Dickens and his facetiousness hard to read.

Mah-jong I greatly enjoyed. We had a very beautiful ivory set, so that just looking at the tiles, chips, counters, and dice was a pleasure in itself. They were colorful and exotic, and so were the names: pungs and kongs and red, green, and white dragons, characters, circles, bamboos, and others. Games were something of a special occasion, as they occurred only when we had a guest. Dr. Goodman, whom Granny later married, was especially fond of the game, but some guests played only out of a sense of duty.

As I was lacking in horticultural talent, so I was lacking in culinary skill. Consequently my invasions of the kitchen were rare. But there was one occasion when we decided to make some toffee. All went well and the preliminary tastings were fully satisfactory, so we poured it into a shallow wooden bowl to dry. It dried, and we tried to get it out of the bowl, but toffee and bowl were locked in so loving an embrace that no one could prise them asunder, and we had to throw both away.

Outside there were often tasks to be done such as weeding groundsel or marking the tennis court. At one point Granny offered me a penny for each hundred groundsel. Finding, uprooting, and counting a hundred adult groundsel took a little while and I earned my penny, but then I came upon a little seed-bed of groundsel, where I could pull up a hundred tiny weeds with a single grasp. It took much longer to count them than to uproot them. I proudly took my little pile along and claimed my penny, which I received; but the offer was then withdrawn. I was also given an archery set: bow, arrows, quiver and target but I never took to archery, partly because when I missed the target, which was usually, I had to trudge after the arrows and search for them in the wasteland behind the target. I would never have made it with my hero, Robin Hood. There were also the swing and hammock already mentioned. To these I devoted much time.

Two events disturbed our lives. First, Olivia was to be married to Professor (later Sir) Ernest Barker. He and I got off to a bad start: I had heard that Olivia would change her name, which seemed to me a bad idea. When Ernest came to tea, and I was five or six, I mused out loud in the middle of tea, 'Barker! That's a silly name, but don't worry, Olivia, when I grow up, I will marry you back into a Horner.' Silence followed, and I may have been banished from the table. Ernest was not amused, and it took me some years to get back into his good graces, but we did eventually become very good friends. I attended both the wedding, where I was bored by the long prayers, and the reception, where I had my first sips of champagne, but did not much enjoy them either.

The other event was the visit of my parents from India. They were in fact not getting on well with one another, and although no one said anything explicit in my hearing, I picked up, as children and dogs will, that something was amiss. They were due in the evening but must have been delayed, and even though we waited long past my bedtime, I was in bed long before they came. In due course they came upstairs to see me, but I pretended to be asleep, and to my relief they decided to wait until the morning. I remember very little of their visit, but it must have during it that my mother arranged for me to make my First Communion, not at the parish church, but at a convent in Haywards Heath, where one of the nuns was Mother's cousin. I do not remember any instruction ahead of time, so I was rather bemused by all the fuss. About the same time, my mother started giving me instruction on the Sunday gospels, passing on to me much of what she had learnt from her Belgian nuns, and arousing in me an interest in the Bible, which, sadly and surprisingly, was not very common among Catholics in those days. Much later I was told by a monastic superior, when I chose the Gospel and Letters of Saint John for my Lenten reading, 'That's not quite what we mean by a Lenten book, is it?'

But I took to the Bible, and one phrase made a lasting impression: 'But he, willing to justify himself . . .' said of the lawyer who asked Jesus what he must do to inherit eternal life. I still have to overcome that 'justifying myself' when challenged.

Also during my parents' visit, we went by car for a holiday at Waxham, by the sea in Norfolk. It was, by the route we took, a full day's drive of about 250 miles. My father drove all the way and became quite cross with some of the other motorists. Fortunately, there were not very many. He did not stay. A farm track ran for a hundred yards or so from the farm we stayed at to the sea. For some reason, Mother insisted that I walk barefoot to the sea. That was fine once we reached the sand-dunes, but the farm track had some sharp little stones, and I dreaded it.

The farm had no running water upstairs, so water for my hip-bath had to be brought up. This bath was full of nearly boiling water when I came running up the stairs, failed to see the bath, tumbled into it and scalded my forearm. We rushed to the doctor who bandaged it and sent us home. When we came back to renew bandage, we found that he had not put any dressing or ointment under the bandage. It took forty-five minutes and much pain to get the bandage off.

Another summer we went to a farm in Northumberland called Rayheugh. I loved life on the farm, even churning butter, where the milk goes round endlessly until suddenly there is a thump, and there's your butter. I was also taken to sheepdog trials and was amazed at what man and dog could get sheep to do. There was a pen of thirty sheep and a prize of £1 for judging the three best. I chose my first very carefully, and then my second. Then some of the boys from the farm wanted me to come and play cricket, so I chose a third almost at random. I still remember the numbers: five, eight, and seven. When the winners were announced, I was one, but so were three others, so I collected only five shillings; but for me that was wealth indeed.

About this time I had my first experience of hospital life, to repair a hernia. I remember having a chloroform mask put over my nose and being told to count to a hundred. I was determined to get to two hundred, but made it only to fourteen. I was to go home in a Rolls Royce and was thrilled at the prospect, but the driver was instructed not to exceed twenty mph and I was bored almost literally to tears, and longed for Granny to be driving.

Next summer we went to Sheringham, which I preferred to Waxham, even though there were no sand dunes. I netted large numbers of prawns and caught five mackerel out at sea, all good eating. The following summer we went to Scarborough, farther north, but still on the East Coast.

The East Coast was believed to be bracing, so I presume I was braced, but I was quite content when we switched to Lyme Regis on the South Coast. We walked often on Jane Austen's Cobb and once were taken for a row by an elderly boatman in a navy-blue sweater. We ventured out of the harbor into the English Channel, but soon the wind rose and there was quite a swell, enough to make getting back through the narrow entrance to the harbor quite a feat. In my ignorance I found it exhilarating, but there was good reason for alarm. Another time we went for a walk to the Seaton Landslip, where we found a bed of springy ivy that served very well as a trampoline. I trampoled until the sun was low, when we set off to walk back to Lyme Regis. We were met by a group of young men from our hotel who feared we might be lost. I was flattered. Much later I came to see that it was a tribute to Mother's beauty.

There were also occasional excursions to London by train from Haywards Heath to Victoria. I loved the trains, which had separate compartments seating four on each side at rather close quarters, and I loved the train-rides. The sound and smell of the tunnels, and the sound of another train meeting us, whistling and changing pitch as it went by, excited me. I remember the huge billboards advertising Carter's Little Liver Pills, and carrying on top a small sign giving the mileage to London. To love London took a little longer. The signs at Victoria Station read 'LONDON where Abdullahs come from'. I did not understand this, and when I was told that Abdullahs were cigarettes, I for some reason disapproved. But I enjoyed the Guinness billboards with their rhymes and jokes and paintings. Our first business was Granny's shopping. We went to Gorringe's, a large department store, to buy her a dress. The floor-walker looked at her and said rather superciliously, 'Yes, madam, Outsize is over there'. I was deeply insulted on her behalf and tried to hit him. Granny was a sturdy woman, but Outsize? We ended with a splendid tea at the Ritz, but when we came out it was raining hard and there was a dense fog, a London pea-souper. We caught a taxi with difficulty because, although you could see a car's lights several yards away, you could not tell whether it was a taxi until it was almost upon you. It was said of a real pea-souper that you could not see your hand in front of your face. Ours, then, was not quite real, but it came close. We also came up to London just after Christmas for the Bertram Mills Circus at Olympia, with fascinating sideshows like coconut shies and Dodgems as well as the main performances; or for the magic shows staged at the Rudolph Steiner Hall under the names of Maskelyne and Devant.

Another annual event was the Old Crocks race from London to Brighton. This was a race for elderly cars, which originally had to be at least twenty-five years old. It started in 1927. The distance is over fifty miles, so it was quite remarkable that any of the cars finished. The road they used was a few miles from our house, and we went to watch them most years. They looked antique to us then, as our car would look now. Their chief trouble was overheating.

After two happy years at the P.N.E.U. school, I was sent to a boys' day-school called Saint Peter's Court, which was only half as far away from home. I was competently taught, and was introduced to Latin, and also to organized games. The first day we changed for these, it was revealed that, because I was a 'delicate child', I was wearing a woolen undervest, when everyone else was wearing cotton. I was despised for this, but soon appeared in cotton. We were introduced to Rugby football, or rugger, and played a match against another school, which we won by the monstrous score of 96-0. One of their players was so slow that I could catch him even though I was wearing wellington boots because of the wetness of the field, and so fat that when I tackled him, my fingers sank into his legs. I can still remember the feeling, both sinking and sickening. I have never really liked rugby; perhaps that is partly why. We also played Cricket, which I loved then and ever since. I caught whooping cough, and during the rather long period of quarantine practised bowling and developed some sort of rhythm, though I do not remember having any coach.

Four

BOARDING SCHOOL

After I had been for two years at Saint Peter's, it was decided that I should go in 1929 to Hordle House in Milford-on-Sea, a boarding prep-school[1] on the South Coast opposite the west end of the Isle of Wight and the Needles, four white rocks of chalk, one hundred feet high. One night there was a great roaring sound. Next morning there were only three Needles. One, having been eaten away by the waves, had collapsed during the night. We saw large liners coming to and from Southampton, and witnessed the Dornier DOX seaplane take off on its flight from Southampton via Brazil to New York. It had twelve engines, and when it passed between us and the Needles was still only a few feet above the water.

I was just nine years old, and boarding school at that age was not uncommon. A friend of my father was Second Master there, and the headmaster was a Church of England clergyman, who held a service for the school on Sundays but had no cure of souls. One consequence of my going to Hordle House was that, after several very happy years, there was no longer a job for my nanny, Polly. We bade her a very sad farewell on the station platform at Burgess Hill. I first felt how good she was when she took a summer vacation and a substitute came, who was not good. Granny made it clear to me that Polly had gone for good, but I could not quite believe that. Olivia, too, had 'gone for good', but she had come back from time to time. But Granny was right. Twenty-five years later I was driving past Polly's home and stopped by unannounced, but she was at work as a nurse.

So in September, 1929, I set out, also from Burgess Hill station on the Southern Line. It had been the London, Brighton, and South Coast Railway and only on January 1, 1923 became by Act of Parliament the Southern Railway; notice boards, platform benches, etc., still had 'LB&SCR' on them, and in about 2005 some still did. I went alone across country to New Milton, Hampshire, with several changes en route. It was a tedious journey, and always after that I went

1. *In England a prep-school prepares for secondary school, not for college.*

26

up to London and down again from Waterloo. My trunk was sent 'luggage in advance', and usually arrived a day or two after me.

Hordle House was my first continuous exposure to an all-male environment. There had, of course, always been men appearing at Bridge Hall and before, but this was the first time they were there all day long every day, and women were almost literally *rarae nantes in gurgite vasto*.[2]

I did not like all the men but I enjoyed the atmosphere of masculinity. The headmaster was a wonderful teacher of Scripture and Mathematics (arithmetic, algebra, and geometry) and my father's friend was an equally good teacher of Latin and Greek. I found out when I went on to Ampleforth for high school that whereas I had a fair acquaintance with the Old Testament, my classmates, who had attended good Catholic schools, had almost none.

If other classes were dull we tried to enliven them. One teacher had the habit of repeating 'D'you see?' several times in a sentence. Two of us started counting and had just reached 130 times. By coincidence, she was saying that the length of some river was 132 miles, d'you see?. I had just lent over to my classmate and said that made 131. She heard me and said, 'No, it's 132, d'you see.' Which it was on both counts.

We were well coached in cricket, soccer, rugby and hurdling, the last by an Olympic trialist; not very surprising this, because prep schools of this kind were often a niche for such athletes, while they looked around for something else. We also swam in the sea, as we were about a hundred yards from the cliffs. Once a year there was, for the whole school, a swimming race in a large public swimming pool in Lymington. I could at that time swim only on my back, and slowly at that. I came in last of all those who finished, to great, derisory, applause. At cricket I did better and played in the first XI for two of my four years.

We had an art class and I was given a prize for drawing, but it must have been for perseverance rather than skill. There was also a class in singing, which I enjoyed, and occasional plays, in which I took part but never shone.

There were about sixty boys in the school. The spirit and discipline were good. Punishment was partly by writing out lines, partly by losing points for your patrol, partly corporal on the backside and known, onomatopoetically, as swishing. The school was divided into six patrols, to whose members points were allotted for academic, athletic or other achievements, or deducted for

2. *Swimmers dotted here and there in the vast, raging waters. It is from Vergil's description of a storm at sea. Aeneid 1.118.*

Hordle House was on the cliffs of the South Coast of England west of Southampton and east of Bournemouth. The sea is the English Channel. The Isle of Wright is at the bottom right hand corner.

'negative achievements'. Points were also given for finding tennis balls after one of our flag games. In this game, each team had to defend a home base where the flags were. They did this by throwing old tennis balls at their opponents. Anyone who was hit was 'captured'. Eventually one team was able to rush the other, break through to their base and take the flags. After the game there were many lost balls. By finding one you scored a point for your patrol.

From country walks and from reading Buckley's *Eyes and No Eyes*, I had developed sharp eyes. It also dawned on me that if someone was sheltering behind a bush and someone else threw a ball at him, a good place to look for balls would be on the thrower's side of the bush, where the ball would naturally drop. Consequently I scored quite a lot of points for my patrol, until someone in another patrol started the rumor that I was taking balls out of the store, dropping them, and then 'finding' them. Unfortunately the headmaster believed him and not me. I was bitter about this at the time, but it had the good long-term result that I tend to believe what I am told, and pounce only if I later find that I have been told a lie.

There was a little bullying but not much, more teasing, and occasional 'peeve-fights'. These were announced loudly round the school by any small boys who happened to be there, They drew both a crowd and, usually, a member of the faculty, so the fights never had time to become very serious.

I was the only Catholic boy in the school. I was picked up by taxi on Sunday mornings and taken to the Catholic chapel in Milford-on-Sea, where an elderly, retired Monsignor celebrated Mass. I was also to receive instruction from the parish at Lymington, but this got off to a bad start and never worked out. The headmaster graciously allowed us the use of his study, and the priest, reeking of tobacco, duly came for the first instruction bringing a copy of the Penny Catechism, a wonderful compendium of Catholic teaching going back to Bishop Challoner of the eighteenth century. It still cost one penny in 1929. The priest told me to learn the first four questions and answers, which I did. Next week he came back and asked me to state the first question; I said, 'Who made me?' 'and what is the first answer?' I said, 'God'. To my surprise he said it was not. 'Yes, it is'; 'No, it's not'. We each said this two or three times. To try to break the impasse I said, 'Then what is the first answer?' and he replied, 'God made me'. Inevitably I replied, 'That's what I said'. 'No, it wasn't'. 'Yes, it was'. This too was repeated several times. It was only about five miles from Lymington, but the road was bumpy and it cannot have been a pleasant chore for him. I thought he was obtuse, and he must have thought I was obnoxious.

One last little incident from Hordle House shows how real the generation gap can be even between those who love one another. I received a telegram from Olivia reading, 'Anne arrived this morning'. I had no idea who Anne was, nor why Olivia would tell me by telegram; and those I asked were equally mystified, so I put it away in my large store of grown-up behaviors that I did not understand. Some time later, when Anne died in infancy, I recognized that Olivia had been announcing the arrival of her first-born, but it was a use of the word 'arrive' that I did not know.

Five

AMPLEFORTH

In those days, when a Catholic married someone who was not Catholic, the latter had to promise that the children would be brought up Catholic. My father therefore agreed that I should now go to a Catholic school. My uncle, Ernest Barker, had, while he was a don at Oxford, tutored and been impressed by two Benedictine monks from Ampleforth Abbey, one of whom was now headmaster, the other a housemaster. Neither of them was a great scholar, so it is all the more remarkable that they made such an impression on him. To Ampleforth College, therefore, I was sent, a school which was beginning to be known as one of the leading public (that is, private) schools.

My first visit there was to take a scholarship examination, and in due course news came that I had been given a scholarship. During the summer we were sent a clothing list. This included an Eton collar and jacket and a bowler hat. Fortunately I noticed that the Eton collar was only for shorter boys, which let me out, but we did buy the bowler. I think I was the only boy in my house (dormitory) who had one. In due course, it was seized and used for a game of soccer in the large room where the younger boys slept.

In September 1933, I boarded the school train at King's Cross, the London terminal of the London and North-Eastern Railway (LNER). There were then about two hundred and fifty boys in the school, of whom roughly one third came from the South of England, one third from Lancashire and one third from Ireland. The majority of those from the South traveled on that train. We took the main London-Edinburgh line as far as York and then our coaches were detached and we took the Scarborough branch line to Gilling. The line to Gilling was closed after World War II, and even the rails and ties were removed, so in 1952 it took longer to get from London to Ampleforth than it had in 1912.

The monks arrived at Ampleforth in 1802. The Community had been founded during the tenth century at Westminster in what is now Westminster Abbey. It was suppressed by Henry VIII in 1540, briefly re-opened by Mary

Ampleforth, monastery and school. Saint Cuthbert's House is the second building from the left: the tall building in centre is the church tower.

Tudor, and suppressed for good by Elizabeth I. The monks scattered, but the community very narrowly survived and was re-established at Dieulouard, near Nancy, about one hundred miles east of Paris. The monks stayed there until ejected by the French Revolution in 1793, when most of them escaped to England. After various stops in the North of England, they settled at Ampleforth, about twenty miles north of York.

The monastery, upper and middle school were on the northern slope of a beautiful valley, which runs east and west. On some days when there is cloud cover, the sun as it sets shines below the clouds and is reflected both off them and off the ground, giving the limestone of the buildings a wonderful honey-like tone. The Abbey owns several thousand acres, some farmed by tenants, some leased to the Forestry Commission, some used for playing fields. There is plenty of room. On the south side of the valley is Gilling Castle, (mostly fourteenth century), which, since 1930, has served as the prep school (grade school) for Ampleforth. West of the castle is a lake, used by the sea scouts for training and by others for sailing, and even, on occasion, for skating. The setting was rural, York was the nearest city and Thirsk the nearest town. East and west of the school were the small villages of Oswaldkirk and Ampleforth. There were a few shops in the latter.

At Ampleforth in 1933 the headmaster, all the housemasters and the majority of the other masters were monks. My second experience of all-male surroundings was much happier than my first. Because my uncle had tutored Father Sebastian at Oxford, I was placed in his house, Saint Cuthbert's. Father Sebastian was well educated but not a scholar. He was a wise and good man, with strong athletic and outdoor interests. At rugby, he played as centre three-quarter and, being of solid build, was often able to crash through the opposition and then pass the ball to another monk, a speedy wing three-quarter, who was said to run like a rabbit and for the same reason. Father Sebastian was also a very effective cricketer. He was a good shot, and during the season, we members of Saint Cuthbert's often feasted on pheasant. His special talent was fishing: not infrequently he would go out when no one else was catching anything and bring back a record fish. He was instinctively in tune with nature, and this included the nature of adolescent boys.

He was also credited with second sight, the ability to see what the eye cannot see. A story circulated among the boys in his House about a lad who used to go out and visit local inns. At the end of one term, the story ran, Father Sebastian sent for the boy in question and presented him with a list of all his visits, and what he had imbibed on each occasion. It may have been in the same class as stories about the Indian rope-trick, but it was an effective deterrent.

Father Sebastian was also a popular speaker with one of the Ampleforth clubs, the Historical Bench, known by the boys as the Hysterical Wench. He would retail ghost stories and stories of second sight, often set in the highlands of Scotland. At one meeting there was a very high-strung boy and sitting next to him an imp. The story was about a haunted house in the highlands. A young lady volunteered to sleep in the four-poster bed in the haunted room. In the middle of the night she heard the door open with a slight creak, and soft steps approached the bed. She felt a slight pressure on her toes, then on her knee, then on upwards to her shoulder, then coming down her arm. Just a it was about to reach her hand, the imp laid his hand very gently on that of the high-strung boy, whose shriek was a more memorable end to the story than whatever was planned.

It soon became apparent to me that many of the boys in the House were of the huntin' shootin' and fishin' type, and had been chosen to match their housemaster, and that I, who was on a scholarship, was out of my depth. They kept ferrets, tied flies, shot pheasants and so on, and I did not, but cricket

All dressed for cricket. The jacket is bright scarlet.

helped me to keep my head above water. There was no riding of horses at Ampleforth, which was a pity, as that too might have helped me. My feeling of floundering was increased by the system of forms then common in public schools. In general new boys were put in the fourth form, older boys in the fifth and the oldest in the sixth. There were also two curiously named forms, upper remove and lower remove. Lower remove was for boys who were too old for the fourth form but not yet academically qualified for the fifth; upper remove was for boys qualified for the sixth form but not old enough (sixteen) to be placed in it. Scholarship boys, however, started in the middle fifth form. That meant that at meals and in church I was seated among boys one, two, or even three years older than I. I expect this was good for my social development, but it was at times uncomfortable.

Saint Cuthbert's, being separate from the main school buildings, had its own kitchen, and so had rather better food than most of the school, and its own chapel, where we had Mass each weekday rather than in the Abbey church. On

Sundays, the whole school attended Mass in the Abbey church. The classrooms were in the main building, and so was the big study, where each boy had a desk where he kept his books and did his homework under supervision. It was also used for examinations, with monks presiding. There was a central gangway, usually patrolled by one of the monks. One day, boys spread sugar on the floor of the gangway, and the monk crunched up and down for the duration of the exam. At the end, he told us to stay where we were while he went and reported the matter to the headmaster. He then left by the door leading towards the headmaster's office. We sat in fear. But instead of going to the headmaster, he went down a flight of stairs and back to the monastery. It was a more effective penance than anything else would have been.

Having been well taught and well coached at Hordle House, I was able to hold my own on the playing fields and even to shine a bit at cricket, and in the classroom I did well in my natural field of classics. By an accident I also won the fifth form prize for Mathematics, which was not my field. I won because one of the problems in plane geometry asked us to prove that AB = AC, with a note under the figure 'remember the median rule'. That seemed to me a clear indication that the median rule was the clue to the proof. I made a guess and it worked first time. I was amazed to learn that I was the only one of the ninety or so boys in the fifth form who found the proof. Father Felix, who was due to teach me classics the following year, was shocked, and came up quickly after the awarding of prizes, anxious to be reassured that I was not planning to specialize in Mathematics next year. One less pleasant result of the hard work in the classroom was that I started to have rather frequent migraines with severe headaches. They lasted until I went abroad in World War II in 1943. My occulist told me that they might well recur when I was sixty. To the day, on my sixtieth birthday they did recur, but with a difference: there was no headache with them, simply the visual disturbance and sometimes mild aphasia. I suffered also from hay fever. That too left me when I went abroad, and has never returned.

The high point of my first year was the cricket season. On the lawn in front of Saint Cuthbert's, Father Sebastian put up a net (batter's cage) for batting practice. Everything was normal except the bat, which was less than half the width of a normal bat. That meant that you really had to watch the ball. I was placed in the Colts (under 16) set and, with my slow left-arm spin bowling, secured a place in the Colts XI. My competition was a right-hander who spun the ball prodigiously but was very inaccurate. He was like a pitcher with a wonderful curve ball who could seldom find the plate. We played half a dozen matches, some at home and some away. I was thirteen, and had two years in the Colts, and then was promoted to the First (or Varsity) XI. Everyone had to take part in all three sports, rugby and athletics (track) being the other two. I got by in them, but was an unusually slow runner, so I tried Cross Country, but did not enjoy it. We had a pack of beagles, and I did on occasion go out with them. I learnt that the hare was apt to run in a circle. Consequently, once the beagles had found a hare, it was not necessary to follow exactly in their tracks.

By way of entertainment, the school provided movies on Wednesday evenings and almost everyone attended. Certainly for my first term, and perhaps for longer, the movies were silent, and Father Felix played on the piano music appropriate to the action. This was especially exciting if the movie was a Western, and the action was a chase. The system for projection was quite unreliable: sometimes the film would break or catch fire, or the projector would fail; sometimes only the sound failed. The boys enjoyed this, leant back in their chairs and yelled 'sound'. Unfailingly this produced the angry face of a monk, who opened the small window in the projection booth and yelled back 'I know there's no sound'. Naturally this only encouraged us to do the same at the next breakdown. Had he kept silence, we would soon have grown tired of the ploy. At the end of the autumn term there was a Christmas dinner for the whole school, served in the Long Passage, which was both long and wide and had a terrazzo floor. Two of the monks, Father Stephen and Father John, sang a duo, which as a young boy I thought hilarious. Father Stephen had a fine voice, and Father John was a natural ham. It took the form 'O Father Stephen, O Father Stephen'. 'What's on your mind this evening, Father John?' followed by some topical comment. Older boys were blasé about it.

In the summer there was Goremire Day. Goremire, about eight miles from the school, was a valley half way down Sutton Bank (dialect for hill) and at Sutton Bank the road was more like a precipice than a bank. There was a picnic there at noon, and we had to get there by any means except a combustion engine. Most either walked or hired a local bicycle. One ingenious group hired a steamroller and came on that. This was undoubtedly contrary to the mind of the rule-makers, but it was certainly not a combustion engine. As its top speed was 2 mph, they were late for lunch. Sutton Bank was notable also as a place for gliders. The cliffs produced updraughts that made for good gliding. It was abandoned during World War II, and several derelict gliders were left there. The authorities decided to make the gliders into dummy wooden aircraft to attract German bombs. German planes duly came over and dropped a bomb, a dummy wooden one.

An entertainment not provided by the school was this: a group of us got together and bought two powerful air-pistols, targets, and little lead pellets. We took these out and practiced on a wooded hill nearby, which was out of bounds, but secluded. We pinned a target to a tree and fired away; and if a rabbit appeared, we shot at that, but I do not remember any hits. When time ran out, we hid the targets in a rabbit-hole and took the pistols home. Naturally we often had to race back in order to be on time, and on one occasion I twisted my ankle badly on a tuffet of grass and had some difficulty explaining that. On another occasion, when we were out on a school holiday and some miles away from the school, one of us held a blade of grass stretched between his fingers and challenged another to shoot it. The other managed to put the pellet into the first one's thumb. After a day or two it was turning septic, and we had to confess. The pistols were confiscated, but the targets remained in their rabbit-hole. Over ten years later, when I was a young monk, some of us were given the task of clearing the brambles and undergrowth that had sprung up on our hill. I happened to be standing by when one of the others in cleaning out the rabbit-hole saw something inside, pulled out a bunch of moldy targets and said, 'Look what I've found; how on earth do you think they got there?' I had no idea.

Another feature of the year, though not one about which I was fully enthusiastic, was that my aunt Olivia insisted that I continue with Carpentry, which I had started at Hordle House. I was competent, but not talented, and made one or two serviceable objects, including a step-ladder. Next year I was assigned to a class on Wednesday afternoon, but as that was the day on which classes stopped at noon and the rest of the day was free, I dropped out. The knowledge acquired has often been very useful, especially when I joined the monastery and one of the monks taught me the basics of working on a lathe. This was to prove invaluable later both as a hobby and as a source of gifts. Monks often want to give gifts, but they have no money for that, and not everyone understands the import of a Mass card. As I grow older, I also appreciate more and more that the lathe does the hard work.

The school year was divided into three terms, with a four or five weeks break at Christmas, three weeks at about Easter, and nearly two months in the summer. The school year ended near the end of July. At the end of each term,

Mother met me at King's Cross, where we had our own version of 'Where did you go?' 'Out'; 'What did you do?' 'Nothing': 'Did you have a good term?' 'Yes, thank you'; 'What happened?' 'Nothing', which seemed to me quite adequate. I suppose it all came out in the course of the holidays.

During one of the summer vacations some friends of my mother took me sailing on the Norfolk Broads. The boat was a fair-sized sailing boat with a small auxiliary engine and quants. A quant is a long, thick pole with a forked end used for punting, especially where the bottom is muddy. The forked end goes into the mud; the other end is rounded roughly to fit the shoulder. With the pole against your shoulder and the other end in the mud, you walk towards the stern. As you walk and push, the boat moves slowly forward. I remember that we had to do that more than once when the wind died. I also remember tripping over a coil of rope on the deck and falling ignominiously into the water. But most of all I remember a ruined, Benedictine Priory near the edge of the water. As we were passing it, a very smart motorboat, steered by a man in a blue blazer, white trousers, and a yachting cap, passed us. He asked what it was, and we told him. 'Oh' he said through his megaphone, 'and are the Benedictines still afloat?' He made it worse by rhyming the last syllable of Benedictines with pines. We assured him that they were still alive and floating.

By this time Granny had married Dr. Goodman, moved from Burgess Hill, and was living in Great Kimble in Buckinghamshire. Dr. Goodman enjoyed village life. During World War II he became head of the Pig Committee. One of the villagers complained, 'What does Dr. Goodman know about pigs?' As the job consisted largely of encouraging two households to keep a pig each to supplement the village's meat ration, organizing the collection of everyone else's swill to feed the pigs, and then arranging for their slaughter and distribution, no specialist porcine knowledge was needed. Later he was asked to judge the wines at the village fair. These might be made from dandelions, nettles, elderberries, etc., as well as from grapes, but could be quite strong. It was a hot day, the wines were in a mostly enclosed tent, and Dr. Goodman only just managed to stagger out of the opening. No one told him to spit out what he had tasted, so he swallowed all his samples.

My parents had now returned from India and divorced, and my mother was given custody of me, but not much to live on. My father lived in London. Having resigned from the Indian Political Service in about 1929, he decided to take up the Law. After the necessary studies and eating of dinners, he was called to the Bar. He practised very successfully as a barrister (trial lawyer), and retired a little indignantly at the age of 87 because they wanted his chambers 'for a younger man', who was in his sixties.

Mother lived at first with her parents in Marlow, (later Great Marlow) in Buckinghamshire. I spent the holidays with her, but with visits to Granny, and to my aunt Olivia in Cambridge. Mother was a good Catholic. I learnt from her example, and prayed fairly often, though more for things than in praise of God. I was not particularly pious. We walked to Mass every morning. I do not remember ever resenting this: I just took it for granted that this was how the world was. Although I had been taught to say my morning and night prayers and had been sent to Mass every Sunday in Burgess Hill, this was the beginning of my serious immersion in Catholic life. There was of course daily Mass at Ampleforth, and the habit influenced me at Oxford to the extent that I was regular at the Newman Chaplaincy on Sundays and attended Mass there two or three times during the week. In the army I attended Mass when it was available. Granny was a practising member of the Church of England (Episcopalian), but, in the English way, God was not much talked about, though his existence was always assumed, and His ways followed. But, as was also the English way, conversation was full of tags which I later recognized as biblical. Allusions to Catholicism were unfavorable but not violently so.

I have three main memories from Marlow: I learnt, rather late in life, to ride a bicycle. It was second-hand, had only one speed and only one brake. When I had mastered it, my father gave me a beautiful new Hercules with two brakes and three speeds. Second, my mother took a long course in first aid. There were tests, and I had to hear her with what she had to learn by heart. In this way I learnt the names of many of our bones, and sundry facts of first aid. At the end of the course there was an outdoor exercise simulating an air raid. Various 'cases' were laid out around the town. One of the 'cases' had to lie on the sidewalk and pretend to be wounded. After 45 minutes no one had come to tend him, so he wrote a note saying, 'Have bled to death and gone home.' The third memory is the Marlow Donk. This was a steam engine on our railway spur; it carried passengers in one or two coaches two miles to and from Bourne End, which is on a mainline to London. It was a sleepy affair, and people used to say in jest, that one day it would forget the coaches. Sure enough, one day the engine arrived from Bourne End all by itself.

In due course my mother, after her parents died, moved to London, where she lived first in Kilburn with two Polish spinsters, and volunteered in a hostel run by the Legion of Mary for homeless young women. Later she moved, with the spinsters, to a basement near the River Thames, south of Victoria station. She also changed her volunteering: she and her friend Joan Cuddon-Fletcher did not agree with some of the restrictions at the first hostel and decided to start their own, with a more open-door policy. It was highly successful, and they opened two or three such hostels for women. Joan tried to do the same for men and failed. Joan left, but Mother stayed on, moved into one of the hostels and spent her later days as a senior counselor in residence.

Ella, one of the young women in the hostel, was dying of cancer. She was from Northern Ireland and had naturally rhythmical speech. She was sent to a hospital in the East End of London and my mother used to make the long journey by tram (streetcar) to the East End. This was time-consuming, so she looked for lodgings near the hospital, and found a Jewish tailor and his family, who would take her in. They were poor, observant, and most hospitable. I was at Oxford, so when term ended, I went to visit my mother and Ella. The Jewish family always gave me a meal. I was once there about Pasch, and was invited to their Seder meal. Mother remained with Ella until she died. I remember well the hospitality of the Jewish family, and my mother's loving care for Ella.

Although I was no longer living with my grandmother, she continued to take an interest in my development. She sent me to take dancing lessons with Gem Mouflet in London, but I was too shy to get much out of them. Later Granny sent me out riding with the local butcher, Mr. Chilton, who used to ride around his territory delivering cuts of meat from an enormous wicker hamper, which he carried on one arm. This was much more successful. I had never ridden before, so for our first ride I was given a gentle nag called Lizzie, with a leading rein. We got on well and there was no further need for the rein. Granny's property was next to Chequers, the Prime Minister's country house, and our rides often took us there. Now that is forbidden. We went through beautiful woods of copper beech and sometimes along parts of the probably pre-Roman Icknield Way. Sometimes we had to get one of the horses shod, and I was introduced to the local blacksmith, to the technique of shoeing, and to a number of words that I had never heard before. We always visited a pub. I was left outside and sent an innocuous soft drink. Mr. Chilton emerged rather later, more rubicund and more talkative.

I fell off once, when Lizzie skidded on a slippery slope, went half down, and I slid gently over her shoulder to the ground. The best part of the ride was when we came to a long field, across which we used to canter. One day I surreptitiously spurred Lizzie on, and she responded with a vigorous gallop, which we both enjoyed. The other horses in the group were taken by surprise and we started with a long lead, but Lizzie was no speedster and they caught up before we reached the end of the field. I was never a polished horseman, but I greatly enjoyed being on a horse, and this hacking stood me in good stead in India, Burma, and Thailand, and later in Montana.

At the age of thirteen I played in a fairly notable tennis tournament. Because of my age and because no one knew me, I was given a high handicap and won the under-eighteen boys' singles, a very unfair result. I played cricket for our village team. In one match there were six members of the Spittalls family playing. Almost unbelievably, our score at one point was six runs for six wickets, all of them Spittalls. We also played and beat the local lunatic asylum. One summer I graduated to playing for Monks' Risborough, where there was a superior pitch, and then for Aylesbury, which was true club cricket.

Not all my exploits were athletic. I spent some time designing the lettering for a sign bearing the name of the house – Pickade House – and then painting it. This was because a lecture at Oxford by Eric Gill had stirred my interest in lettering. Some sixty years later, the sign, though weather-beaten, was still in use.

There were variations in my round of visits. At the end of my second year at Ampleforth, I was staying at Kimble. We invited Father Felix, who had been my principal teacher that year, to stay for a night or two. He arrived driving an old Bean car, which he had hired from Appleby's garage in Ampleforth Village. The car, which had ceased being produced about six years earlier, was a castaway, which Appleby had bought cheaply and refurbished. It managed the journey of perhaps two hundred and fifty miles from Ampleforth to Kimble without mishap but with some strain. Father Felix and I took off for Crawley, in Sussex, a comparatively short and easy journey. After a little while, to my surprise, Father Felix stopped the car, raised the bonnet (hood), bent over and started puffing vigorously. I got out too, to see what he was doing, and saw that all the exposed wiring was either smouldering or actually on fire, so I joined in the puffing. When we had extinguished the smoke and flame, he pointed out to me that the car had a gravity-feed gas tank, which was just above the fire. We then had to decide what to do. I naively suggested that we could only drive to the nearest garage, which we did, and no explosion ensued.

I was to stay with a cousin near Crawley. I went to see the Australians play cricket against Sussex at Hove, my first experience of first-class cricket. At the other end of the scale, I played cricket with a friend sometimes in his garden and sometimes on a tiny, bumpy, and very little used grass airstrip behind his house. It had a windsock, and nothing else. While playing in the garden, my friend made a big hit which left the garden and broke the windscreen (windshield) of a passing car. We were made to go for several days to pick wild blackberries until we had covered some of the cost of a windscreen. While playing on the airstrip, we were unknowingly playing on what may well now be part of one of Gatwick Airport's runways. It was certainly on what is now the airport's property.

For my second year at Ampleforth I was placed in the Upper Remove Form, which was for boys of Sixth Form ability, but under sixteen. There, we concentrated on Latin and Greek languages and civilization, continued with English and French and perhaps History, but dropped Mathematics and had no Science. It was a bit lop-sided, but we were well taught. Like Mr. Johnson at Hordle House, Father Felix had a remarkable talent for teaching young boys, but I still found him interesting when I was older, whereas when I met Mr. Johnson later in life, he had lost his magic. Father Felix had a distinctive and quite imitable way of talking. Many did try to mimic him, but there was only one, by far the best schoolboy mimic I have ever heard, who captured his style and mannerisms almost perfectly.

Father Felix rightly felt that I was not fully exerting myself. He sent for me and said, 'Horner, I think you are letting things slide'. (at Ampleforth, boys were addressed by their last name by the masters and by their fellows, and they addressed both monks and laymasters as 'Sir'. I soon found out at home that most priests did not expect to be so addressed.) Father Felix spun out the last word, 'slide', to considerable length and accompanied it with a sliding gesture of his hand. It made an impression on me and led to greater diligence. He was a man of wide and varied interests. One period a week was devoted to what he called 'ology'. In this he would talk about any topic that had caught his interest: a kind of very free-ranging general knowledge, but with no tests attached. He might talk about one of the arts, or natural history, or climate, or politics, or even something scientific, though that was less common. His influence was not restricted to the classroom, which is one of the advantages of a boarding school. He and I sometimes played golf on our local, rough and ready, nine-hole course, and as I was learning at the time to write Greek and Latin verse, I was moved by a victory on the links to address some elegiac verses to him which started:

Haud bonus est golfor golfo quem vincere possum
(He is not a good golfer whom I can beat at golf)

To my chagrin and amazement, at the end of that school year, he was sent to serve on one of the parishes around the country that were staffed by monks from Ampleforth, and I seldom saw him again.

Three of my other most accomplished teachers at Ampleforth were laymen, and yet it was undoubtedly the monks who had the most influence on me, so I should say a little about them. It is hard to express precisely what impressed me, and hard, too, to disentangle the impressions made on me as a boy in the school from impressions made later. There was no monk who struck me then as being egregious, in the literal sense of standing out above the flock. Abbot Edmund Matthews we hardly saw except at Pontifical High Mass on major feasts; Father Paul Nevill, the headmaster, was nearly as remote. He did teach me Victorian history for one year but it was only later that I saw his true greatness. Yet, although I had more very good teachers who were laymen, even as a boy I felt that the laymen were teaching more for the sake of their job and the monks more for the sake of the boys.

I was not spiritually mature enough to appreciate the spirituality of the monks or even to know in what it consisted, but they did strike me as good men, who were in no way phony, 'in whom there was no guile', or, as Samuel Johnson might have said, no cant. Later I would call it a kind of spiritual commonsense, and later still I would see that they were very much in line with the wisdom books of the Old Testament, and that Saint Benedict's Rule is itself very much in that tradition. Having seen them at close quarters in a boarding school, I was never tempted to set them on pedestals, but I did see them as men having likes, dislikes, and needs just as other men do, but trying to be holy in a life that reminded them several times a day that God is the centre of their lives. That perception became clearer as I became older. They were fair, which was very important to me then, and still is. They were versatile, and had a wide variety of talents and interests. It certainly impressed me as a boy that the monks could produce a cricket team that could threaten a strong MCC side, and at rugby could beat the Duke of Wellington's regiment. One of the soldiers was heard to mutter as he left the field, 'Fancy being beaten by a pack of parsons'. He need not have been ashamed.

There were artists and athletes, though more of the latter; musicians and mechanics, though more of the former; those who liked to read and those who did not. Each was different and yet each gave the impression of being very much part of the monastic community. The tale is told that Father, later Abbot, Herbert Byrne was on holiday and spotted a man who, he thought, must be a Jesuit. He approached him and asked, and was delighted to find that he was indeed a Jesuit. His delight was lessened when the Jesuit said to him, 'And you must be from Ampleforth'.

Monsignor Ronald Knox, when he was Chaplain at Oxford, said that if you were holding a dinner you could count on support from Downside boys; if a Mass, Ampleforth boys. That reflects the monks' influence, but perhaps the best summary is that I felt I would be quite pleased to grow up to be like them. The thought of becoming a monk did in fact enter my head, but quickly left again, as I was determined to go to Oxford under my own auspices as a layman, and not as a monk.

At that time, as noted, monks held all the key administrative positions in the school. The headmaster, housemasters, games master (Director of Athletics) and heads of departments were all monks, and major matters of discipline and policy were in their hands, but there was also a monitorial system in the hands of senior boys.

The punishments were of several kinds. For small offences there were lines. One had to write out in large letters twenty or thirty, or even more, lines from some book and hand them in within twenty-four hours. The first time I had to do this, I wrote out twenty lines of Virgil with great care in a rather cramped hand, only to have them contemptuously rejected and doubled as being too short. I was too shy to protest. The second time I was far less careful, far faster, and wholly successful, from which I learnt something, but not what was intended. There were also Penance Class and Detention Class, the former for thirty minutes, the latter for longer. These were for bad work, or bad behavior resulting in bad work, and entailed appearing at a predetermined place and time to do whatever academic work was set.

Finally there was corporal punishment, which had two forms: stick and tanning. Stick was the prerogative of housemasters, to whom boys who misbehaved in class were sent. It was administered with a ferula, a flat piece of laminated leather about fifteen inches long and about half an inch thick. You held out your hands and the housemaster smacked them. It stung for a few minutes. Tanning was much more serious and much less common. It was the prerogative of boys who were head either of the school or of their house (dormitory) and was administered on the backside with a corps cane, or officers' swagger stick.

It was a time when corporal punishment was taken for granted as the way things were. In such circumstances most boys preferred it to a lengthy detention. Anyway I did, partly, perhaps, because I incurred it seldom. I give one example of each kind, stick first: We had for Greek an excellent teacher, Mr. Bamford, who was a product of the famous Manchester Grammar School and spoke with a broad Lancashire accent. A member of the class was translating softly in a low voice. Mr. Bamford said, 'Ah wish tha'd spake oop, Taylor; tha voice is nat'rally low,' making the last word sound almost like 'law'. A few days later the same boy was translating in German class, and I could not resist quoting Mr. Bamford's words and, I hoped, accent. For this I was sent to my housemaster. I told him my tale and he grinned, but I did not escape the ferula. The cause of the tanning was that two of us were accused of fooling around in church at the school Mass. We were talking and giggling and evidently distracting others from their prayers. It did not seem very grave to me, but it did to those who counted, so I received six of the best, and a hard chair was a hardship for a day or two. My psyche was untouched, and I felt no animosity, nor can I remember it having any effect on my future monastic calling, either for or against.

Having been born in late August, I was only just thirteen when I went to Ampleforth and not quite eighteen when I left. I had five years there, and in my last two years, was taught Classics predominantly by two remarkable men, both excellent teachers but in entirely different ways: Walter Shewring and Laurence Eyres.

Mr. Shewring was a man of rather frail physique but of great strength of will and intellect. He could easily have been an Oxford don. I once did a Greek prose for him in which I was evidently over-ambitious. I proudly handed it in. It came back with a single word at the end: 'mephitic'. I had to look that up.

44

Mr. Eyres was quite different. He had served in World War I in what was then Mesopotamia. He was a very good and very steady tennis-player. He was accurate, too, in his teaching and expected the same of us. Later, when I was myself teaching, I asked him whether, for purposes of the School Certificate examination, the Latin adjective, *plenus* (full), could ever be followed by a genitive. All I really wanted by way of answer was Yes or No. I received three typedpages, which listed all the possibilities and illustrated them with quotations in red type, and that was in the days when to type in red you had to alter the setting of the ribbon, and then change it back again when you had finished.

Their teaching took place in the pleasant surroundings of the small, half-paneled, Classics room, furnished with Thompson furniture of solid oak. The paneling had a little ledge at the top, just wide enough for a mouse to run along. There was, too, a mouse that did run along it, sometimes in class-time. We saluted it with a Latin poem, which started:

Musculus hic aderat, seu muscula verius audit?
(A little he-mouse was here, or is it more accurately called a little she-mouse?)

There was also, written on the solid oak table, *Hic dormiebat olim Patricius O'Donovan* (Here Patrick O'Donovan once used to sleep); so we put our knowledge of Latin to practical use. Patrick later became the London *Observer's* correspondent in Washington.

I have mentioned Thompson furniture. Robert Thompson was the village carpenter of a village a few miles from Ampleforth. Soon after Father Paul Nevill became headmaster, he invited Thompson to submit a sample chair for the school library. It had to be boy-proof. Thompson came back with two men carrying a massive throne all of solid oak several inches thick – quite impractical, but undeniably boy-proof. It is still intact in the library over eighty years later. A more practical design has evolved over the years, and Thompson's furniture is now famous throughout England.

With Messrs. Shewring and Eyres, Father Felix and Mr. Bamford, I was very well taught in my field of specialization. This is not to say that I was not well taught in other fields. My comment there is that I studied no Mathematics after my first year and no Science at any time. There was a plan to introduce us to Biology, but nothing came of it. This absence of scientific and paucity of

Under-Officer Horner may be the nearest in the row of three.

mathematical knowledge was quite a disadvantage when I found myself in the Artillery in World War II, but not insuperable. I also acquired a fair reading knowledge of French and an introduction to German, both of which were useful at Oxford and after.

Ampleforth used the monitorial system, which was then normal in Public schools. It gave the boys some practice in the art of leadership. Some learnt from leading their peers, others from being led. House monitors had limited jurisdiction in minor matters over members of their house (dormitory) and school monitors had rather wider jurisdiction over members of the whole school. The head monitor of each house had wider powers within the house, but always subject to the housemaster; the head of the school and school monitors had wider powers over the whole school, but were always responsible to the headmaster. I was head of my house and a school monitor, but never head of the school. In my last year I was quite busy enough. I was preparing to take the scholarship examination for Christ Church, my father's college at Oxford; I was captain of cricket; and an Under-Officer in the Officers' Training Corps (OTC). The last was by accident. The OTC met twice a week. Its officers were monks, but there were from the regular army a Sergeant-Major and an instructor in weaponry to make sure that all was well. The latter was a wonderful example of one kind of teaching in the army. He knew the manual by heart. He was once lecturing on shooting a rifle and aiming off for wind. He started, 'you estimate the wind speed and double it' and so on. At the end he asked one of us how to aim off. The cadet started, 'You estimate the wind speed and multiply it by two'.

'No, sir'.

'But sergeant, that's exactly what you said'.

'No, sir'.

'But sergeant, you said you estimate the wind speed and multiply it by two, you double it'.

'That's right, sir, you double it'. It reminded me of my learning the catechism.

We did a certain amount of drill and a certain amount of theory. As a corporal I was lecturing to my group, as many others were lecturing to theirs, on some rather dull military topic, and the class was laughing and getting somewhat out of hand. At that point the Commanding Officer, a monk who had been in the Grenadier Guards, came into our classroom, stayed for a bit and went away. I thought I would be in trouble and, sure enough, I was sent for. To my amazement the C.O. said, 'I want to congratulate you; you were the only one who seemed to have captured the interest of his class.' This was the accident that led to my promotion to Under-Officer. I think I had already learnt by then to accept undeserved blame, and consequently to accept also undeserved praise.

Each year the OTC was inspected by some very senior regular soldier. I learnt that when standing on parade in the sun for a long time it was possible to avoid the ignominy of fainting on parade by letting circulation come to my heel by raising the heel slowly without disturbing the creases in my uniform. Little did I think that I should find that technique useful some seventy-five years later when concelebrating at Mass.

About that time we all took, and almost all passed, a test in military knowledge called Certificate A. We were told that this would guarantee us a commission if there were ever a war. We did not believe this even at the time, because, had it been true, there would have been almost more officers than men in the army, as most independent schools had an OTC and offered this test, and most boys passed.

The major event of the first term of my last year was the Oxford scholarship examination. When Father Paul, the headmaster asked Mr. Shewring about my chances, the latter replied, referring to two boys who had recently won scholarships to Oxford, 'Horner has less knowledge than A and less taste than B.' In transmitting this opinion Father Paul said, 'Horner has more taste than A and more knowledge than B'. Typical of both of them.

About two months before the examination I caught a severe chill. I tried to ignore it, but after a day or two, I passed out in class and had to recognize that it had developed. It had in fact become jaundice (hepatitis). I spent the next six weeks or so in bed, not in any great pain but with very little interest in anything. At least it meant that, when I went off to Oxford, I was not nervous, but indifferent, and still a bit yellow.

At Christ Church after dinner on the first day of the examinations an Old Boy (alumnus) of Ampleforth took the two or three of us who were from Ampleforth to the buttery and gave us large glasses of port to imbibe. I had a very good excuse for confining myself to just one. Not surprisingly I failed to get a scholarship, but I was awarded an exhibition, which carried less prestige but had the same cash value. As it was my father's college, and I liked the look of it, I accepted readily. I think Father Paul Nevill was disappointed, but I was very content. The London County Council added a very generous award, of which I had to give an annual account. Each year, therefore, I put on my 'poor but honest' suit and trudged off to City Hall. In those days it was possible, though not easy, to live at Oxford and during the vacations for £300 a year.

I remember also one event from the athletics (track) season of that last year. I was standing at a fair distance from another boy who had a javelin in his hand. I challenged him to throw it at me, which he did. I thought I was well out of range, but was mesmerized by the flight of the javelin, which landed about 18 inches in front of my foot.

In cricket, in my third year I was fifteen and should have been still in the Colts, but the school was very short of bowlers, and I was promoted to the First (Varsity) XI, and remained for my last three years at Ampleforth. Our most exciting match was against Durham in my first year. We batted first and made the modest score of 128. I had to bowl the last over with Durham on 128 for nine wickets. Their last batsman lost his nerve, took a wild swipe at the second or third ball and was easily stumped.

In my last year, when I became captain, I noticed that we did not play the Jesuit school, Stonyhurst, the other prominent Catholic boarding school in the North of England. I discovered that in the year before I went to Ampleforth there had been a match in which our umpire was thought to have given a wrong decision, which affected the outcome of the match. The row escalated until Old Boys (alumni) of the two schools would not greet one another when they met, say, in London, and the match was cancelled. This seemed to me disproportionate, and I wrote a one-paragraph letter to my opposite number at Stonyhurst suggesting that we renew the match. He showed my letter, as I am told, to his Games Master (Director of Athletics) who showed it to the Headmaster, who showed it to the Local Superior, who sent it to the Provincial in London. It may even have gone to the Jesuit General in Rome, but in due course back down the chain of command came the answer, 'No'.

Years later, after World War II, when Father, later Abbot, and then Cardinal, Basil Hume was coach of our First XV (Varsity) rugby, we did renew our schedule with Stonyhurst, but only for rugby. The first game was at Stonyhurst, who won. Everyone was being very polite all round, and in showing our team their school they took our boys into the Squire Waterton Museum. Waterton (1782-1865) was an eccentric, adventurous naturalist. In Rome he climbed up to the angel on top of Castel Sant'Angelo, and then up to the lightning conductor above the cross on top of Saint Peter's, and left his glove on it. When the Pope said this might harm the lightning conductor, he climbed up again and removed his glove. He also rode on a crocodile. He collected flora and fauna of all sorts and gave many to Stonyhurst, where he had been educated. Among them were many heads of animals. Father Basil took our team to the bus and said goodbye.

They stopped en route for a meal. At the end of the meal, one of the team asked Father Basil if he remembered the Museum. 'Yes'. 'And all those heads?' 'Yes.' 'Well, one of them is on the bus'. Father Basil headed back to Stonyhurst and, with many apologies, returned the head. They then set off on the eighty miles back to Ampleforth. En route, Father Basil thought he would say the rest of his prayers and reached for his Breviary, which should have been in the pocket of his raincoat. It was not: he had taken their Games Master's raincoat instead of his own. He did not turn the bus again.

In due course the summer term came to an end, and with it my career at Ampleforth. There was no ceremony, no equivalent of the American graduation. We said goodbye and left. Most of us in fact went to OTC camp, and then dispersed. I remember nothing from that summer, but Oxford must have been uppermost in my thoughts.

Six

CHRIST CHURCH

hrist Church was the largest college at Oxford, some four hundred men under graduates. It is noted for Tom Quad (Oxford's largest quad), Tom Tower by Sir Christopher Wren, and Big Tom, the bell that tolls 101 times at 9.05 p.m. Its chapel is also the Cathedral of the Bishop of Oxford, the smallest cathedral in England but far from the least beautiful. The fellows are called Students, and whole college is often called The House and never Christ Church College. It is alleged that a young man of the House was engaged to a young woman who wrote to him at Christ Church College; he said that if she did that again, he would have to break off the engagement. She did, and he did. Perhaps she was lucky.

Our undergraduate body included 'bloods', men whose primary interests were social and sporting rather than academic, but also a great majority who were there to further their education, at least in a broad sense. All this was long before the advent of league tables, so it was hard to compare the men of the House with those of other colleges. Although there were still special links between certain schools and certain colleges, Westminster-Christ Church, Winchester-New College, Eton-Balliol, and others, the university as a whole was already drawing more undergraduates from schools run by the state.

At Oxford, undergraduates live in college for their first two years, and then live out. Cambridge does the opposite. As a freshman I lived in Meadow Building, a Victorian edifice with spacious rooms, high ceilings and a pleasant view over the Christ Church meadows to the Isis, but with no running water. There was a collection of baths on another staircase. On each staircase there was a 'scout', who brought breakfast and hot water, and arranged lunch when one entertained in one's rooms. Lunch was also available in the Junior Common Room and dinner was served in hall. This hall and its kitchens, which are still in use, go back to the time of Cardinal Wolsey (1475-1530). The hall is known for its collection of portraits and for the very beautiful stone staircase, with fan vaulting, by which it is approached. The food was good. There was a special guests' table, where it was

dragon at least eighty feet long on the bed of the trailer. I was fascinated and staring, but two worthy burghers of Oxford were walking ahead of me. One looked up and said quietly, 'there's a dragon.' The other replied quietly, 'so there is' and they resumed their conversation. A slightly similar incident occurred when I was a young monk at Ampleforth. On the lane down to the village was the piggery. I was scratching the back of a pig with my cane, and Mrs. Woods from the monastery kitchen came by. I said, 'I like pigs'. She replied, 'Yes, they are nice, aren't they?'

Seven

CRY 'HAVOC'

I did, however, in the second half of August, take a rest from reading. A friend and I decided to visit Normandy. We were gone for seventeen days, and it cost us less than £10, including the fare across the Channel for ourselves and our bicycles, and a full bottle of Benedictine at the end. Christ Church kindly contributed to my trip, and I drew out of the bank a ten-pound note, which in those days was about the size of a pocket handkerchief, and I had some change left at the end.

I bicycled from London to Newhaven, met my friend, Michael Riddle, and crossed the Channel. We then bicycled round Normandy, visiting cathedrals and cities and Paris itself. We stayed at the *Auberges de Jeunesse* (youth hostels), which were very cheap and where the company was cheerful. On one occasion we bicycled to Chartres on a hot day and on arrival asked if there was a bath. No. A shower? No. Any water? Oh yes, there is a pump in the yard. So we stripped to the waist, took our soap and towel and started to wash as much as we could. We soon saw that the rest of the youth had gathered round to watch, wondering what *ces fous Anglais* (these mad English) were doing. Indeed they asked us as much, and seemed surprised at the answer.

Not quite all our stops were at Youth Hostels. Michael taught at a boarding school on the South Coast of England, to which came a few boys from France. Two of these were sons of M. le Comte de Vogüé, who had invited us to stay. We bicycled in our shorts up the long drive leading to the Château, whose front must have been several hundred yards wide. We were welcomed by the Comtesse and shown to our rooms. Our only luggage was what we could carry on the bicycle's rather small carrier. I think we each had a pair of long trousers but no coat, so we came down to dinner dressed as formally as we could. Behind each chair was a footman with long white gloves waiting for us to be seated. We had soup, with sherry; fish, with white wine; a meat course, with red wine; and then, with the main course, the very best champagne. M. le Comte was a champagne king, and this, he said, was champagne that you could not buy on the market: he kept it for his special friends – and I was lucky enough to be a friend of one of his special friends. It certainly was special, not too sweet, not too dry, but just right. Then we adjourned (the ladies did not withdraw) for coffee and port. When we were all ready for bed, we asked if there was any chance of a bath. There was an ominous silence until Mme. la Comtesse said sadly, 'I'm afraid tonight is the maids' night for the bath.' In all the château there was only one bath.

After that we ate mostly at roadside cafes and drank the local wine, which was almost always good on the spot. We often had to protest that we did not want *bif-tek*. We could get all the beefsteak we wanted in England. One friendly innkeeper wanted to tell us that he had lived in London and had served in the Great War. Would we like to see his wound? As he had been wounded in the hip, we tried to decline, but neither that nor the fact that we were right by the side of the road, could stop him.

We visited many cathedrals, and were surprised how many were in areas still paved with cobble-stones, which a cyclist notices. Rouen, despite all our efforts, we could not see as Monet saw it; Notre-Dame de Paris' lovely rose window was lit by the sun; La Sainte Chapelle was our favorite for a while; Beauvais, even though incomplete, was impressive; and there were others. But none rivalled Chartres in our affection. We first saw it across fields of golden corn in the late afternoon sun. We could only get off our bicycles and gaze. When we reached the cathedral itself, the building, the sculptures and the stained glass left us wordless. We were able then to climb a stairway and emerge not on the top roof but on a lower roof. At various points on our climb we found ourselves face to face with some of the statues and gargoyles, and so were able to study them at very close quarters, and to admire their craftsmanship. As usual, even the parts of them that would not normally be seen were finely finished. We allowed too little time, and had to leave Chartres, longing to stay longer.

We then headed for Paris, where, we had heard, there was a brand new Youth Hostel, all sparkling and clean. The first part was true, but shortly before we arrived, the pipes had become blocked, had backed up, and the place was flooded. Duckboards had been put out, so we only occasionally got wet. The sparkle and cleanliness had gone and did not return during our stay, but at least it was open, and far cheaper than anything else.

We bicycled round Paris, including a circle round the Arc de Triomphe, and visited many of the usual sites. What has remained longest with me is the Jeu de Paume, where the Impressionists were all in one room, and much more compactly displayed than now in the Musée d'Orsay.

Then we wanted to visit Cologne. This was on the 25th or 26th of August 1939. We were completely out of touch with current affairs. We had not been reading the newspapers nor listening to the radio. We went to the appropriate train station and asked what the fare would be for us and our bicycles. The man at the ticket window looked at us strangely and said 'Sir, you should buy a newspaper not a ticket.' We did so, and saw why. The clouds of war were gathering, indeed had gathered, and France was mobilizing for war with Germany. Cologne was on the border with Germany.

We thought better of it, jumped on our bicycles and headed, via Beauvais, Amiens, and Abbeville, for Dieppe. We were in Beauvais on that Sunday and attended Mass in the Cathedral. The Bishop preached a fiery, patriotic sermon on Faith in La Belle France, Hope for the outcome of the war, if there was one, and Love for our soldiers. He concluded his harangue rather incongruously, 'and now let us pray for peace'. We reached Dieppe and, after each of us bought a bottle of Benedictine liqueur for the equivalent of fifty cents, crossed to Newhaven early on the first of September, and bicycled to my friend's home. There we sat and listened to a recording of Mozart's oboe concerto. It was during this that we learnt from the wireless that Hitler had invaded Poland and that the allies had sent him an ultimatum. I presumably telephoned Mother, and then left and bicycled straight to London, where I was now staying with two Quaker sisters, friends of my Aunt Olivia. On September 3 at 11 a.m. Mr. Chamberlain, the Prime Minister, announced in the House of Commons that we were at war with Germany. At 11.15 a.m. the air raid warnings sounded and we all marveled and trembled at this example of German efficiency. We need not have: it was a false alarm, and the 'all clear' sounded after a few minutes. Had we had them, we would all have been running for our gas masks, but they were not issued until a week or two later.

Eight

PHONEY WAR

The outbreak of war posed two related problems: should I volunteer? And, what about Oxford? I did volunteer, I suppose through the Oxford ReserveOfficers' Training Corps (ROTC). The next event makes me blush: Having convinced myself that it was my duty to forward the war effort by doing so, I wrote a letter to the War Office suggesting that my classical brain would be better employed in cryptography or some such than in the artillery. It is just possible that this was true, and several classical scholars were so employed, but I never received a reply. Presumably, some wise old clerk either put my letter in an inactive file, or simply threw it away. Soon after that I received a notice from the Universities Joint Recruiting Board asking me to appear for an interview in Oxford. I came before a board of middle-aged to elderly professors, who must have seen service in World War I. They asked what I wanted. I asked for a commission as an officer in the Royal Artillery.

'Oh, Mr. Horner, are you reading Mathematics?'

'No.'

'When did you last study Mathematics?'

'In my first year in high school' (We reached quadratic equations and the use of logarithms)

'Don't you know that the artillery requires extensive use of mathematics? We think you would be far better suited for an infantry line regiment.'

I was downcast and about to creep away, but fortunately I stayed, and said, 'Well, I am in the artillery ROTC.'

'Oh, are you?'

'Yes, and I did attend camp this summer.'

'Oh, did you?'

'Yes, and I was awarded certificate B.'

'Oh, were you indeed?'

'Yes, and in fact, I am an instructor in the ROTC.'

'Oh really? Well that does make a difference.'

They then put their heads together and came to the conclusion that I could and should serve in the artillery after all. I felt I had had a narrow escape. They said I would hear from the appropriate authority in due course. I asked how due the course might be, and they replied, sagely enough, that this would depend on how the war went, which no one could yet predict.

So I went home and waited. I forget whether the first air raids were during this period before the Oxford term started or afterwards. I was certainly in London for a fair number of them, which occurred while I was staying with the Quaker sisters, who also offered shelter to Jewish refugees from the Nazis. One such refugee, who had come over before the war, managed to make the most extraordinary noises breathing in and out while wearing her gas mask, which she insisted on wearing all the time during a raid. Most of us had the masks with us, but not on. There was, especially until we got used to bombs, a fair amount of tension when we were in our shelter, so her noises either irritated us considerably or reduced us to helpless giggles. As the war went on, many householders built a shelter in their garden. The shelter would not have survived a direct hit, but it did provide protection from blast and bomb splinters. Most shelters had at least a light of some sort and something to eat and drink and read. Some even had cots. After the war, many were converted into potting sheds. The raids were noisy. Three noises remain with me most clearly: the lugubrious wail of the sirens, the hand bells rung in the streets by the air raid wardens, and the whistling of the bombs.

Once the air raid was on a Saturday night. We heard some bombs come whistling down quite nearby, but no explosion. On Sunday morning we looked around but could see no sign of damage. On Monday there was pandemonium: Everyone was told to evacuate immediately as the Bomb Disposal Squad was coming to deal with unexploded bombs (UXBs). They did so, and when it was all over we were allowed back. The two bombs had fallen in the garden of two elderly spinsters three or four houses from ours. When we remembered that there had been no raid on Sunday night, we asked the old ladies why they had not said anything sooner. 'Oh', they replied, 'we couldn't disturb our dear police on a Sunday, could we?' Is that why we won the war, or why it took so long?

I was not in London for the raid when much of The City (the business district) was set on fire. I had three dominant feelings about the raids: relief that there was not more damage done; admiration at the alacrity with which things went on next day – there were signs in shattered shop windows reading

BUSINESS AS USUAL; perplexity at the freakishness of the blast from the bombs. It was like Saint Luke's description of the day of the Son of man, 'Two will be working at the mill: one will be taken, the other left'. The effect on morale was slight compared with that of the V.1s and V.2s later in the war, but by that time I was far from London.

Early in October, the Oxford term started and I duly returned, to find that the university was offering, more or less at once, examinations in an abbreviated form of Honour Moderations in Classics. The normal length of the course was five terms, with examinations around Easter of the second year. I had to decide whether to take the examinations now and have something to show for the work of the three terms of the previous year, or to wait until Easter, complete the full course, and hope that I would not be called up before then. Thinking of the bird in the hand, I chose the less laborious course (less laborious because there was no time for intense last minute preparation), but because of the 'phony war', during which there was no major offensive in France, I could in fact have done the full five terms. One could be awarded a Pass, Honours, or Honours with the Distinction. They kindly gave me the last.

Then the university offered to the majority, who chose as I did, snippets of Greats, the second, seven-term part of the classical course, formally called Litterae Humaniores, but often reduced to Lit. Hum., or Greats. Both the sections I chose were on philosophy, which at that time I preferred to Greek or Roman History. One was on political theory and included Hobbes, Locke and Rousseau, the other on epistemology and included Descartes, Hume and Berkeley. As my tutors in philosophy were Gilbert (*The Concept of Mind*) Ryle and Freddy, later Sir Alfred, (*Language, Truth and Logic*) Ayer, my recent encounter with Saint Thomas Aquinas was well tested. I do remember trying to establish with Freddy Ayer an argument from infinite regress by asking how he came to be. To my surprise he blushed and said, 'Well, er, from my mother, in the usual way, you know'. I went on with 'And where did she come from?' I forget how far we got. I do know I was not satisfied by his final answer, but to my chagrin I cannot remember what it was.

I also started to read Plato's *Republic* with Michael Foster, but he went off to the war before we got very far. I kept on, attending a fine series of lectures on it from Mr. R.C. Cross, of which I took copious notes. At the end of the term, I put them with other notes in my suitcase, which I took down to the porter for delivery to the station, but the suitcase was stolen. The thief must have been nearly as disappointed as I was. There were examinations, too, in these sections, on which we were awarded Pass or Distinction. They gave me the latter.

My second year at Oxford was somewhat unsatisfactory, but this was due to Hitler not to Oxford. It was harder to focus on philosophy when I did not know when, or even whether, I would be called up. One brighter spot was cricket in the summer. I became captain of our rather depleted college team, and was also asked to play for the Authentics Cricket Club, which might be described as Oxford's Varsity squad, and later was made a member. I had promised myself that in the summer of my third year I would try all out for a blue and play against Cambridge at Lord's, the seat of English cricket. But there never was for me that third year. I suspect I would not have succeeded, because, although I was accurate, my spin was not sharp enough, like a pitcher who could throw strikes but without much on them. But I would have enjoyed trying.

Soon after term ended, I bicycled seventy-five miles or so from Oxford to the Forest of Dean in Gloucestershire to work in a forestry camp. A friend, who taught in the City of Oxford High School, was taking some boys to work there and lured me into joining them. We slept in tents, and prepared pit-props. Fellers felled the trees with axes and crosscut saws, then trimmed them and left them for us. We had an instrument called a scriber, with long nails sticking out from it at specific intervals. We started from the base of the tree to where the diameter came down to nine inches. We sawed off that butt and left it. From there the aim was to get as long a piece of trunk as possible with a diameter of not less than so many inches. Possible sizes were 9' by 7", that is 9 feet in length by seven inches in diameter; then 6 ½" by 6 ½". And so on. The adults marked the logs and then joined the boys in sawing and stacking. It was hard manual labor.

At the end of the day we washed as best we could, had dinner and walked down to the local pub, where we drank the local draft cider. That West-country cider is stronger than most beer. A couple of pints of it were enough, and sometimes more than enough, especially if we were playing a treacherous game called Cardinal Puff: I drink to the health of Cardinal Puff; one sip; one tap on the table with one forefinger and then one with the other; one tap with one forefinger on one side of your nose and then one with the other on the other side; and then the killer, half rise from your seat and slump down again once. Next round: I drink to the health of Cardinal Puff-Puff, two sips; two taps with two fingers; and so on. There were penalties, too. It was not always easy to walk home.

It was a hot period of the summer, and one day we were working in an area where there had been a forest fire, and there was a layer of ashes left, several inches deep. They retained and reflected the heat. We had taken off our shirts. Next day I had on my back blisters several inches long. They were not especially painful when I kept still, or even when I moved gently, but sawing was close to agony. In due course they popped, and nothing turned septic.

We had an excellent supervisor. It was said of him that he had once estimated the number of cubic feet of usable timber in a fair-sized wood and had been only nine cubic feet out in his estimate. He must have given the authorities a good report on our work as we were asked back to do another two weeks a little later. That was the time of the retreat, gallant and often heroic, from Dunkerque, but even that prompted no immediate call-up.

At the end of our second stint, my friend and I bicycled up to North Wales to explore Snowdonia. He had to return suddenly and I went on alone, spending the nights in youth hostels, which were clean and had running water, and the days scrambling up the various mountains. Each evening those who had been truly climbing, tramped in with their ropes and climbing irons, exuding moral superiority to us scramblers. But it was otherwise when I walked and scrambled to the top of Snowden and sat down to rest. Out of the mist came a train, which disgorged its passengers into a hut where there were hot refreshments, and I could feel morally superior.

Another day I tried to scramble up the Devil's Kitchen. At one point I came to a difficult part, which took many minutes to climb. To get down meant a perilous leap onto an unsure landing ground, so I knew I could not safely return that way. Unfortunately, when I got close to the top, I could see that cliff was sheer, if not leaning back towards me, and quite beyond my capacity. I had to go back the way I came. It's wonderful what you can do when there is no alternative. When I got back to the youth hostel and said where I had been, they told me that someone had been killed recently attempting that. They added that I should never have gone there alone. True, but I was nineteen and immortal. The immortality stood me in good stead during my military service.

I bicycled back to London for a week or two. I then spent some of the rest of the summer in Kent. It was during the Battle of Britain, so we could see this event in the sky over our heads. We recognized the valor and the skill of the young pilots involved, but not, as I remember, the full import: that on it depended the German invasion of Britain. We certainly did not know how meagre was our equipment, nor how much of it had been lost at Dunkerque. Only later did we hear of the Local Defence Volunteers, or Home Guard, being armed with pikes consisting of a long metal tube with some sort of blade on the end. A single machine gun would have mown them down. Even the following summer, as I was to find out, our artillery on the South Coast was quite inadequately equipped.

Nine

SERVICE IN ENGLAND

The long-awaited letter arrived, and I was summoned to report in October, 1940 to 121 Officer Cadet Training Unit (OCTU) at Alton Towers, a victorian pluto-castle in Staffordshire, which is now a Butlin's Holiday Camp. It was built partly by Pugin. We slept in huts in the grounds but had our meals in the great hall, with a stately wood-burning fireplace. The OCTU had the reputation of being the most gentlemanly of those training officers for the Royal Artillery. The Commanding Officer was a good soldier, an amateur military historian, and had a pack of beagles. I was glad that I had sometimes hunted with the beagles at Ampleforth.

We arrived in the afternoon, and spent the rest of the day drawing uniform, equipment, and bedding and learning what to do with it. The key object was a palliasse, which is a big bag, which you stuff with straw and lie on. We received two blankets, no sheets, and had to improvise a pillow. One could fold, and then interleave, the blankets, it being important to have as much under you as above. Later on, our sergeant came in with instructions for the following day. He said that there would be a test in Trigonometry in the morning, and that those who failed would be RTU. That was the first time we heard that threat, which hung over us all our time at the OCTU. It meant 'Returned To Unit'. I was not sure what that would mean for me, as I had no previous unit.

I kept my mouth shut, and when the sergeant had gone, turned to one of my friends from Oxford and said, 'George, what is trigonometry?' He said it dealt with triangles, and asked me if I could read log tables. Fortunately I could. He then introduced me to SOHCAHTOA, explaining that it stood for 'Sine = Opposite over Hypotenuse; Cosine = Adjacent over Hypotenuse; Tan = Opposite over Adjacent'. I had just enough mathematics to follow that. He said this would enable me to deal with all right-angle triangles. He added that there were also two other rules, Sine and Cosine, but I said they could come later. Come the test, I went in armed with this fragment of knowledge and full of confidence. The first two questions simply tested our ability to read log tables; the next few dealt with right-angle triangles. All those I could answer. Then there were one or two dealing with obtuse-angle triangles. While I was thinking about these, time ran out. I was relieved to learn that I had gained a pass.

We did a fair amount of drill, in the course of which I learnt that the sergeant, who was short, tended to pick on those who were tall; we went for route marches through beautiful countryside; we learnt our gun drill, and enough about mechanics and hydraulics to know why the gun, when fired, recoiled and then recovered; we studied electricity and magnetism and applied the knowledge to our wireless sets. We practised our driving, and as it was a very prolonged, cold winter, we were driving mostly on snow and ice. One of the cadets left the truck with one wheel hanging in midair over a railway cutting. We all had to get out on the landward side. But the only person who hit another car was our instructor. Then we had an introduction to 'Accident Reports'. They almost always started, after the date and time, 'I was proceeding at 15 mph on my own side of the road . . .'

We learnt something about choosing gun positions and observation posts, much about fire orders, but never actually fired any guns. We had one lecture from a cavalry officer, recently converted to tanks. He was very well dressed, had a fine moustache, and started thus: 'I am going to talk to you this morning, gentlemen, about tank-proof localities. A tank-proof locality is a locality proof against tanks.' I remember no more.

When we had time off, we could bicycle over to Dovedale, a truly beautiful valley in the Peak District of Derbyshire, or go out with the beagles, or go for a walk. Once with the beagles on a rainy day, we were on a rough farm lane. I was trying to pass our colonel, slipped on a rut and barged into him, said I was very sorry and ran on. That may have been one of my most significant acts at the OCTU.

After Christmas we were given a weekend off. A fellow-cadet invited me to go with him to visit his family, who lived nearby, where we were regally entertained. When, after five months, our course ended and we were posted to various regiments, we were shown our reports. Mine made no mention of any technical abilities but read in full 'This well-mannered cadet should make a good officer'. Thank God for that rut in the lane.

After a short leave, during which I visited my mother and friends, I reported in May, 1941, to 136 Field Regiment in Sussex on the South Coast as troop

2nd Lieutenant Horner, RA joins 136 Field Regiment, RA on the south coast in May, 1941.

leader of F Troop, its four guns, and about thirty men. It was a territorial regiment from Liverpool, and many of the officers and men had been together for years before the war. It was due to be equipped with 25-pounder gun/howitzers. When I joined, it had the right number of guns, 24, but of the wrong types. Eight were converted 18-pounders, which had been bored out to take the 25-pounder's larger shell of about 3.45 inches diameter; eight were French 75 mm. guns, firing a slightly smaller shell; and eight were ancient 4.5 inch howitzers. Our task was to repel any invasion, and in particular to cover the beaches with fire. Of our 24 guns, eight could fire onto the beaches. The 75s, which were excellent guns, could not do so because of their very high muzzle velocity. If they were to clear the high cliffs on our front, they could hardly land their shells nearer than two miles off shore. The howitzers would have been perfect, except that they had, stamped on the breech-block, FOR DRILL PURPOSES ONLY: NOT TO BE FIRED, followed by a date of manufacture in the 1880s or 1890s. To test them, we took our eight out onto an open space on the South Downs, and put down a round of gunfire. For a troop of four guns, this should fall within a zone 50 to 100 yards wide and perhaps a little more in depth. Ours covered literally miles in each direction. We never even saw some of the bursts. We never fired those guns again, and before long they were replaced.

Then we took our replacements onto the Downs and fired them out to sea. All the officers took their turn, and even some potential officers. One of these was a fine upstanding bombardier (= corporal in the infantry) with a splendid moustache. He looked every inch a soldier, but his looks were his best qualification. There was a wreck not far out to sea, and we had been instructed on no account to hit it. His first round was a direct hit on the wreck. Nonetheless, he was sent to an OCTU, but he did not make the grade. The army, with sensitivity for his, and our, feelings, sent him to another regiment.

We lived in commandeered houses but ate in Mess tents. Each officer had a batman, or soldier servant (the army's phrase), who tended to his personal needs. We spent the days in the normal army ways – parades, inspections, drills, training, maintenance etc., – but each night one officer took three men down to the coast and kept watch in a Martello Tower for a possible, and, at first, quite probable, invasion. These towers had been built early in the nineteenth century so that watchmen could give warning of the approach of any Napoleonic invaders. The towers were sturdy and had, to all appearances,

This is the tower most like ours, but we had a single not quadruple tower, rocks around us, not sand, and no bridge for entry, just a ladder to the opening as in the photo.

survived well. We climbed in by ladder, slept on that floor, and watched, one at a time, from the floor above. The officer usually took the dawn watch. The principal difficulty was keeping awake, but no Germans came. One morning another group woke to see a small fleet anchored in the bay in front of them. They immediately gave the alarm, but it was soon cancelled. It was a group of merchant ships that had sought calm water on a stormy night.

The only other excitement came when the fire we had made spread from the fireplace and set the floor on fire. We managed to beat it out, and just as well, because the twenty-foot outside ladder was taken away by night. We did not set the tower on fire, but had we done so, we would have had a twenty-foot jump onto rocks to reach safety. After that, we hauled in the ladder, and were given some sand and a length of rope.

Our CRA, the brigadier Commanding the Royal Artillery in the Division, came to talk to all his officers. He said this and that, and made a great point of our responsibility for the vehicles in which we traveled. If our vehicle would not start, that was our fault. As I was in charge of our troop's vehicles, I listened closely. He left the lecture, got into his staff car, and it would not start.

Nonetheless, he endeared himself to me by being a keen cricketer. He organized a tournament for the artillery regiments, which our regiment won. The artillery then challenged the rest of the division and beat them. We were then invited to take part in a charity match on the Sussex county ground in Hastings. We had one man who had played in a Test Match for England, one county player, roughly the equivalent of a baseball all-star and a major league player respectively, and then the rest of us. Our opponents also had a Test Match player and a county cricketer, and the rest of them. I only remember that in the first over I dropped a catch off the bat of their Test Match player, later had him dropped off my bowling, and finally caught him by the sight screen (on the track) after he had made a century. The match was drawn.

When winter came and invasion was improbable, we withdrew to Yorkshire and spent a bitterly cold winter in Scrayingham, a small village eleven miles north-east of York and only about fifteen miles from Ampleforth. We were to repeat this procedure, south in the summer and north in the winter, the following year. By now, I was in charge of the vehicles for the whole battery and spent most of that cold winter underneath our vehicles testing the serviceability of the ice-cold prop shafts and other parts. This was the second strain on my scientific knowledge, the first having been at the OCTU in the fields of mechanics and hydraulics, electricity and magnetism. Fortunately engines, controls, and the whole chassis of an automobile were very much simpler then, and the army had a very comprehensive form (1098), which listed all the parts that had to be inspected. Also, I was interested, and had absorbed most of what the OCTU taught us about vehicles.

Besides inspecting vehicles, I had to instruct our recruits how to drive them. Some could already drive very well. I was instructing a young man who was very nervous, and when rebuked became even more so. I took him driving, and for some small error, cussed him out. I then asked him to pull over, and explained to him that officers were going to do this to him, sometimes even unfairly, and he had to get used to it. It was nothing personal, and might be no more than that the officer was having a bad day. We smiled at the end of it, and I think he improved.

Like other junior officers, I had to talk once a week to my troop about current affairs, about which I knew very little. The Army Bureau of Current Affairs produced weekly news bulletins and I simply followed them. Unfortunately one of my men had been a journalist before the war, and knew far more than I did. He was gracious enough not to ask too many difficult questions. Once when our fortunes were low, he asked whether I really thought we would win this war. My opinion was almost valueless, but I answered with great and genuine conviction 'Of course we shall', and I think all my fellow officers would have said the same.

Soon I was moved to Battery headquarters to be Assistant Command Post Officer, because I had impressed the Battery Commander with my mathematical skill. That happened fortuitously. We were out on exercise, knew the map reference of our guns and of the 'target' and had to work out the orders for the guns. The Battery Commander set a bombardier mathematician and me to work. As we were working, there was a loud noise and he was distracted. I was curious too, but went on with the problem. I finished before the bombardier, but our answers did not agree. We checked them and mine was right. I suspect that, had we done that ten times, he would have been right he other nine.

At Christmas, one of the celebrations was a game of soccer, in which the 'other ranks' of the battery confidently challenged the officers. There was reason for their confidence as they had one professional and several other very proficient players. I had attended Mass and arrived just after half-time. Almost as I came on, our centre forward broke away and had a shot at goal. Being, as no one else was, quite fresh I followed him. His shot hit the crossbar and rebounded right at my feet. Quite undeservedly, I scored the winning goal. Not long after that our professional, who had played for a Yorkshire club, was released by the army for several of that club's home games, and some of us were invited by the owners to watch one of their matches. We were seated in the owners' box. To our eyes, our man seemed as nimble as quicksilver on the field, but we heard one of the owners say to another, 'Poor McGarry, the army has really slowed him down.'

During our time in Scrayingham, Field Marshal Sir John Dill, Chief of the Imperial General Staff and our top soldier, was to inspect our Division. Among many other preparations, we re-painted our trucks. Late in the afternoon before the inspection I was checking the trucks and their numbers, freshly painted by our sign-painter, Gunner Jupp, a nice lad from the West Country. To my horror, and fury, a truck that should have borne the number Z 4181425 actually read 5241814 Z. I summoned Gunner Jupp, rebuked him, asked him what he had been thinking of, and told him to re-paint it at once. He completely defused my anger by replying, 'Well, zur, I tell you what: the truck must have been facing the wrong way'. Even at that rather tense moment we all laughed.

We had two major military exercises, one in the Midlands and one in Southern Scotland. Returning from the former, we were on the Great North Road and the three or four inches of snow had been beaten down to ice by the commercial lorries. I was on a motorcycle and trying to move up the column, which meant going a little faster than was safe. I came off and on the slick surface the bike spun round and round, with me attached to it. I was wearing a military greatcoat and the surface offered no resistance, so I was unhurt. Soon after that they decided to put all motorcycles in a big truck, and I spent the rest of the journey in a quad, or gun tractor vehicle, which was warmer and safer. However, it sprang a leak in its radiator and we had to stop in Doncaster to put in more water. The house we stopped at invited us all in for high tea, which was very welcome. They would accept no payment, though I did give them something 'for their children'.

On another occasion, I had to leave my motorcycle propped up by the side of the road while I helped some vehicle in the convoy. While I was away, it fell over and the carburettor leaked, so when I started it, it caught fire. Fortunately I was wearing heavy gloves and was able to beat out the flames before the whole thing exploded. It would have been an ignominious end.

The other big exercise took place in the south of Scotland. We were billeted in farm buildings near Kirkcudbright. I was in a stall next to a powerful bull. During the night he became a bit restive, and started to kick the partition between us. It was clear that he could easily kick it down, and I became a bit restive too, but after a few kicks he ceased, and presumably went to sleep, as did I.

In the spring we went down south again and watched for the Germans, but by then invasion was improbable, though the German barges were still there. It was much like the previous summer except for two incidents, each involving a gunner who happened also to be one of the few Catholics in the troop. The police called one evening to say that they had this gunner in jail in Eastbourne, and would someone come and fetch him. He had been urinating in the street. The army permits you to do this against, if I remember, the rear, near wheel. Our gunner had chosen the wrong wheel, and the military police took him in. I went down, and found him in the furthest cell singing at the top of his voice, 'I am a little Catholic; I love my bloody faith.' I had to assure the officials that, despite all appearances, he was a respectable citizen and that I would take him in charge.

The other incident was not so easy. The same gunner was the driver of one of our 15-hundredweight trucks. He and some others were out driving on the Seven Sisters, high chalk cliffs on the coast. To drive across them parallel to the sea was like a switch-back, or roller-coaster. He had left the truck facing down the slope not in gear but with the brake on. The brake had failed, the truck went down the slope, partly up the other side, hit a rock and fell over the cliff into the sea. I was not there. The Battery Transport Officer called me, said what had happened and asked me to do something about. He had been giving me some trouble and I thought he was pulling my leg, so I hung up. But it was true, and trucks at that time of the war were not only costly but rare.

Next day we took a crew with an acetylene torch, a boom and pulley, and so on. One party set up the boom on the cliff above the truck while the rest of us drove on till we came to a place where we could get down to the shore. But the place was also a minefield. There was, however, a light railway running through the minefield, and we saw some men pushing a light truck along it. We followed them, turned along the shore and reached our vehicle, which, with the acetylene torch, we divided, like Caesar's Gaul, into three parts. These we sent up by the pulley. But all this took time, and by the end the tide had come in and cut us off. The only way back to the world was up the two hundred foot cliff.

First we sent the cylinder of compressed air, hoping it would not fall and explode, and then ourselves, one by one. None of us knew anything about rappelling, so our ascent was not elegant, but we all reached the top safely. I was the last to leave, by which time the tide was over my ankles. We then had to face the question, why the brake had failed. I had inspected the vehicle, spotted and reported the weakness, and so we were in the clear.

Later that summer we went to Larkhill, the artillery training headquarters on Salisbury Plain. It was after Dunkerque, and so the emphasis was on speed rather than on total accuracy. We did not use live ammunition. My troop was moving from one position to another. The guns arrived, but the signals and headquarters truck with all the instruments of accuracy did not. I was on my motorcycle. Bearing in mind the need for speed, I used my oil compass, to give the guns their zero line. When our Regimental Sergeant-Major, arrived, he asked how I had laid out the guns. I said I had done it with my compass. He was of the old school, snorted at such inaccuracy, and checked the angle with the proper instruments. To his chagrin, I was about half a degree out of 360 from the true line.

In due course we returned north. Shortly after we arrived, I was sent for a six weeks Signals Course to the Signals Corps Headquarters at Catterick. I am grateful now to the Army for filling in these gaps in my scientific knowledge, but I was not grateful at the time. But, knowing that I would be responsible on my return for the signals efficiency of the battery, I applied myself, and was rewarded with the top grade of D (Distinguished) at the end of it. I then trained up our signallers to a high degree of theoretical proficiency, but when we went for our first exercise, it was a shambles. Gradually they increased their practical proficiency, and we had a good outfit. I remember now little of what I learnt then, except the morse code and $E = I \times R$, but I still have a very clear picture of young women in the Auxiliary Territorial Service being trained at Catterick to drive three-ton lorries. There were at least ten lorries stationary at the road-side. The Instructor gave the sign for them to move. They must all have let in the clutch with a bang, and all ten lorries started to hop forward, almost in time with one another.

Ten

BOUND FOR THE EAST

There followed a trying time of rumors: we received a warning order that we were to embark for service abroad, but, after we had sent off our guns, it was cancelled. That was just as well, as our guns arrived in Singapore just in time to be captured by the Japanese. In the end we did embark in the *Mooltan*, on January 14, 1943. The *Mooltan* was a vessel commandeered from the P. & O. line and converted into an Armed Merchant Cruiser. She had two nineteenth century six-inch guns mounted at the stern and several excellent

P&O liner Mooltan, converted to armed merchant cruiser, took us from Liverpool to Bombay.

Oerlikon 20 mm. anti-aircraft guns. Her length was 625 feet, her top speed sixteen knots, her capacity between 700 and 800 passengers. There were nearly 5000 of us on board. The single cabins now had four officers in them, but that was nothing compared with the conditions below decks. The total capacity of all the lifeboats was 1500, and we thought there might be rafts etc. for another 1000, enough for about half of us. Initially there were twenty-nine ships in the convoy, but some left us at Gibraltar, and more at Capetown. We finally disembarked at Bombay on March 19, but much happened before that.

As the ship was being loaded at Liverpool with our guns and the limbers that carried the ammunition, the door of one of the limbers swung open, revealing the live ammunition. The longshoremen at once stopped working and demanded danger money. This did not sit well with us, who worked daily with these dangerous objects.

Once we sailed, our first threat was not from U-boats but from the ocean. We steamed into a major North Atlantic storm, which lasted for several days, and by which even the regular seamen were impressed. I remember being on the top deck and being able to see water above me all the way round. The tops of the biggest waves crashed over our bow. One evening during the height of the storm I was duty officer and was walking rashly down the deck on the windward side when a monster wave flooded the deck and sent me rolling toward the side. Providentially there was a rail, and I was wearing an army greatcoat, so I was not swept overboard nor was I soaked to the skin. I clung to the rail, and when the wave had passed over me, fled to the other side. There I saw the ship next to us apparently coming straight at us. I watched for a while and wondered whether to tell those on the bridge. At first I thought there was no point, as they must have seen it. Then I thought that, if by some chance they had not seen it, it would be very stupid, not to say fatal, to be responsible for a collision in a storm at sea. I went up to the bridge, and partly to my relief and partly to my horror, they said, 'Oh yes, her steering gear was disabled yesterday by the storm.' She never hit us, and when the storm finally abated, her steering gear was repaired.

We soon came to our first port of call, Freetown in Sierra Leone. We anchored about a mile off shore in a large bay, out of range of land-based mosquitoes, and were there for two days, but without shore leave. It was hot, humid and windless. We were happy to get back to our ocean breezes.

After that on our way to the Cape of Good Hope, we spent one day making a full circle to avoid German submarines. Our six-inch guns had a little target practice, but the target was unscathed. So were we, thanks to the vigilance of our naval escorts and their airplanes, and this although there was one pack of five U-boats operating around the Canary Islands and another of six around the Cape at about the times when we were steaming through, in addition to a lone German cruiser in the South Atlantic.

We crossed the equator without any festivities, partly because we did not know where it was and no one told us, but there were numerous other activities, some instructional and some not. We learnt to use the heliograph, a device using the sun and mirrors to communicate up to considerable distances by morse code; there was a course in unarmed combat in which we were shown a potentially lethal handshake, one or two other lethal tricks, and how to disarm a man attacking you with a knife. I had no occasion to use them during the war, and since then, although as a monk and schoolmaster I have been tempted, I have not yet succumbed.

There was also bingo, bridge and on some evenings a concert. I was passing a bridge table in the officers' dining room at which sat our colonel, second in command and adjutant looking for a fourth. They asked if I played bridge, and when I rashly said 'Yes', they invited me to sit down. All went reasonably well until the man on my left opened with one spade, which, with all the surrounding chatter, I did not hear. My partner continued with two hearts, which, I took for a forcing two, meaning, in those days, a very strong hand. I had a good hand too. We reached a slam in hearts, doubled and redoubled, and went about six down. My truthful excuse that I had not, because of all the noise going on around us, heard the opening bid was not well received. I was not asked again, nor would I have accepted again. Thereafter I tended to spend the evenings on deck watching the spectacular displays of summer lightning and wondering how the four stars of the Southern Cross could be so enchanting.

It was not long before we reached Capetown and had the famous Table Mountain on our port side and spouting whales and flying fish to starboard. Half our convoy left us, and we steamed on to Durban, where we had several days of extremely welcome shore leave.

We walked into one hotel for lunch and found in the middle of the table a bowl piled high with fruit. As there had been strict rationing in England for some time, we assumed that they were of wax, but they looked very real. Eventually one of us took one, felt it, and bit gingerly into it. It was real.

The next day, two of us took the train towards Pietermaritzburg. It was a steep climb up into the hills of the beautiful hinterland, and the curves were tight. It was the first time I had seen the tail of a train I was in level with the carriage I was in, but going in the opposite direction. Our short stay in Eden came to an end, but as we left the harbor, the Lady in White (Mrs. Gibson) sang farewell songs to us, moving some to tears.

Eleven

WE TRAIN FOR THE JUNGLE

We arrived at Bombay on 18 March 1943, and had a day of shore leave. I remember the heat – each time we thought it could not get any hotter, it did – the smell, and my nearly paying a rupee for a daily paper which cost one anna (there were 16 annas in a rupee). We returned to the ship almost with relief. Next day we disembarked and got on our train for Ahmednagar, a hundred miles or so inland from Bombay. It was a military encampment with tents, mess halls, facilities, parade grounds, and so on, and a large number of civilians around all the time. There we met and killed our first snakes, a cobra and a krait, both poisonous; we found a scorpion in one of the beds, and learnt that it was wise to tap on the ground the heel of any boot we were to put on, in case there was a scorpion inside. After the war, it was over a year before I shed the habit, so much had it become a routine. We were robbed by kite-hawks. These large birds, with a wingspan of around four feet, were amazing aerobats. We had to pick up our meals from the cookhouse, and then walk across an open space to the mess-tents. At our first breakfast more kites got fed than men as the kites swooped down and snatched the food off the plates, hardly brushing the men.

There were medical parades for inoculations, for which needles were in short supply. This meant that, although the needles were disinfected between stabs, the same needle had to serve up to one hundred men. It was worth being up in the front of the queue. I have seen tough sergeants faint at the sight of the needle. Even so, the inoculations were worth it. There were also quinine pills, mepacrine, and later quinacrine, to prevent malaria. The pills were unpleasant but the malaria was much worse. Not to take them and not to make sure your mosquito-net was securely in place with no mosquitoes inside, were penal offences. Prickly heat, an intense itch caused by clothing rubbing against sweaty parts of the body, could not be prevented by any pills, and there was ringworm too. We were warned to drink liquids, especially hot liquids, to keep us sweating and for 'loss of heat by evaporation'[3], and to eat salt, as guards against heat-stroke and heat-exhaustion. Even so, some succumbed. Popular liquid was provided by the char-wallahs, or tea people, who carried on their backs great urns of scalding, sweet tea.

I learnt here that for communication in a foreign language grammatical and syntactical accuracy were desirable, but confidence trumped them both. I wanted someone to tell the water-carrier that I needed some hot water for a bath. I found an Indian soldier and said to him, halting between words, '*Bhistiko bolo ke sahibko kuch garam pani chahiye guslkewasti*'. (Tell the water-carrier that the Sahib needs some hot water for his bath). The man looked blank, so I repeated it. Blank again. A British Sergeant of many years in India came by and asked if he could help. He said with great confidence and little regard for grammar '*Bolo* the *Bhisti* to *pakkaro* some *pani jeldi*' (tell water-carrier bring water quickly). The soldier said '*Thik hai, sahib*' (OK, sir) and rushed off to do it. The key words plus conviction did the trick.

More important than all this, we were reunited with our guns, and were able to do some training with them, but if they were out in the open sun, they soon became too hot to touch. After six weeks of fairly gentle introduction to army life in India, we entrained again for the journey of about five hundred miles to Chhindwara, in the central plain nearly half way between Bombay and Calcutta. Train journeys in India were then, and may still be, quite different from any in England or US. There was an unhurried air about them. Whenever we stopped, enterprising soldiers jumped out, rushed up to the engine and asked for boiling water to make tea. Early each morning, stewards came round to take the officers' orders for breakfast. These were telegraphed ahead to the next stop, where the train paused for an hour while we went and ate what we had ordered. I suppose the same happened for the other meals, but I remember it only for breakfast. When we arrived at Chhindwara, there were many Indians squatting on the platforms, with both their feet flat on the ground, a position that most Europeans find almost impossible. They were waiting for the next train. When we asked when the next train was due, we were told 'tomorrow'.

We joined the Seventh Indian Division, which consisted of three infantry brigades, each of three battalions, one British, one Indian and one Gurkha. We had one Indian and three British artillery regiments, and the majority of the

---

3. *The army was good at coining such sound bites. Another was that hand- grenades had 'segmentation for fragmentation'.*
See also page 144.

other units were Indian, but mostly with British officers. Of the top British officers the General, the Chief of the Artillery, the Chief Administrative Officer, and either the Chief Engineer or the Chief Signals Officer were Catholic, so we were sometimes referred to as the Pope's Own Division. The divisional badge was the golden arrow, which we came to wear with great pride. I think it was at Chhindwara that I was put in charge of a store to supply our battery with soap, sweets (candy), tobacco, etc. I was told to keep the accounts in the double entry system. Someone explained this to me, and I followed exactly what he said. At the end of a week or two, my account book showed a profit of about 50%. The cash box did not. I was fired, which was fine by me.

Our guns had rejoined us but our vehicles had not, so any training was done on foot in an area where tigers, bears, ferocious wild pigs, snakes, and scorpions were common – it was in fact the country depicted in Kipling's Jungle Books. If we had had transport, it would have been a very good area for training, but we were not to be there for long. It was long enough, however, for us to meet our new General and our new CRA (Commander, Royal Artillery). The latter was one of very few senior artillery officers of the Territorial Army (National Guard) who not only retained his rank but was promoted during World War II. The meeting with him was momentous for me. He met each officer individually, shook his hand and asked where he went to school and university. In my turn I answered, 'Ampleforth and Christ Church'. There was no comment, but when he got back to HQRA (Head Quarters Royal Artillery), he sent for his Brigade Major, who had had the same education, and said, 'There's a young man in 136 Field Regiment who went to Ampleforth and Christ Church, just like you.' Before too long I was transferred to HQRA. My Battery Commander wanted to forward the career of another officer, who was a regular soldier and to send him, but he was overruled. I was not sorry, as my superior officer at the time was one of only two men that I met in the whole course of the war whom I really disliked. I owe it to him to add that he gave me one of the best pieces of advice I have received, 'Never be rude on paper: if you have to be rude, be rude verbally, face to face. What you write may seem very clever and appropriate at the time, but if read years later, when all the circumstances have been forgotten, it will look simply ill-bred.'

But first we completed another train journey, this time of six hundred miles to Ranchi, another military base, and within two hundred miles of Calcutta.

Soon after our arrival there, we were told that the monsoon was approaching and therefore we should dig a trench eighteen inches wide and equally deep all round each tent. Some thought that excessive, but when the monsoon broke, those who had skimped had their tents flooded. I had never seen rain like that in even the severest thunderstorm in England, or since in the United States.

My transfer to HQRA as Assistant Staff Captain took place almost at once after our arrival in Ranchi, and carried with it promotion from Lieutenant to Captain, and a little more pay. One advantage of being in the Indian Army was that we were on Indian Army rates of pay, which, though still below those of most of our allies, were higher than the British Army's. It was quite a switch from gunners, guns, vehicles and wireless sets to files and telephones; and also to inspecting rather than being inspected. The Brigadier was a man whom I very quickly came to admire greatly, and his Brigade Major, the Amplefordian, was a hearty extrovert, who played rugby at Oxford, came within a hairsbreadth of getting a blue, and who became a lifelong friend. I learnt a lot from each of them, but especially from Brigadier Tim Hely. who made it very clear that the job of the staff was to guide and serve the troops, and not to boss them around; a useful principle not only for staff officers, but also for headmasters and pastors. While we were at Ranchi, I also learnt to like two new fruits: mangoes and litchis, especially the former.

At Ranchi, an elderly, bearded, Belgian Jesuit had charge of the Catholic parish. The church was pleasant, with a dirt floor. There were no pews, but at Sunday Mass, chairs were put out by the Communion rail for the four of us from HQRA. Men were on one side of the church and women on the other. All sang all through Mass what must have been a Litany. I could catch only the word *Swami* (*Lord*). At first it was distracting, but gradually became for me prayerful and meditative.

Our time at Ranchi was our first opportunity since we had been in India for real training, and lasted for about three months. We knew by then that we were bound for the Arakan on the north-west coast of Burma, so we had to learn all we could about jungle warfare as quickly as we could. Our General, Frank Messervy, endeared himself to us at a meeting of his officers by asking if anyone knew anything about Jungle warfare. Nobody did. 'Neither do I,' he said, 'so we shall learn together'. He had been captured in North Africa by the Germans and had ripped off his badges of rank. When asked why he was still

80

a private at his age, he said his general had a grudge against him. They took him off in a truck, but he jumped out, rolled into a ditch, and escaped.

My duties as Staff Captain included legal matters, for which my only training was that my father was a barrister. One case concerned a gunner who had spoken unprintable words to his sergeant. As I read the papers, I noticed that one witness said this had happened on such and such a day, another witness, on the day after. I sent the case back to his regiment and, no doubt to everyone's relief, it was dropped, and they could turn to matters of more pressing concern.

While we were at Ranchi, and as we were clearly soon to go into action, I was given two weeks leave and went to Delhi, where successive conquerors, including the British, had built edifices that were intended to impress, and on the whole I was impressed. But I was also chagrined to learn later that I had been within 120 miles of the Taj Mahal and had not visited it.

Just as I was becoming accustomed to the new job and surroundings, I was posted again, since there was no mention of an Assistant Staff Captain in the War Establishment for an artillery headquarters. I was sent off to Divisional Headquarters as a Liaison Officer on the Operations staff. Almost immediately afterwards, we received orders to make for Madras by train, and there embark for a short sea journey across to Chittagong, north of the Arakan. We embarked without difficulty but were somewhat apprehensive on the journey, since we had little naval and no air escort on the way and knew that the port of Chittagong had been subject to Japanese air attack.

We arrived in Chittagong at night, and the ship was unloaded at night, presumably because of the threat from the air. I was somehow involved, but had little idea of what was going on, and the same was true the next day, when we met a train with more of our stores, and had an equally chaotic unloading. Had I followed the rule for a young officer and asked the advice of the sergeant, the chaos might have been less. I felt badly when it turned out that the portable altar set of our Roman Catholic chaplain had been damaged.

We were now a little over one hundred miles north of our destination, and for the rest of the way we traveled by road, that is, over an earth surface with many potholes. The surface also rapidly became corrugated because once there was any unevenness, the trucks, especially the bigger ones, would bounce and so enlarge and extend the unevennesses. Nonetheless the journey was pleasant: we stopped for a day or two at a camp by the sea and were able to stretch our

The singer, Dame Vera Lynn, DBE, the "Forces' Sweetheart," successfully entertains troops in the Arkan in NW Burma within a mile or two of the front line.

legs and swim in the sea, which we all enjoyed except a quartermaster sergeant who was stung by a jellyfish, and was laid up for a couple of days.

In due course we reached Bawli Bazaar and went on to set up our temporary headquarters a little south of that. During our brief stay, Vera Lynn came and sang to us in a *basha* (bamboo hut) within a mile or two of the front line. She was deservedly called the forces' sweetheart. It was also from Bawli that Colonel Wagstaffe, my best battery commander when I was still with 136 Field Regiment, was sent home. He had been in India before and contracted most of the local diseases. The doctors in India sent him back to England and told him, for medical reasons, never to return to India. He did return, but the diseases won: he was within easy range of the Japanese, climbed out of his slit trench one night, waved a lighted cigar at the Japanese and challenged them in picturesque language to shoot at it, which they did. We did not remain at Bawli long, and I remember only three events from that time.

I was sent to meet a VIP from Delhi to bring him to our headquarters. I took a jeep to Bawli Bazaar, but just north of the village was a river. There was no bridge and no power-boat apparent. I asked the engineer in charge for a boat for the VIP, and he replied that the only boats were the local sampans. In my innocence, I believed him, and even thought that the VIP might rather enjoy and appreciate the skill of the boatmen. I hired two sampans, crossed the river and waited. In due course the VIP and his retinue appeared, and I explained the situation. Grumpily they got in. When we were half way across, the engineers chose that moment to cross in front of us in the only power-boat within miles. I was annoyed with them and the VIP was annoyed with me.

The second event involved what was rather grandly called the Goppe Pass, which ran east and west over the Mayu Range and came down on the east nearly into the Kalapanzin River. The pass was an earth track traversing the dense jungle of the Mayu Range. From almost sea-level, it climbed about 2000 feet over the range. Men and mules could cross, but no vehicles. Our chief medical officer was an Indian full colonel from the Punjab, who prided himself on his walking. He established his record for the walk, and I set out to beat it. I was successful, and also wise enough to keep my time to myself. After all, he was a full colonel.

The third event was that I had a very mild attack of malaria, but it was unpleasant enough that I became scrupulous about taking our daily ration of mepacrine. It was also drilled into us again that if at night you heard a mosquito inside your mosquito net, you did not go to sleep until you had destroyed it. I never had malaria again.

The terrain needs some description. We were then just west of the Mayu Range and advancing to the south. The mountains ran north and south, and the rivers flowed south. Some way off on our west was the Bay of Bengal. Between the Bay and us was flat marshy land, then the river Naf. Between the Naf and the Mayu Range was a mile or two of flat land, then the Range, dropping on its east to the valley of the River Kalapanzin. On the far side of that were more flat land, mountains, the River Kaladan and then still more mountains. The flat lands were mostly paddy fields, but there were occasional ridges of higher ground, which, like the mountains, ran north and south. The ridges and mountains were covered with dense jungle. If you had to make your way into the jungle at its thickest, you could, with a machete, (which we rhymed with hatchet) cut your way in at the rate of about two hundred yards an hour. We and the Japanese both kept mostly to the jungle on the higher ground by day, and patrolled both the jungle and the flat ground by night. The Artillery, and, *a fortiori*, Divisional Headquarters, were spared this patrolling. But as we had arrived during the monsoon, activity of any kind was at a minimum, with each side preparing an offensive for as soon as the monsoon was over.

Twelve

ACTION IN THE JUNGLE AND BEYOND

Our whole division soon moved east over the Mayu Range into the Kalapanzin Valley, leaving the Fifth British Division on the west of the range. In the valley, when we first moved over, there was no mechanized transport and no electricity except what our generators provided for our signaling equipment. This meant that stores and equipment were carried by mules, and if you needed to go anywhere, you either walked or rode a horse or went by sampan, a small boat that was a cross between a punt and a large canoe, propelled by a single oar at the stern. The boatmen were skilful but not speedy, a few knots downstream and one or two upstream. All cooking was over a fire and lighting was by oil lamps with a hurricane *batti* (Coleman lamp) in the lucky office-tents. Because of the mosquitoes, ticks, and leeches, and despite the heat, we wore bush-coats, or olive-green battle-dress with long sleeves and tucked in at the ankles, and had to dye our underwear and everything else olive green. We never wore shorts nor went about in shirt-sleeves, and invariably slept under a mosquito net. We had collapsible, canvas camp beds, and often put the legs in tins filled with kerosene as a guard against ants. We had also collapsible canvas baths and basins. One's orderly brought hot water for these. We had a cook, an Afghan rogue, whose name was Dhost Mahommed (friend of Mahommed). He used henna to dye his beard orange. Give him all the ordinary facilities and he would produce a very ordinary meal. But let there be pouring rain, and us in the jungle with the bare minimum of equipment, and he would go out and catch some jungle chicken, dig a trench to act as an oven, somehow light the wet wood, and produce a banquet.

We took a variety of precautions against leeches, which, if you were walking along a path in the jungle, heard the footsteps or sensed the vibrations and hurried down to the ends of the branches to meet you. Mostly they were small, an inch or so long, but they could suck quite a lot of blood. There were leeches, often much larger, in the streams, too. One such invaded Major Leach when he was swimming. He became known as Major Leech-Leach, or the

Hyphenated Major. Whenever I took a bath (in the canvas basin about thirty inches square), I made a careful inspection of my body for leeches and ticks, and burnt them off. Ticks you could also smear with margarine or ghi (Indian butter) and wait for them to come out for air. It was not good to pull off either leeches or ticks, as then they left their heads in you to go septic. The weather was hot and humid, the rain torrential, but not so severe as it had been at Ranchi.

Our headquarters were tucked into the eastern foothills of the Mayu Range. We walked in single file along the path leading to the area because that was the width of the path and there was dense jungle on either side. We were concerned when at one point we found in the middle of the path a one-foot-high pile of elephant droppings, still warm. We hoped the beast would keep going, as there was no room to pass. When we needed to turn off the path, we had to hack our way, which was when we learnt how far you could hack in one hour. For each office we had either to find a level patch or, more often, dig one into the side of a slope. This was good exercise and kept the perspiration flowing, always hygienically, though not socially, desirable in hot weather. For cover, we stretched tarpaulins over the spaces where we worked, ate and slept. At this stage, we had camp beds and other camp equipment. We were soon to lose those, and then we slept on the ground, always scooping out a hollow for the hip bone, and washed and bathed as best we could, until we recovered some of our equipment.

We arrived during the monsoon and the ground was soaked, so the main aggressive activity was patrolling, resulting sometimes in fire from artillery or mortars. This period lasted for nearly six months, and during it I was promoted from Liaison Officer (or dog's body) to GSO III O (CW)[4]. This stood for General Staff Officer of the third (and lowest) grade for Operations and Chemical Warfare. Somehow CW was extended to include camouflage. Gas was never used either against or by us, and camouflage was not much of a problem in the jungle. There was one rumor of a gas attack, but otherwise I was entirely involved with Operations.

The most significant event during this lull was the visit of Lord and Lady Louis Mountbatten. He was the Supreme Allied Commander, South-East Asia (SACSEA). Our Fourteenth Army had been on the retreat from the time of

4. *A Division's Operations staff consisted of a GSO I (Lt-Colonel); a GSO II (Major); a GSO III, Operations and a GSO III Chemical Warfare (both Captains). There was a similar staff for the Intelligence branch.*

Lord Louis Mountbatten addresses troops from the top of the 40-gallon oil-drum he asked for.

the fall of Singapore in February, 1942, and it was now September 1943. The morale, at least of those who had been continuously retreating, was low. Lord Louis came round to change that. Churchill had, by words, changed the spirit of Britain three years earlier; Lord Louis and General Slim did much the same for us. Lord Louis made a point of wanting to be informal with no elaborate preparations, 'just an oil drum or two to stand on'. So we gave him just that. I think he was a bit miffed, but he could hardly complain at getting what he had asked for. His best line was, 'Just let me know what you need, and I'll send a telegram to my cousin the King, and we'll fix it'. We all knew that those two could do nothing, but the bravado gave us heart and the troops loved it. His wife, who took a keen interest in medical supplies, had a very good reputation for sending the troops what she was asked for. We complained about the abundance of soya links, a type of ersatz sausage, and they got them removed from our rations. Their visit was a great success.

Meanwhile both sides were planning an offensive for as soon as the monsoon ended. During this period, the Engineers improved the Ngakyedauk Pass (known to the troops as 'Okeydoke') over the Mayu range into the Kalapanzin Valley. We then moved over into that valley. What had been little more than a mule path, the Engineers made temporarily passable for tanks. One troop of tanks came over; they were to be invaluable.

As the monsoon petered out, the Japanese got their offensive in first by a day, and we awoke very early on the morning of February 5, 1944 to find ourselves with Japanese to our rear and on one flank, as well as in front. We dressed very rapidly, left everything behind, and escaped with General Messervy by the back way out. One quick-witted officer went back and destroyed as many of our files as he could, then left by the front way in and met no Japanese, but one of our tanks, which took him on board. The rest of us climbed up a narrow path and were shot at. The bullets coming through undergrowth and bamboo made an astonishing, and quite unfamiliar, noise. No one was hit and we went on uphill and down, sometimes quite difficult going even for the young and agile.

After several miles we came to a chaung (stream) which led to what came to be called the Administrative Box, or Adm. Box, where all stores and supplies, including food and ammunition, were kept, and maintenance was done. We waded down the chaung and eventually came to that area; but we did not know whether the Japanese had already arrived there. When we reached a place where it was possible to climb out of the chaung, I volunteered to do so. I was wearing rubber-soled shoes, which, being wet, gave me no traction and I got stuck half-way up. Someone else who, like a good soldier, was wearing his boots. climbed up easily and gave the all clear. I was left looking foolish, and cowardly. Picturesque but untrue legends grew about our escape: that the general marched down the chaung in his pyjamas with a grenade in his hand and his hat at a rakish angle, and so on.

Our other two brigades – the third was mostly in our box – had also formed themselves into boxes for all round defense, but did not know where we were. We were soon able to organize a makeshift system of communication, and told them that we were alive and well. We set up the rudiments of a headquarters, but while we were doing so, a Japanese fighter, a Zero, dived towards us. It was only when I saw spurts of dust from the path on which I was standing that I realized that it was an enemy plane and was firing at us, and I had better stand aside. The only casualty was a wounded mule, which I had to finish off with a shot from my revolver. By chance someone had told me that in such a case one should imagine a line from each ear to the opposite eye and put the bullet at the intersection. Fortunately, with very rare exceptions, we had complete command of the air.

We also had to provide ourselves with somewhere to sleep. This meant digging a slit trench for two, with room for one man to sleep somewhat curled up while the other stood on guard at one end. There was a small chaung and ravine between us and the Japanese, and they were thirty to fifty yards away from our slit trench. There was plenty of Japanese firing that night, but, to our surprise and relief, no attack. The Japanese had either a good English speaker or, possibly a prisoner under duress, who kept calling out, 'Sergeant Smith, Sergeant Smith, come and help me; I'm wounded'. This was eerie and nerve-wracking, and was part of the attempt by the Japanese to locate our positions.

It seemed odd that there was no actual assault that night, but the Japanese had no idea how many of us there were, and may have been in no hurry, since up to that time, every allied formation that they had surrounded had in due course surrendered for lack of food and ammunition. We were able not to do so, because General Slim, who commanded Fourteenth Army, had foreseen this and had arranged for supply by air to any troops in our predicament. Very soon supplies came to us by Dakotas (DC3s), some flown by the Royal Air Force but most by the United States Army Air Force. To those intrepid pilots and crews, flying low through mountainous country and often in bad weather and poor visibility, we owe our lives. A few days later, our fighters gave us a grandstand view of their dive-bombing of a high point in the Mayu range that seemed to be serving as a Japanese observation post.

That first night there was much firing, and the Japanese had bullets that made a crack when they left the rifle and another later if they found no target. Thus it sounded as if they were all around us. Those bullets doubled the noise and the scariness. It was an uncomfortable night.

In an account published in England in the Northern Edition of *The Daily Mail* on June 23, 2001 during a Burma reunion at Blackpool, John Leyin wrote, 'The opening attack was an eruption of unbridled violence so intense that my mind could barely cope. Curtains of tracer bullets poured out of the darkness from seemingly every angle, mortar bombs rained down and the earth shook with the explosions of screaming shells.'

It was risky and pointless to fire back because we knew the positions neither of the enemy nor of our own troops. Nor did we want to give away our own positions. The Japanese had at least one piece of artillery – 105 mm we thought – but must have had little ammunition, as they fired it only at dawn and dusk. On one occasion I was passing a row of empty metal oil-drums when a shell landed a little way off. I thought I heard shell-splinters hitting the oil-drums both ahead of and behind me. I also thought it would be bad for morale to be seen running for cover. I soon learnt better.

We survived the night, and next day established a rather ramshackle command post, with a wireless set, in a bren-carrier, a light, armored, tracked vehicle with half-inch steel sides and floor. From this we made contact with the brigades each evening. It was thought that my voice penetrated the Burmese evening static well, so this was usually my task, until the General wanted to speak. A little later on in the siege, I was in the middle of a transmission, when there was in my headset the very loud noise of an explosion nearby. As there was nothing I could do about it, and as I was still alive, I continued with what I was saying. But I was eager to have the General take over and to discover what had happened.

I was told that a small missile had indeed exploded right under our bren-carrier, but had not been able to pierce its armor. So we joined the fairly small group of those who have been within a foot or two of an exploding missile and been unscathed. It must have been a very small shell, but it was appreciably more than a bullet.

We were in a very unsatisfactory position as there was high ground all round us, either the Mayu mountain range or little conical hills. The Japanese naturally tried to occupy these, and our infantry had to charge uphill again and again to dislodge them, but besides our British infantry, we had the first, and presumably best, battalion of the Sikh Regiment and other very good Indian and Gurkha battalions, plus the troop of tanks. The Japanese made a night attack on the area of our Main Dressing Station, where the wounded lay, and brutally shot many of them, but in the end they were repulsed.

Both sides suffered casualties, but logistics, for the first time in this campaign since the fall of Singapore, were on our side. The Japanese were short of food, ammunition, medicine, and all stores, and had very long lines of communication. They were counting on capturing our supplies. Probably more of their casualties came from hunger and sickness than from any action of ours. We had the stores, especially of ammunition, already in the Adm. Box, plus what came in by air. Even mail was delivered, a great boost to morale. Most of the airdrop was by parachute, some by free drop, but all had to be collected, often under fire.

The initial shock of being surrounded was severe, but we gradually came to see that we were able to hold the enemy at bay, and, gradually after this, we became convinced that we were going to win. This conviction was sealed by the news that another division was on its way down from the north to our support. After nearly four weeks, they reached us. By that time the Japanese must have ordered a retreat as I do not remember any fierce fighting. But then, neither do I remember where I slept all the time of the siege. The first few nights we certainly spent in slit trenches. Whether we spent every night there I cannot say, nor where we slept if not in them.

Shortly after the siege ended we were relieved and sent to Central Burma, where the battles for Imphal and Kohima were still raging. But before leaving we had a reconnaissance and picnic a few miles south of the Adm. Box on the tunnels on the road from Maungdaw on the coast to Buthidaung on the River Kalapanzin. It's the only time I have picnicked with two generals and other high-ranking officers. We were also able to recover much of the equipment that we had to abandon when we left our former positions rather hurriedly. Among other things that I got back was my now blood-stained Missal, or prayer book, which was of special value to me, because my uncle, Ernest Barker, had given it to me when I left England, not knowing where we were being sent. In it he wrote a stanza from Horace:

Sive per Syrtes iter aestuosas
Sive facturo per inhospitalem
Caucasum vel quae loca fabulosus
Lambit Hydaspes.

(whether you will journey through the turbulent Syrtes, or through the inhospitable Caucasus, or the places lapped by the legendary Hydaspes). As the Syrtes are notorious quicksands and sandbanks off the north coast of Africa, the Caucasus mountains are east of the eastern end of the Black Sea, and the River Hydaspes (now Jhelum) is a tributary in Pakistan of the Indus; and as our three most likely destinations were North Africa, the Middle East and India, this was a piece of real classical virtuosity, but hardly likely to be appreciated by the Japanese. I was also glad to recover the Missal, since our Catholic chaplain was invalided out and never replaced, so we never had Mass again until Thailand.

We made our journey to Kohima by road, following, because of the mountains, a route which was far from direct and where the surface varied from acceptable to risky. For some of the way, there was a strip of tarmac about the width of one vehicle, with a wet, sloping dirt surface on either side. Oncoming traffic was a problem, and overtaking was difficult. In trying to pass a slow-moving vehicle, I had to leave the tarmac and was soon sliding into the ditch. We were pulled out, but my passenger hurt his nose, and the jeep suffered a bent stub axle of the off-side front wheel. Luckily we were near an Ordnance workshop, and they fixed it.

We arrived at Dimapur in Assam, our railhead, and after a day or two set off up the winding, mountainous road to Kohima. Here the battle, which had been most ferocious, was still fierce but had passed its peak of intensity, because here too the Japanese had long lines of communication and were running out of food, ammunition and medicine. They had, however, dug themselves into bunkers, which were almost impervious to mortars and artillery. The surest way of destroying them was with a Bangalore torpedo, an explosive charge on the end of a pole. If you could get on top of the bunker and thrust the pole through its slit, there was little hope for those inside, but as the bunkers were arranged so as to cover each other with fire, that could be done only at night, and even then at great risk since the Japanese had Verey lights, or the equivalent. By the end of the battle, the ground was denuded of all cover and the trees had lost not only foliage but most of their branches. It looked like a bleak painting from World War I. By now, it was June, 1944.

These three battles, the Arakan, Kohima and Imphal marked the turn of the tide. From then on, although the Japanese still fought with amazing tenacity and ferocity, we were sure we would win in the end. The end could have come much more quickly, but we were low on the priority-lists for reinforcements and supplies. We were called 'the forgotten army', and so it often seemed. On VE (Victory in Europe) Day, May 8, 1945, Lord Alanbrooke, Chief of the Imperial General Staff in London, wrote in his diary, 'Thank God the war is over', but it was still three months to VJ (Victory over Japan) Day, and, but for the atom bomb, would have been very much more.

From then on we were in pursuit of a fleeing enemy, the path marked by discarded weapons and equipment, and often by the dead and dying, both seen and smelt. But the living were still capable of ferocious resistance. We were mostly retracing the path of the allied retreat after the fall of Singapore.

The central plain of Burma is completely different from the jungle of the Arakan. Once we were south of the mountains round Kohima and Imphal, it was mostly flat. Some of it was even like English park-land, with clumps of beautiful, shady, hardwood trees with rice paddies between them. There were also clumps of bamboo. It seemed strange, after the jungle, to be able to see for miles. To have a road, one merely had to break down the *bunds* (low earth walls) between the fields and there was a smooth surface for a while. Once a single irregularity broke the smoothness, it was soon multiplied by supply trucks, and the road soon became corrugated and inches deep in dust. I was usually in a jeep but sometimes on a motorcycle, and both felt every bump and I was exposed to every particle of dust.

Our headquarters had its share of jeeps and motorcycles but only one big vehicle, a three-ton lorry (truck), which housed the clerks, typewriters, duplicating machines, etc. The offices were simply flat spaces, covered by a tarpaulin, as were our eating and sleeping spaces, except that these seldom had a tarpaulin. There was some office furniture, but very often we had to make our own from bamboo. We had one Gurkha orderly who used his kukri (an enlarged fighting knife with a curved, razor-sharp blade) so skillfully at making tables that we nicknamed him '*Mez banao*' (make a table). The files were kept in Yakdans, large, heavy, leather containers. These Gurkhas were ferocious soldiers, of whom the Japanese were truly afraid. They got on well with the British troops, who called them 'Johnny', were full of courage, and always obeyed orders. There is a story, which may well be true, that a Gurkha battalion was converted into paratroops. They trained and were then taken up for their practice jumps from 400 feet. On the order 'jump', they all jumped except one. The officer ordered him again, and he refused. As the plane circled, the Gurkha said he would jump if they came down to 200 feet. The officer said that then there would not be time for his parachute to open. 'Oh', said Johnny, 'do we have parachutes?'

Late one evening just before a major attack, an interesting scene took place. Our office was a flat area dug into the side of a small hill and just below General Messervy's similar flat space. The general sent for his head Gunner, Brigadier Tim Hely, and said that he wanted the artillery to neutralize the mountain that we were going to attack. The CRA said quite rightly that it could not be done with the guns available. 'Then you must get some more from Corps.' 'Even with them, Sir, it cannot be done, but we will do what we can.' The discussion, which was plainly audible to us, became more and more heated, and ended with the general saying, 'Well, it has got to be done. Now, get out of my tent, you bad tempered Irishman.' The CRA saluted smartly, said, 'Yes, sir; good night,

Sir, but it can't be done', and disappeared into the darkness. Next morning I happened to be alone at breakfast with the general, when the CRA came in. I dreaded a renewal of the row. Instead, the general said, 'Good morning, Tim; did you sleep well?' 'Yes, Sir, thank you; I slept very well.' And no more was said. I learnt a lot from that.

Soon afterwards, the Division was in reserve for the first and only time, and Air Supply asked for volunteers to help with their drops. Several of us volunteered. We set off in a Dakota (DC3) and were flying up a valley towards a mountain, which lay across our path. Our valley ended in a T-junction with another valley. We flew closer and closer to the mountain, and I assumed the pilot was going to turn either left or right. Instead he kept straight on, and at the last moment pulled back the stick and we started to climb. We were fully laden, and I thought we would not make it. We did, but the undercarriage of the plane brushed the trees on the mountain-top. The pilot thought that was funny: I, who was sitting at the time in the cockpit, did not. Having made it to the dropping zone, we had to work hard. The worst items were one-hundred-pound gunny sacks of rice for free fall without parachutes. When it was over, all our fingertips were bleeding. The pilot, having probably miscalculated on the way there, played no games on the way back.

Then two of us were sent on a month's leave. We decided to go to Kashmir, but to Gulmarg at nine thousand feet rather than to the more famous, and notorious, Srinagar by the lake. We went by road from central Burma to railhead at Dimapur, and then embarked on the five day rail-journey to the far corner of India. But first we had to cross the Brahmaputra, a turbulent river that many have never heard of, but which, at eight knots or so, must be the fastest flowing large river in the world. It is fed by snow from the Himalaya range and shifts 400,000,000 tonnes of suspended sediment a year. We and our baggage crossed it by boat – the railway bridge had been carried away by the water – and then got on another train on the far side. When we reached Lahore, they made a fuss about our travel warrants, but the head of the railways had a son in my old regiment, so we mentioned Griffin Sahib's name, and the fuss ended. At Rawalpindi we left the train and took a taxi for the last sixty miles or so to the foot of the steep ascent to Gulmarg.

The scenery was astounding as we climbed up between snow-covered mountains, with the peak of Nanga Parbat (26,660 feet) visible from time to time in the distance. For the last part of the journey we walked, climbing a thousand feet or so. Our baggage was on donkeys. When we arrived at our lodging, our landlady looked horrified. Her first words to us were, 'Didn't you get my telegram? I told you there was no room. And anyway I thought there was only one of you.' She had read 'Captains Horner and Henderson' as 'Captain Horner-Henderson' hyphenated. We slept the first night or two on the floor, which was no worse than the jungle, and soon she was able to make room for us.

We relaxed, walked, played a little golf, enjoyed the wonderful views, and ate and drank well, a change from army rations and our half-bottle of spirits and three bottles of beer a month. We joined a party and rode our horses up the mountains to above the tree line, sixteen thousand feet. At the top we paused and admired the view. When we were ready to go down again, one of the ladies said her spirited horse was giving her trouble, and could someone else ride it down for her. I gave her my gentle nag and took her horse, which behaved well. It liked my red hair, which was much the same color as his.

Kashmir seemed like Shangri-la, after the Jungle, and two weeks among the Himalaya mountains was a tonic. They are majestic and beautiful, but also rugged and relentless. I had no desire either to climb them or to live among them, and yet I was sad to depart. But our leave expired and we had to face another few days on the train. After the cool temperatures of Gulmarg, the heat of the train was more oppressive than when we had come from the heat of Burma. There was no air-conditioning in the train: instead they sold us an eighty-pound (one maund) block of ice and played a fan over it. This certainly reduced the heat in our compartment, but did not make it cool, and sleeping was hard. This was a regular passenger train, and the majority of the passengers must have traveled by the cheapest means available. The train's coaches seemed to have people in every possible space, and on the roof, and sometimes literally hanging half out of the windows. But in due course we arrived back at our unit.

During our absence the Division had advanced southward. I soon had my first flight in an airplane, an L5, a single-engine monoplane with seats for the pilot and, behind him, one passenger. I was astonished at seeing palm trees from the top down rather than from the roots up. I always watched the pilot with great care, in case I ever had to take over, and came to the conclusion that I could probably land an L5 in good weather, and perhaps even take off again, but I have never done so, except in dreams.

On one flight we were returning home over Japanese held territory when the pilot asked if I would like to go down and have a closer look at some Japanese dug in on a hilltop. He said it was quite safe as the Japanese were told that they had complete command of the air, so they would never shoot at us. Stupidly I agreed, and we went down to a few hundred feet. At our speed, we were a simple target. I have seldom felt so defenseless, so I bombed them with my one hand-grenade, and was delighted when we were out of their range.

Also at some point in this advance I was sent on a course in Chemical Warfare and Camouflage, which was fair enough, seeing that this was my title. It was held at Shillong in Assam, where most Indian tea is grown. The annual rainfall at Shillong is 92 inches, and at Cherrapunji, 50 miles to the west, 450 inches. At the end of the course, another officer and I were asked to put on a brief tactical exercise to illustrate some of the points made during the course. As the exercise was to use thunderflashes (small fireworks made for such exercises to simulate gunfire), and as the other officer was an engineer and used to explosives, I asked him if he would deal with them. In the course of the exercise, as our troops were creeping through the undergrowth, my colleague lit his thunderflash and waited for the moment to throw it. He waited too long, and it exploded in his hand. He lost two or three fingers and the exercise came to an abrupt end.

I do not remember much about chemical warfare or camouflage, but I do remember that any time I had a drink in Shillong I developed horrible hiccoughs, possibly because of the altitude (5000 feet) or perhaps I was just out of practice. I received a 'D' (Distinguished) for the course. I hope they did the same for my colleague, but, after visiting him in hospital, I never saw him again. I never had the chance to use my new knowledge, partly because neither side ever did use gas, and partly because I was switched from that job to GSO III Operations, and someone else took care of the camouflage and chemical warfare.

Our next major action was the crossing of the River Irrawaddy. At over a mile, it was the longest opposed river-crossing of World War II. I was a member of the planning team. On our way towards the river, we were given an 'earthquake', a demonstration by bombers and artillery of a concentrated attack on a small target. We were kept at a distance of one thousand yards. The bombing and shelling were accurate, but only a direct hit with a heavy bomb was fully effective against a Japanese bunker.

The success of our crossing of the Irrawaddy was due largely to surprise.

Our division's advance down the Gangaw Valley was under wireless silence, and the Japanese had no air reconnaissance. We made it look as if our crossing was to be either to the north, or to the south, of our real crossing at Nyaungu. At about 3.45 a.m. on 14 February 1945 a company of the South Lancashire Regiment rowed across the Irrawaddy and established themselves on the far shore successfully.

Then everything started to go wrong, largely because we had not been able to carry out tests of the outboard motors, because the noise would have destroyed the surprise. As dawn broke, the engines of many of the boats failed. The occupants were drifting helplessly downstream within easy rifleshot of the enemy. We recovered, however, and by evening the situation was nearly as it had been planned. It helped us that the enemy troops facing us were largely Indian National Army, who had no heart in the fight, and also that the boundary between two Japanese armies was on our front, so the enemy's communication from one part of the front to another was slow. We soon established a bridgehead secure enough for 17 Indian Division to pass through us and advance to capture Meiktila, in Central Burma and its railway junction, thus seizing a key point on the Japanese supply lines. This cut off Japanese forces in the North from their base at Rangoon in the South. There ensued a ferocious battle, in which 17 Division prevailed, but in which we were not involved.

Our engineers constructed a pontoon bridge across the Irrawaddy – quite a feat in view of the width of the river and the speed of the current – but as it was for single line traffic one way, there was usually a wait of some hours. One day we needed to get a chaplain across the river for a burial. I called our airforce base to see if they could send a light plane and received the reply, 'Don't you know there's a war on?' I then called the Americans and received the reply, 'Sure, and would you like a plane for each of the burial party?' Of course they had far more planes than we did, but even so the contrast was striking.

Our Headquarters were not far from Old Pagan, the first capital of Burma, now a city of over two thousand ruins, of which nearly a thousand are wats (temples) or stupas (monuments). One evening when there was a full moon, we walked down the broad, dry, sandy bed of a stream running down to the Irrawaddy. The sand was bright silver in the moonlight, and the Temples ghostly in the background.

There was any amount of beauty around. I saw a flock of bright green parakeets flying. Then all as one bird turned so that the sun shone on the sheen of their feathers, like an enormous emerald. There was Mount Popa too, a 5000 foot volcano rising strikingly straight out of the central plain. There is a famous Buddhist monastery on the slopes nearby. The monks are said to be protected by king cobras, from whose bite they are themselves immune.

Either while we were at Pagan or soon afterwards, I was promoted from GSO III to GSO II, still in Operations, with the rank of Major. That meant that I received a considerable pay-raise, and also that I became a field officer. It did not make much difference in war, but in peacetime it would have been quite significant. I also walked into a slit trench and sprained my ankle quite badly. They wanted to evacuate me, but I refused, knowing that it would cure itself in time, and that almost anything was better than traveling back to the rear in pain.

Next we set off southwards through the oilfields of Yenangyaung, and on down roughly the course of the Irrawaddy nearly to Rangoon. Some twenty miles north of Rangoon we turned back northeast and came to rest at Pegu. That journey took us several months, as the Japanese were still fighting energetically. Somewhere near Prome there was a standing Buddha about eighty feet tall. It was placed behind a small hill, which had steps cut into it. We climbed the steps and came to the top just about level with the Buddha's lips. It was humbling to stand there and gaze into this enormous, serene, stone face. It was also quite different from the lying Buddha we were to see at Pegu, which was 120 feet long with ears about twenty feet long.

One evening during this journey to Pegu we were in the Officers' Mess (a tarpaulin over the top and a table and chairs beneath) when a benign-looking visitor came in. We gave him dinner, and then most people drifted away and I was left alone with him. Our monthly liquor ration had just arrived, but he looked unlikely to be a hard drinker, so I offered him a drink, which, slightly to my surprise, he accepted. He introduced himself as Colonel Grant-Taylor, and when I asked him what he had come for, he said that he was to run a short course on close quarter combat with small arms up to and including a tommy gun. His background, given his appearance, was incongruous. He had been a police officer in England, was seconded to the American police during the time of the gangsters and was present at the death of Dillinger in Chicago. Before World War II he was sent to Palestine to train their police in dealing with disorder and proto-terrorists. In the war, he trained officers, especially Commandos, in the proper use of small arms.

In the course of our conversation, and as we finished off the liquor ration, he made two hair-raising remarks: first, if you are chasing a terrorist and he goes into a house and you pursue him, and if you go upstairs and find someone in bed, shoot him. This was based on an incident when a terrorist had fled into a house, gone upstairs, jumped into a bed and shot his pursuer through the covers. The second remark was based on his experience in training a commando officer to land on the north coast of France, to take a German headquarters by surprise when they were taking their ease at the tavern, and shoot them all. The remark was, 'If someone puts up his hands, shoot him first'. When I said that this was hardly cricket, he replied that if an enemy were to walk in, it would be about ten seconds before most people realized what was going on. The man who puts up his hands has realized, and is therefore dangerous. He added that he had trained the commando, had given him two revolvers (twelve bullets) for the ten Germans, and the mission had been successful.

About a dozen of us signed up for his five-day course. On the first day he said that there would be a demonstration at the end of the course to display to the top brass what we had learnt. My assignment was to put two shots with a Colt 45 automatic into a playing card thirty yards away. That seemed very unlikely, but his instruction was such that, at the end of the course, all of us achieved what we had been assigned. After my turn, he walked down the range and returned with the card with two holes in it. I should have kept it to frighten away intruders.

There was a curious sequel to this. Nearly fifty years later, I was given a copy of *To War with Whitaker* by Countess Ranfurly. In it she described being trained to shoot a revolver by a man who sounded very like Grant-Taylor. She called him Abercrombie. As she also mentioned the names of some men with whom I had been at school at Ampleforth, I wrote to her. I described my encounter with Grant-Taylor and asked whether we were referring to the same man. I also mentioned my slight connection with Stirlings, Frasers, Lovats, and others at Ampleforth. I received a delightful letter back, confirming the identity and making some gracious comments about the need for monastic life.

By the end of June, Divisional headquarters was approaching Pegu, a little north of Rangoon. I was sent ahead to plan the general layout. The monsoon was starting and the soil was largely clay and very slippery when wet. I consulted the engineers, who said that if we dug trenches each side of the tracks into our area, this would leave the tracks dry. I was doubtful, and reported my doubts back to our general before the move. They moved nonetheless, and the heavy office lorries (trucks) slithered all over the place. Heroically, they finally reached their allotted sites, but had the Japanese had any air power, they could have wrought havoc. This and another incident to come later have left me with a distrust of 'expert' advice, which is still with me more than sixty years on.

By this time we had cut off very large numbers of Japanese from their escape route. They were in hiding, but often strongly dug in, west of us in the jungle-clad Pegu Yomas (low mountain ridges running south) and needed to cross the Sittang River, which also ran south, about twenty miles away to our east. We, who were weary, but had more ammunition and supplies, and were in much better health than the Japanese, held those twenty miles. Mostly the Japanese tried to escape by night, but we set up searchlights and machine guns. Some certainly did escape, but in the morning the area was a grisly sight, and bulldozers were needed to dig trenches to bury the dead and stop the spread of disease. Although they must have known that they could not win, those Japanese who escaped still fought fiercely. One small force of ours advanced well ahead of our lines, and was in danger of being surrounded by the enemy. We had to order them to withdraw, disable their four 25-pounder guns, and leave them behind. It was the first time in our whole campaign that we had lost guns. We for our part, although we could see that the Burma campaign was ending, were expecting to be sent to Malaya to continue fighting there. And that was indeed the plan of the high command.

Then came the completely unexpected news of the dropping of the atomic bombs, followed on 15 August 1945 by the surrender of the Japanese and the armistice. Our reaction was one of great relief. We knew very little about the bombs, but we did know that instead of our having to invade Malaya, and then probably Japan itself, we would fight no more. None of us at that time doubted the value of the bomb.

Thirteen

WE OCCUPY THAILAND

At this time I had two very interesting conversations, one with General Evans, who had taken over from General Messervy a little earlier, the other with our CRA, Brigadier Tim Hely. They each asked me the same question, 'What are you planning to do now that the war is over'? To the general I replied that I did not know, but I certainly was not planning to stay in the army. He looked at me without a smile and said, 'But why not, Michael; you play cricket; you'd do very well in the army'. To Tim Hely, when he asked me, I made the same reply, but added that I knew that I wanted to do something that I really wanted to do twenty-four hours a day, and not something that I did from nine to five, so that I could afford to do, out of hours, what I really wanted to do. He made no comment; but when I joined the monastery, I wrote to inform him. In reply he asked me if I remembered that conversation, and added, remarkably, that his insight at that point was that I was going to be a monk. I did not then know it myself.

Soon after the armistice, the colonel of the Royal Signals and I were given some leave. We set out by jeep for Maymyo, a hill station and beauty spot in the north of Burma. We drove some 400 miles on very bumpy roads. On the way, we visited Mandalay but saw no flying fishes. The city was not at its best, but even so, its site was impressive. After two or three days in Maymyo, we decided to go to Mogok, and make our fortunes from the ruby mines there. We were within fifteen minutes or less of departing when a signal came through that all leave was cancelled, and we were to return to base at once. It may have been as well, since our route would have taken us and our jeep over at least one swinging bridge made mainly of bamboo.

The reason for the cancellation was that we were to move to Bangkok, and to occupy Siam, as it was then still called. It changed its name to Thailand (Land of the Free) soon after our arrival. There were around 120,000 Japanese troops in Siam, and we were not quite sure whether they knew that the war was over. We set off from Rangoon in several DC3s, with the general and about sixteen of us in the leading plane. We were armed with a revolver apiece. There were about 16,000 Japanese guarding Don Muang, the airport for Bangkok: we did not know how they would receive us.

But there was another problem first: we encountered some very dark, torpedo-shaped clouds, which often had extremely vicious air-currents in them. There were stories of planes flying into them and only bits coming out. We plunged down, and for a time the plane was skimming the waves. Then we had to fly over the mountains, and there we met more bad weather. The plane carrying our office equipment and files had to jettison much of its cargo. This was the second time we had lost many files and much equipment. Later, it was a wonderful excuse when we were asked by Corps Headquarters for reports and returns. 'That information must have been in one of the files jettisoned in that storm'. But curiously, I cannot remember any occasion later when the loss of information in those files caused us any inconvenience. Perhaps it would have, had we still been at war. We arrived in due course, were warmly greeted by the Japanese, taken to their Officers' Mess and offered drinks. This was just what we needed, but the general said firmly, 'No fraternization!' so Instead we were shown to a large, empty hangar, where we spent the next few days.

The hangar was more or less empty, but at one side there was a long row of electric light switches. As evening fell, the hangar grew darker and we lit our oil lamps and the few hurricane lamps as usual. We had not seen electric light for over two years. We may even have thought that the switches might have booby-traps. Eventually I went over and turned on several of the switches. The blaze of light that ensued is something I remember still. It brought home to me, as nothing else quite had, that the war really was over.

The airport was at that time about fifteen miles out in the country from Bangkok. Now there is development all the way in to the city. In a few days we moved from our hangar into a palace in the city. The government sent a fleet of three elderly Rolls-Royces for the general and his immediate staff. We asked why they needed three for so few people. We were told to wait and see. After a few miles, the first Rolls overheated, and we had to stop and transfer to the second. After another few miles, that did the same. The third one got us there.

Our palace was grand but not very convenient. There were many palaces in Bangkok because a recent King had had four queens, many wives and at least seventy-seven children. All of the children were of princely rank, but there were gradations of princeliness, and each generation went down one grade; so eventually they melted into commoners. But meanwhile, they needed palaces. I was on the fifth floor of our palace in a suite with a walk-down marble bathtub, a cube of about eight feet, but without running water. My orderly and I agreed that we must have one bath in this, and he duly filled it with a few inches of hot water. I presume the prince had used it every day. I had my bath, and left it for my orderly to use if he wished.

Bangkok is also a city of temples, many of them very beautiful. In the temples in the cities, and also in monasteries throughout the countryside dwell Buddhist monks. It was very noticeable both here and in Burma that these men were well respected and that when they appeared with their begging-bowls, they were treated with gentleness and generosity. When we were in Thailand most young men spent at least a few months in a monastery. This must have given them a common background of belief and an introduction to contemplative life. There must be some connection between this and the impression that Thais make on visitors of being a happy and smiling nation. The respect felt for the monks by the Burmese too was shown during the uprising in Burma in 2007.

Our GSO I, the staff officer above me, held a daily meeting with the senior Japanese Liaison Officer, a colonel, to learn what had been done by his troops and to instruct him on what still needed to be done. One day we sent for him after our evening meal. It soon became evident that he had had too much saké. When we said this, he denied it. Our G I drew a chalk line on the floor and asked the colonel to walk along it. He put down his head, charged down the line and dealt the G I a sharp blow in the stomach. Even the ranks of Tuscany could scarce forbear to giggle. He was sacked and we found a more docile and less bibulous successor.

Each morning the General held a meeting with his principal staff officers. At a very early meeting General Evans asked about the state of the bridge across the wide Chao Phraya river. It was then the only bridge; now there are seven. It was a critical link in our land communications and it had been bombed during the war. We urgently needed to know from our Engineers whether it was safe, and if not, what could be done. It was vital to have this link in operation AS SOON AS POSSIBLE. The Commander of the Royal Engineers (CRE) was to report to the meeting next morning.

His recommendation was to build a new bridge at a much more satisfactory site about a mile upstream. He estimated that the bridge and the necessary roadways leading to and from the bridge could be ready in six to twelve months.

The General was nearly apoplectic, and indicated that he was thinking in terms of days, not months. Fortunately, further inspection determined that the existing bridge was fit to use in its present state. This was my second reason for being wary of expert advice. But gradually I came to recognize that it was not the expertise of the experts that I mistrusted, but their application of their expertise to the practical needs of the matter in hand.

Not long after our arrival in Bangkok, our Staff Colonel (Operations) was sent to command his old regiment. Because all the fighting was over, and the task of the Operations Staff was now administrative and not military, I was promoted to succeed him. And so there I was, aged 25, in what would normally have been a very senior position. Apart from the liaison with the Japanese, it was mainly routine staff work, which was within my capability. I did this for just under five months. By army regulations, one receives the pay and acting rank for any job that one does for three months or more, but in this case they sent my predecessor for a month's leave with rank and pay, and then my successor from Delhi on a month's leave. They deducted the two months from my tenure, thus reducing my time to just under the necessary three months. Had it been otherwise, I might have bought more of the beautiful Siamese silk then on sale, at a time when silk was almost unobtainable in England. Perhaps it was as well, because colors that looked radiant in the bright sun of Siam looked garish in England, as those friends for whom I bought them, 'uncertain, coy, and hard to please', made clear on my return.

The Thais were in an awkward position because of their co-operation with the Japanese during the war, so they were very anxious to show us that their co-operation was due to *force majeure* and not to any love for the Japanese. Thus they made us honorary members of an elegant club and in general were most hospitable. As the young Thai women were mostly beautiful, this was very agreeable. We fell in with a most interesting family. The father was a politician who had been sent to Australia with a large sum of money to buy racehorses for the royal stables. He spent the money on lavish entertainments and then reported back that he had really put Thailand on the map, and could he now have some money to buy horses. He was recalled in disgrace, and to repair the family fortunes he bought and managed, with the help of his two beautiful daughters, a circus. They all spoke English, and were very interesting company. We all went to the circus one night and saw our first Siamese boxing. On other nights at the club there were highly stylized dramatic performances with ritual dancers in elaborate costumes and fingernails, and any amount of noise.

There was also our favorite restaurant, the Hoi Tien Lao. On the ground floor it served the best Chinese food I have ever had, better even than in China, because so much of the raw supply comes from the Gulf of Siam: sharks fins, birds nest soup, roast sucking pig, and countless courses more. As the floors of the restaurant went up, the quality went down. We took Lord and Lady Mountbatten there when they came to visit us, and I had the good fortune to sit at a table for eight with him and our general. He was a fascinating talker. At the meal we had, amongst other things, one hundred years old pigeons-eggs. They were small, hard, and very slippery. The aim was to pick up with one's chopsticks one egg from the bowl, dip it in the sauce, and convey it to one's mouth. We soon had pigeons-eggs all over the floor, but I did achieve the aim.

When I took over as GSO I, I learnt, in my interviews with the Japanese liaison officer, more about the bombing of Hiroshima and Nagasaki. It gradually became clear that the bombs had not simply caused destruction far more wide-spread than was possible with conventional weapons, but had also caused radiation injuries of a kind that we did not then understand. That caused great distress, but I do not remember any moral indignation at the time.

Just before Christmas, General Evans told me we were going to make the complicated arrangements necessary then to visit the ruins of the twelfth century Temples of Angkor Wat in Cambodia. I was delighted and said I had always wanted to go there, but he added that we could not both be away at the same time, so I would not be going. As a consolation, a friend and I later went to Hua Hin, then the King's seaside resort for the summer, and now a popular spa. We rode horses along the shore, a five mile gallop on hard sand with occasional inlets from the Gulf of Siam – clippety-clop and splash, splash, splash. Truly exhilarating. We also played golf, each of us for the first time in several years. There were caddies and two small boys as fore-caddies to spot the ball. Our first drives to an invisible green were both to the edge of the green. This went on until one of us sliced the ball into the rough. But when we caught up with it, there it was on the fairway. Then we realized what the fore-caddies were doing. They could hardly believe that this was not what we wanted. It was a pleasant trip, but it was not Angkor Wat.

We also arranged some cricket matches. In one I made as good a catch as I have ever made, and then bowled as badly as I have ever bowled.

Fourteen

THE END OF MY SERVICE IN THE ARMY

owards the end of my tenure as acting GSO I, a signal came from London advertising a course in England on Combined Operations. It was limited to officers of field rank. No one volunteered, so I suggested to the general that he put my name forward, and I was accepted.

The journey back to England was more exciting than the course. The first leg was in a DC3 from Bangkok to Rangoon. When we touched down in Rangoon, the plane suddenly veered sharply to the left and then back onto the runway again. When we stopped, we asked the pilot what had happened. He said there was a large truck coming down the runway towards us, and he had to try to raise our right wing so that the truck could pass under it. We flew on to Calcutta without incident. In Calcutta, we found that riots were occurring daily in favor of Indian independence, and cars were being burnt on Calcutta's main street, Chowringhee, where we were put up at a grand hotel. Next morning I had to go to convert my travel warrant into a ticket. With a group of civilians, men and women, I went to the travel agent to do this. When we had all completed the lengthy transaction, we learnt that a riotous crowd had gathered in a square on our route back to our hotel. We had an experienced British driver of our three-ton lorry (truck), who suggested that the civilians get in the back and keep their heads down. I was to sit in front with him. When we came to the crowd, which was already throwing stones, he charged straight at them, braked violently as he came to the edge of the crowd, which then parted, and he accelerated through the gap. We harmed no one. They threw stones at us, one of which, but only a small one, hit my hand. Now when I read accounts of stoning, I really empathize with the victim.

We got back to the hotel safely to find all kinds of rumors already flying around. The riots went on all day and into the night, with many more cars being burnt. There was looting and rape. We were told to be ready at any time, and in fact were roused in the middle of the night and taken to a Sunderland seaplane, waiting on the river Hooghly. It took off in the early hours of the morning. It was my first flight in a seaplane: both take-off and landing were wonderfully smooth, and the bow-wave as we landed was most graceful. This, with stops at various lakes en route, took us to Karachi, where I saw a large four-engine plane landing. As it did so, suddenly all its engines roared. I thought there would be a horrible accident. It was my first encounter with reversible-pitch propellers.

From Karachi a Liberator took us on to Lydda, near Jerusalem. The Liberator had, right above my head, a small hole in its fuselage. We flew at about 10,000 feet mostly over desert. It was, no doubt, uncomfortably hot down there, but where I was it was miserably cold. We landed at Lydda, but soon learnt two pieces of bad news: the first was that although we were only about twenty-five miles from Jerusalem, because of unrest in the country, we were confined to the transit camp and would not visit the holy city. The second was that there was almost no transport back to England. Providentially, the officer in charge of transit at Lydda had been an officer in 136 Field Regiment, and we knew each other. He recognized my voice and came out from his inner office. I explained that I was due back in England for my course, and he asked me whether I would be willing to become the draft-conducting officer for a group of RAF men going back to England. I agreed gladly and became, for a few days, Squadron-Leader Horner.

We flew from Lydda in a DC3 southwest over the southeast corner of the Mediterranean to the North African desert. We were to land at Sidi Barrani to refuel but the airstrip was in fog, and we were sent on to Tobruk. At fogbound Tobruk we were sent on to Benghazi, but that too was fogbound. By this time we were running out of fuel, and were told to fly on to a disused strip in the desert, and they would send us fuel and something to eat. This they did, but when we were ready to take off again, the pilot came to me, as draft-conducting officer, and said that he had been measuring the strip, and it was about 390 yards long. He added that with a full load of fuel and personnel, such as we had, he needed about 750 yards to take off. In addition, there were telephone wires at the end of the strip. I asked his advice, and we agreed that there was not much alternative. He took the plane back to the extreme end of the strip, opened up full throttle with brakes still on, and we then sprang forward, leaving the ground just before the strip ended and carrying with us some of the telephone wires. We hoped they were as disused as the strip.

We crossed the Mediterranean and landed in Sicily at Catania, near Mount Etna. Next morning when we took off, the cloud base was at about four thousand feet. We climbed up through the cloud and there was the top half of

Etna sitting on clouds turned pink by the rising sun, a magical sight. After that, the last leg of our journey was uneventful, and we landed safely in England, and were taken by coach to London. En route we all agreed that a pint of ale was just what we needed. We had forgotten that the temperature in February was around freezing, and we soon had to stop again and line the roadside.

The course was interesting, but I remember little. The officer in charge asked me to talk about the war in Burma, and introduced me as having come from Bangkok, the capital of French Indo-China, now Vietnam.[5] Here too we were the forgotten army.

After the course, I had some leave, after which I was due to rejoin the division, which had moved to Northern Malaya. I went to join Mother, who had spent the war at her charitable work, but now came to stay with our Quaker friends in London. Also staying with them was their cousin, a medical student, Elizabeth Rutherfoord. We fell in love, or started to do so. That was an agonizing complication, as I was by then thinking about what I would do after the war, and the first decision I had to make was whether or not to ask the Abbot of Ampleforth if I could join his Benedictine community. I could have done this at the end of my schooldays at Ampleforth, but did not, because I wanted to go to Oxford as a layman. Then came World War II, and I spent the next six years in the army. Now in 1946 was my first opportunity to ask.

Then, quite unexpectedly, came a telegram from Malaya offering me a Class B release. This was for those wishing to return to their university, and I did not so wish. Also, I wanted to rejoin my friends in Malaya, and I wanted to travel. I managed to get into the War Office in London, and to persuade a signaler there to send a telegram back to the division to say that I was neither eligible for, nor desirous of, a Class B release. Meanwhile, Elizabeth and I had decided that we needed some time for thought. I told her I was thinking of going to Ampleforth, and we agreed that marriage would never work if she felt all the time that she was keeping me from what I really wanted to do, and I felt all the time that I was not doing what I really ought to be doing. We did also see that if I tried my vocation at Ampleforth and it did not work out, there was a chance that she might still be unmarried, whereas it could not work the other way round. It was an agonizing time for both of us, but we spent some very happy days in London, and then she went off to Kenya, where her parents planted coffee, and I flew to Malaya.

5. *Bangkok is the capital of Thailand, formerly Siam, not of its neighbor, Vietnam.*

The flight to Singapore was uneventful compared with our flight to England. When we took off from Cairo, the pilot kindly circled round the Pyramids, so I had my first view of them and the Sphinx. We were delayed at Colombo, Sri Lanka, but finally reached Singapore. I made the rest of the journey up to Ipoh, in the north of Malaya, by train.

I was looking forward to rejoining the division, as war does lead to male bonding. It is an incentive to friendship if your life depends on the men around you. But my return was a bitter disappointment. Not only had so many of the familiar faces gone, but the whole spirit was different. The rumor was that the new general had said, 'Thank God the war is over: now we can get back to real soldiering'. I hope he never did say it, but there was something of that in the air. The spit and polish side of the army made little appeal to me, so I kept my head down, did my job as well as I could and ached for discharge.

One day we went out and ordered a dinner for that evening: my order had to be translated into five successive languages, but strange to say, we got what we ordered. Another evening, a group of us drove over some low mountains to have dinner with friends on the far side. After the dinner our jeeps raced back. While we were driving the twisty road over the mountains, one of the headlights on our jeep was flickering. We did not want to stop, so I climbed out onto the bonnet (hood), fixed the bulb and clambered back in again. My guardian angel was with me.

In due course, the longed for discharge came through. My friend, Ian Stemson, and I were discharged together, and were allowed to take a jeep and driver to drive the length of Malaya to Singapore to catch our boat. On the way, we spent a night in Kuala Lumpur with Chinese friends of Ian's. Their young daughter came home from school. She had wooden clogs that played two slightly different notes as she walked melodiously across the stone courtyard. She soon settled down to her homework, took out her brush and ink-pot, started at the top right-hand corner of the page, and worked her way down the right-hand margin. Then she went back to the top and started again a little to the left of the first column. I do not know how many characters she knew, but her calligraphy was pleasing to watch. The family was most hospitable, and gave us a full Chinese dinner. But there was some mix-up and as we were finishing, the phone rang, and another of Ian's friends was wondering whether we had forgotten that we were to come and dine with them. We had two full Chinese dinners that evening, well over twenty courses.

We reached Singapore and stayed in the transit camp to wait for a ship. We kept the jeep, and that enabled three of us to make a trip up the east coast. We found a beautiful beach with an apparently abandoned hotel. There was a caretaker, who said we could camp in one of the rooms. We took a midnight swim (a full moon and no jelly-fish) and had a good night's sleep. Next morning we found the caretaker, gave him something, and thanked him warmly. He replied, 'Please do not say anything about it.' We thought he meant that we could get him into trouble, but in fact it was his version of the then conventional reply to thanks: 'Don't mention it'.

A week or two later, the ship came and we embarked. I started to reflect. I had already decided not to remain in the army, a decision that I could make very easily. I was grateful to the army for taking me to places far beyond my reach: India, Burma, Kashmir, Thailand, Malaya, and for fascinating, exciting, and sometimes dangerous, journeys by sea, land and air. I accepted the rigors and, in the early days, the spit and polish and drill of army life, so long as there was an obvious purpose in them, as there was at the OCTU. In the Burmese jungle not only was there little scope for spit and polish, but anything polished was dangerous, as it might reflect your position to a watchful enemy. I was able to revise completely my opinion of regular army officers, and to enjoy my association with other ECOs (Emergency Commissioned Officers) and with a wide cross-section of men who were not officers. All that was a broadening experience, which has proved useful in countless ways, but it was not the life for me.

The journey home by way of the Suez Canal was serene, with no storms, no untoward events, and no distractions from reflection. I had thought about monastic life while I was still in high school, but then Oxford and World War II took care of the next eight years. And yet it was not true either that during those eight years, I had given these matters no thought. I wanted, as I have said, to do something I wanted to do all the time, and not something that I did just from nine to five; but it was not until we were on board the ship that there was plenty of time to speculate; in fact there was not much else to do.

The idea of some sort of religious vocation to serve God explicitly and closely had been at the back of my mind from my later days in high school, and still was. One way of clarifying the idea was to look at other possibilities. I knew that I would not stay in the army, but I could perhaps follow my father as a barrister. We both agreed, however, that I should not do so: he thought I would not be a good one, and I had no real desire to be one, for much the same reason as I did not want to be a politician. I attached then very great value to the truth[6], – I hope I still do – and felt that both those callings might often put me in the position of defending or voting for what I thought was untrue. I thought of trying to be a professor at Oxford, teaching ancient philosophy and history, and even of trying for an All Souls Fellowship, but neither quite kindled my enthusiasm. I was not attracted by banking or business or journalism. I did not think of architecture, though that might have suited me quite well. So, having eliminated these other possibilities, I came back to religion. Then it was a question of what kind. I had seen quite a lot both of the Jesuits and the Dominicans at Oxford, and had friends among both; but in both orders the older men seemed to me to be somehow eviscerated. I assume they were not in fact, but so they seemed to me in my youth. I did not have the same feeling about the monks at Ampleforth. I found them, whether young, middle-aged or old, to be human, humane, and possessed of what I came to call later spiritual commonsense.

And so in the middle of the Indian Ocean, as I was walking round the deck, admiring the sunset and its afterglow, I found that I had made my crucial decision: I would ask the Abbot of Ampleforth if I might join his community. At several important points in my life I have noticed that it is not so much that I make a decision as that I recognize that I have already made the decision; and so it was this time. There were no spectacular circumstances about this call from God, but it was quite definite.

It is very hard now to say more about the reasons for this decision without inserting ideas that have come to me much later. I believe there were two basic thoughts: that this, in some form, was what God wanted me to do, and that, if I were to do it, Ampleforth was the place. I knew Ampleforth best and it was quite clear to me that if Ampleforth regularly produced men such as I had met there, I was very content to try to be like them.

This was my second trip through the Suez Canal but I was an infant during the first. Port Said was unattractive, but while we were there I had the wild hope that Elizabeth would somehow appear from Kenya. Of course she could not and did not, but I watched nonetheless.

When we left Port Said, the Mediterranean was sunny and a brilliant blue. After we passed Gibraltar, the skies became somewhat overcast; then, the closer

6. *I have always disliked exaggeration, distrusted fundamentalists, and been wary of enthusiasts. Kahlil Gibran wrote that exaggeration is truth that has lost its temper.*

we came to England, the less attractive the weather became. We reached Liverpool in chilly mist and rain.

And then came Customs. I was in the queue, behind a young woman of ENSA (Entertainments National Service Association). She was in her uniform, but I was wearing a khaki pullover and khaki trousers, as we had been wearing all the voyage. The Customs Officer was giving her a hard time, and I made some remark in her defense. He rounded on me and said, 'You're her husband, and you're in ENSA too; you keep out of this.' I denied the honor, but thought I might do better in one of the other queues. I went and put on full uniform and decorations, went to another Customs Officer, and then presented myself to the first, to show him that I was what I said. He must have been having a bad day, but it was not exactly a hero's welcome home. I had a bit more sympathy for him when I learnt later that one passenger said he had nothing to declare. They had been through his trunk in the hold and found 750 pairs of silk stockings, and told him so. 'Oh! I'm sorry' he said, 'I quite forgot about those.' I have a high regard for ENSA. I have mentioned that Dame Vera Lynn came within a mile or two of the front line to sing to us; and Noel Coward later did much the same. Many of his audience had a rather low opinion of him beforehand, but completely changed their minds.

We then went through a warehouse, where we given a complete set of civilian clothes, and a ticket to our home. Then the war really was over. I made for London, where my mother and our Quaker friends were awaiting me. I was warmly welcomed, but Elizabeth was not there and it was not the same.

Fifteen

BECOMING A MONK

Almost at once, I wrote to the Abbot of Ampleforth a (now) embarrassingly military letter, starting
'I submit this my application' and ending:
I have the honor to be,
Sir,
Your obedient servant . . .
but nonetheless received a friendly and favorable reply: I was to come early in September. Father Abbot also observed that the only kind of monk it was worth being was a whole-hearted one. It was then the end of July. That gave me about five weeks to make a tour of the family and tell them what I planned.

I asked myself what I had learnt from the war. I had entered the army, after two years at the university, with a rather supercilious attitude about regular officers. There was a joke going around among us at Oxford: there was once a cavalry officer who was so stupid that his fellow officers noticed it. I then thought it was funny and contained at least a grain of truth. By the time of my discharge, the grain of truth had become infinitesimal. Many of the officers or other ranks that I met had, before the war, been either in the Territorial Army (National Guard) or, like me, civilians. Of the regular officers some, naturally, were more intelligent than others. They usually were brave, calm under fire, had plenty of horse sense, and intense loyalty. The last could easily lead to a coolness or even disrespect towards other units, formations, branches of the service, (Signals, Artillery etc.) or even for the whole Navy or Air Force. The best of them were magnanimous, the opposite of petty, and bore no grudges. If they cussed you out on parade in the morning, they could very easily see you in the Mess that evening and stand you a drink. By the end of the war, my superciliousness had turned into admiration. Perhaps I should add that the more I read of accounts of other campaigns in World War II, the more I think was very lucky in the officers I met.

I also learnt much about men of many sorts and nationalities, whom I would not otherwise have met at such close quarters. I learnt about the way they thought and spoke. A Cockney may say 'Mikes yer fink donit' (makes you think, doesn't it?'). He may even on occasion lapse into Cockney rhyming slang: "'Ow's yer pain and godfers?' where 'pain' stands for 'pain and strife' which means 'wife', and 'godfers' for 'God forbids' and means 'kids'; but that is rare. A Northerner can say 'Oh aye, t'war barn b'far t'warr, t'war' and expect you to hear 'Oh yes, it was born before the war, it was,' and a man from the West Country will say 'Wal, zur; de trook moost 'ave bin facing t'wrong waay.' (Well, Sir, the truck must have been facing the wrong way.')

I picked up knowledge about guns, revolvers, cars, wireless (radio), and a fair amount about administration. I learnt how to drive almost anything from a motorcycle to a tank-transporter, including tracked vehicles. I tell myself that I drove a tank-transporter on the twisting mountain road between Dimapur and Kohima. That may have been in a dream, but it remains a very vivid memory. I learnt much about teaching, some of it misleading, because in wartime the men really wanted to learn material that might save their lives, but boys in school are not always so keen. I acquired a love of travel by land, sea, and air, and, by visiting other countries, and also by my own experience, some understanding of quite different ways of living.

In the course of the war I was shot at, shelled, strafed, and bombed; I had stones thrown at me by an angry mob, but I was never torpedoed nor shot down, so God spared me the worst, and, at least in retrospect, I was grateful. I never thought I would die in the war; no one of my age did. But I do think the possibility was in some way present at the back of my mind. My relief on hearing that the war was over certainly suggests that. All those experiences were valuable, yet I find it hard to express why. Man's inhumanity to man? Intimations of mortality? Fear experienced and overcome?

There was also one very tangible benefit, about which I learnt from Brian Barry, a member of our faculty. He had been in the Royal Navy and in conversation referred to his pension and asked if I had one. He said they started at age 65 and had to be claimed before you were 70. Fortunately I was under 70 at the time. I wrote to the source of pensions and found that the deductions made from my pay did not quite qualify for a pension, but if I sent them £200, I would qualify. This was a bargain our treasurer could not resist, and for over twenty years I have been drawing it.

I was awarded an MBE (Member of the Order of the British Empire) and twice Mentioned in Despatches. For the MBE, I was summoned to her

Majesty's presence at Buckingham Palace, but by then I was in the novitiate at Ampleforth and not permitted to go.

I would not have chosen to spend that time at war, but I can think of some worse, and many better, ways of spending the years from age twenty to age twenty-six.

It remained to communicate my decision about Ampleforth to those who needed to know. Mother was sad from one point of view, but mostly glad; my father acquiesced graciously but did not understand, and must have been disappointed, as I was his only child and he had a very strong sense of the family name. There had always been a known male Horner since Little Jack Horner in the first half of the sixteenth century, but I was the last. Of my other close relatives, the most sympathetic was my uncle, David, who wrote elegant novels and was a friend of the Sitwells. He was the most light-hearted of his siblings, his mother's favorite, and later became a Catholic. He once told me that when he woke up at 5 a.m., he used to think of me getting up at that hour, perhaps say a prayer for me, and go contentedly back to sleep.

Then there were the Horner Aunts. They lived at Mells in the South-West of England, not in the ancestral Manor House but in a house nearby. None of them ever married, and they lived to be 99, 99, and 92. The most lively at the time was Aunt Muriel, who expected, and received, regular letters from me, even from Burma. I once told her that my Muslim batman, when he was late one day, explained that they had been celebrating the near-sacrifice of Isaac by Abraham. Aunt Muriel passed this on to the rest of the family in the form, 'Isn't it nice that Michael and his batman have the Old Testament in common?' In due course she asked me what I was going to do now that the war was over. I said that I was going to be a monk at Ampleforth. I waited for her to express shock, but in fact she replied, 'A month, dear; that's a very long time to stay there'. I tried again with 'I am going to be a priest'. Again I was surprised when she said, 'A priest, dear. That's wonderful: there has always been a priest in the family'. She was referring to the Horners' advowson, or right of presentation of a rector, to the Church of England (Episcopalian) parish of Mells. The family often presented one of its own members. It was not a large parish, so its rector was not unduly busy. One Horner rector discovered a complicated method of extracting square roots, and another compiled a Coptic dictionary. I had been expecting anti-Catholic expressions of disapproval, so I was relieved that I was quite wrong.

In general, though, the family's comments were more 'rebound from the war: it won't last' or 'escapism'. To Elizabeth, who was still in Kenya, I had to send a sad letter, which took me a long time to write and a long time to get over.

After making the rounds of the family, I packed up what I needed, including a considerable number of books, mostly classical texts that I had had at Oxford, and which I was told to bring with me to Ampleforth. They went into a tea-chest, and joined my old green trunk, a tin trunk from the war, and a suitcase. These were joined later by an ammunition case, which I had left in store in Calcutta under the care of Messrs. Cox and King. At first Cox and King denied its existence, then said it had been looted in the riots there, but finally produced it and most of its contents. It was useful because almost indestructible. Then in due course I took the train via York to Gilling, where I was met, and driven the two miles to the abbey.

Sixteen

BACK TO AMPLEFORTH

We arrived just in time for supper. I was standing near the Refectory (dining-room) with the monk who had driven me to the abbey from the station, when the whole community emerged from Vespers in church and came towards us. The approach of this black phalanx was too much for me, and I fled, but not very far. I was recaptured, given a napkin and a place, and started my first monastic meal. The monks had just finished their annual Retreat and their Conventual Chapter, (annual general meeting) and were now celebrating with wine and a few speeches. Abbot Herbert Byrne was an excellent and witty speaker, and I thought that monastic life might not be so austere as I had feared. But it was not a typical monastic supper.

Abbot Herbert was known for elegant and economical turns of phrase. There was also in him a vein of pessimism. He was once in a railway carriage with two other monks with a similar vein. They were reading their newspapers. One said, 'The news is grim'; the second said, 'Grim but true'; the third concluded, 'The grimmer, the truer'. Many years later I was standing by the abbey's barometer, which was a rotating cylinder with a pointer that marked the reading as the cylinder rotated. Abbot Herbert came by, looked at the pointer and, taking all three parts himself, said, 'The glass is low; I think it is as low as it can go; I think it would go lower, if it could.' Once, after rugby practice, he was walking back with one of the boys, who was uttering a string of complaints. At the end, Father Herbert, as he then was, said simply 'Practise praising, Perceval.'

There were several Junior monks who had been in the school with or after me, who greeted me and the other postulants (men 'demanding' to be monks) with great friendliness. That was flattering until I discovered that part of the reason for their joy was that during the later years of World War II no one had been allowed to join a monastery. Consequently these juniors had, for several years, been doing all the sacristy work and other chores around the monastery. Now at last they saw the prospect of shedding the chores; we, the new novices, were the prospect.

We started with a Retreat from the Prior, Father Laurence Buggins, and were then clothed as novices. Ten of us started the novitiate; six were aged from eighteen to twenty-one and four from twenty-six to thirty-six. The community betting was that the young would survive and the older 'war rebounds' would go on their way. The exact opposite happened.

In those days (1946), the novices, except when on business, spoke only to one another and to the Abbot, Prior, and Novice Master or his *socius* (associate), so it was a blessing that there were ten of us. Coming from the army, I did not find the idea of obedience strange, even though the army's motive for obedience is quite different from the monastic motive. But, also because of my time in the army, during which we had been constantly on the move both from place to place and from country to country, I did find the idea of being in the same place for life very strange. Nor did I relish the prospect of getting up at 5 a.m. for life. When I told the Novice Master that, he said, 'but you don't have to' and my heart leapt. But he went on, 'all you have to do is to get up at 5 a.m. tomorrow'. That was a let-down, but also a wise piece of advice, which helped my future outlook on many things.

Some of the monastic practices also seemed strange. One was the 'confession of faults'. This entailed kneeling out in the middle of choir in front of the community and stating not sins, but faults, such as breaking the rules of silence or looking around in choir. One of our novices had a rather peculiar hairstyle, and the monks, unknown to us, had nicknamed him 'the witch'. He and I were given the job of beating the coconut matting, which served as a carpet for the novitiate gallery. We rolled it up and threw it out of the window. It shattered a shrub below. We then found two brooms, removed their handles and started beating the matting, he at one end and I at the other. When we met in the middle, we both struck at the same time, and that was the end of his handle. At the next confession of faults he, the witch, shattered monastic decorum by saying he had done thus and so, and concluding, 'And I broke my broomstick.'

Another much more welcome custom was the Month Day, a day on which the novices had a day without classes, and any monks who were free could join them. We often went over to our lakes and sailed a 14-foot, Bermuda-rigged yacht called Anne. It was interesting sailing partly because Anne was too big for the lake, and partly because the lake was surrounded by trees, but with gaps. Through the gaps could come a sudden, violent gust of wind. One such did come and snapped the mast. We carried the mast two miles back to the carpentry shop, where Father John, an expert carpenter, planed the two ends, made a beautiful diagonal joint and glued it with what was then known as airforce glue, a two-bottle glue. One applied glue from one bottle to one side of the cut and from the other bottle to the other side. We carried the mast back to the lake, re-fitted it and set sail. Exactly the same happened again and the mast snapped again; but the break was not in the same place but an inch or two higher. The joint and the glue were stronger than the wood itself.

We read the Rule of Saint Benedict several times and discussed it; we studied the Psalms in the late-Latin of the Vulgate, and had other classes; but it was not, and was not intended to be, a year of intense mental work. The Prior, not a great Latinist, taught us the Psalms. On one occasion he opened his Latin text at Psalm 71 and his English translation at Psalm 70. After a verse or two, we, the most junior members of the monastery, suggested to the second senior monk that something was amiss. Without fuss or crossness he said, 'What a duffer I am', turned his English translation to Psalm 72, and started again. We did not learn a lot about the Latin, but much about monastic behavior. I also quickly learnt how little I knew about the life I had chosen.

Our manual labor was partly indoors and partly outdoors. One of our first tasks was to clean up the novitiate gallery. I have already alluded to the coconut matting. For several years there had been no novices and so the novices' gallery was unkempt. Bats had invaded a loft at one end of the gallery. They also emerged from their loft and flew up and down the gallery and even into our cells. The ceiling was high and they were out of reach, but with billiard cues we could intercept them. We swung our cues at them, but a flying bat is an elusive target. We did hit some and the rest were either discouraged by this or removed by the janitors. We learnt how to deal at night with a bat in the bedroom: turn out the lights, open the window, get a flashlight and hold it at arms length in the middle of the window. The bat will go toward the light, and so out of the window.

Indoors, our other manual labor was mostly sacristy work, mine being initially in the Abbot's chapel, where the abbot and an elderly monk celebrated Mass. I asked the latter if all was well, and he told me a number of things that were wrong, ending with, 'Look at this alb: no gussets.' Having no idea what a gusset is, I duly went to the main sacristan and asked if he had any. Together we searched all the drawers and found none. I corrected the other things that were wrong, and then told the old monk I was sorry that the sacristan had no gussets.

He replied, 'You idiot, don't you know what a gusset is?' or words to that effect. He explained, and I took the alb along to the seamstress.

Outdoors, we worked in the monastic garden or in the monks' wood, or in the orchard. Picking raspberries was the most popular job. The tasks were often hard work, but after six years in the army, I was quite fit. I also worked in the monastic library.

We did our half-hour of Spiritual Reading, as it was then called, which was less centered on the Bible than now, and our half-hour of Meditation, or Mental Prayer. We learnt about the various forms of prayer. I once told Father Abbot that I was reading a book called *Difficulties in Mental Prayer*. 'It must be a very long book,' he replied. We did our sacristy work morning and evening. The fewer there became of us, the more each one had to do.

We also discovered that the reasons for many monastic customs or rules are hard to put into words. It is only after a monk has observed them for twenty years or so, that he appreciates their value and wisdom. One of our novices asked me whether we really had to keep all these pettifogging rules, and most novices feel that way at some time. It is an act of obedience and of faith to observe them and to trust that experience will show their wisdom. But most parents and teachers have on some occasion used the phrase, 'because I say so', which is the much same idea.

Life in the novitiate was so different from what our life was to be afterwards that we sometimes questioned how good a preparation it was. But monastic superiors have, more recently, been concerned about young monks making Solemn Vows or receiving priestly Ordination and then, soon afterwards, departing. It now seems possible that the stricter novitiate somehow militated against that more effectively than the gentler novitiates of today. Neither way is perfect, but the older way had its points. It focused almost entirely on the spiritual side of being a monk, and left most of the practicalities for later.

One quite unexpected phenomenon was novitiate giggles, a result, probably, of the enclosed nature of the novitiate at that time. It is less common today. Another novice had been a wing-commander in the Royal Air Force in World War II. He and I were in the middle of the choir, reading the readings and responses of the second nocturn at Vigils. He suddenly began to giggle. It was infectious, and soon both of us were helpless, and had to return ignominiously to our seats. He had suddenly started to wonder what our respective commanding officers would have thought and said if they had seen us. It does not seem hilarious now, but it was early morning and long before the first cup of coffee.

Reading aloud in public could be problematic, but singing aloud and solo in public was much worse. When I first had to sing the epistle at our monks' Mass, the tune was a plainchant tune, which was to me an unfamiliar style of music and has a special melody for questions. It is not particularly difficult, but I had four questions in a row. By the end, my knees were knocking together, the only time in my life that I can remember that happening.

Christmas brought a vacation for the novices as well as for the boys, though not for so long. After Midnight Mass, each priest celebrated privately two other Masses. Lunch was the big meal, worked off, by those who felt like it, by a game of touch rugby. Then, on December 28, the Feast of the Holy Innocents, the novices were required to entertain the community. This took place in the Calefactory (warming place, common room). At one end was a large open fireplace, facing which was a semi-circle of chairs. The novices had the other half of the room as their stage, so they started with their audience having their backs to them. If the entertainment was good enough, the audience would turn their chairs round, but this did not always happen. We were lucky enough to secure their attention with a series of songs and skits, but it was touch and go. Another novice was reading to me from a fictitious letter from me to my former Commanding Officer, saying that I had joined a community of Black Monks, which is one way of referring to Benedictines. Taking the role of the commanding officer I broke in, 'Black monks! BLACK monks? I hope they have British officers.' This was long before political correctness.

At the end of the Christmas vacation, the novices had to clear away all the holly and other decorations from the Calefactory. It seemed easier to burn them in the large fireplace than to lug them outside. The holly made a wonderful crackle and blaze, which we were all enjoying, when the Prior appeared. The chimney went up past his room, and he had heard a strange roaring in it. We had set the chimney on fire, but in due course it went out of its own accord.

Every three months there was a 'perseverance', which is a kind of spiritual inspection. The abbot and his Council of Seniors, with the help of the Novice Master, discuss whether each novice should be given another three months. The novice, for his part, is free to leave at any time. Five of the six novices who left did so of their own accord, but the threat of dismissal seemed quite real: it was like the threat of RTU (Returned To Unit) when I was at the OCTU, as I mentioned above, and quite real enough to cause, if not panic, at least apprehension. At the end of our first year, the four of us who were accepted made our Simple Profession: that is, we vowed that we would be monks for the next three years. That was a serious commitment for those three years, but we would be completely free to leave at the end of them, should we so wish.

Although in the second year we were still novices and sequestered from the other monks, we did start our course of ecclesiastical studies: Scripture, Philosophy, and Church History. These were taught by resident monks, all of whom had a heavy load of work in the school. Although they were knowledgeable and made the courses interesting, it was not an ideal arrangement.

Our philosopher, Father Raphael, was also the housemaster of a house (dormitory) some little way from the main building. We wrote essays and then took them up to him and read them. He would then comment and discuss, very much as in an Oxford tutorial. One snowy day, Brother Gervase had done all this. At the end, Father Raphael, who was a little hard to understand at the best of times, put his pipe in his mouth, wrapped a scarf over it, and his cloak over both. They walked down together to class in the monastery, with Father Raphael continuing the discussion. Brother Gervase, who could hear nothing intelligible, answered yes and no alternately. When they reached the monastery, Father Raphael took off the outer layers and said, 'Brother Gervase, I would never have thought that you would believe that.' Brother Gervase never discovered what 'that' was.

Father Raphael was devoted to Aristotle's *De Anima*, of which he kept the library's copy in his room for many years. When I gently suggested that it might be returned, Father Raphael replied that 'his' copy had fallen to bits and we should buy him another one. There were joyous moments in his class, too. He complained one day that there was a draught in his room because the door would not stay closed. Brother Benedict suggested a door closer, of which the main parts were a cylinder with a piston inside, and a spring. The gadget worked, and next day he was all smiles. Several days he later, he was not, and we asked him why. His reply was 'Do you know what the boys did? They put treacle (molasses) in the cylinder'.

At the start of the third year we emerged from the novitiate and were allowed to talk to the other monks. We also started to have some contact with the boys in the school: a little teaching and a little coaching of the sport in season. But a bombshell was on its way. A senior Classics teacher had to go home to care for his sick mother. The Prior summoned me and told me to take over his classes, 28 periods a week, ranging from the Junior House (eighth grade) to the scholarship sixth form (seniors). This was quite demanding, especially as I had studied no Classics for the last eight years. As I left the Prior's room, he said, 'and you must not let it interfere with your ecclesiastical studies.' 'No, Father' I said. This lasted for six or eight arduous weeks. It was also my first classroom teaching of Ampleforth boys. I had done a fair amount of teaching in the army, but that was to men to whom what I was teaching might prove literally vital.

I had a lively set in the Junior House, one of whom had a little collection of farthings[7]. He often dropped one in class. When I collected the eighth farthing, I said, 'That's eight: how many more do you have?'

He claimed I had only seven. I made a deal. If I had only seven, he would get them all back; if I had eight, I would get the rest of his collection. There was a small upright piano in the classroom. Next class I brought my eight, and counted them out resonantly on the lid of the piano. He handed over his residue, but he got them back when I stopped teaching the class. During the Christmas break I was sent over to Gilling Castle to catch up the ecclesiastical studies that I had missed.

Gilling Castle was acquired by the monks in 1929 for their Junior (grade) School. It is late-medieval, though parts may be earlier, and some of the stone doorways of the basement still have the grooves where the soldiers sharpened their spears as they went out to battle. The late-sixteenth century Great Chamber is one of the most complete Elizabethan rooms in England.[8] The castle was a pleasant milieu for study, but I did not really catch up.

At the start of my fourth year, I was sent back to Oxford to fill in, as far as possible, the parts of Greats that I had missed before World War II. I focused on Greek History, which I came to love, and more philosophy, which too I found fascinating. For History my tutor was Mr. Robin Dundas of Christ Church, who had also been the tutor of Father Felix, who had in turn taught me. I lived at Saint Benet's Hall, Ampleforth's house of studies, but was still a member of Christ Church. At Saint Benet's we lived a modified monastic schedule, which left much more time for study than life at Ampleforth did. My life was much less social than when I was at Christ Church before the war, but I did manage in the summer to

7. The farthing was a tiny coin worth a quarter of a penny; it ceased to be legal tender in 1960.
8. Its paneling, stained glass, fireplace, and the dado showing Elizabethan musical instruments, are all of great artistic merit and historical importance.

spend some time bowling in the nets in the Parks with the Varsity cricketers of that year, one of whom, D.B.Carr, later played for England.

Tutorials with Dundas were always interesting. Lewis Carroll had lived in Dundas' rooms previously, and the tiles around the fireplace are believed to have inspired some characters in his writings. Once when I was reading my essay, Dundas took off his shoe, and then his sock, produced an old wooden mushroom, a needle and some thread, and started darning the sock. I went on reading. When I had finished reading, Dundas had finished darning and gave a detailed critique of what I had written. He was very good at that but, curiously, was not a good lecturer, and he hardly published anything. But he did fan my interest in Greek History into a flame, and I taught it with joy at Ampleforth for several years. I had one pupil who very much wanted to get a grade of 'Distinction' in the Higher Certificate examination. I told him he was unlikely to do that in Latin or Greek language but might do it in Greek History, if he worked hard at it. He did, and all three predictions came true.

I came up for membership of the Marylebone Cricket Club, the Mecca of English Cricket, but, to the chagrin of some of our Old Amplefordians, Father Abbot decided No.

One of the monks at Saint Benet's had a tandem bicycle. On a day off, the two of us decided to visit the Benedictines of Priknash Abbey, a ride of about sixty miles each way. We arranged this with Priknash and set off. We arrived late in our cycling costume and said we were expected. They replied that they were expecting two monks but they had never shown up. Nonetheless, they fed us and showed us around. When we left, the tandem broke down and we had to dump it in someone's back garden. This was on a Saturday, and when we reached Gloucester, there was neither train nor bus to Oxford until Monday morning. We called Saint Benet's and said we would start walking and hoped to hitch-hike back. A man kindly picked us up, but said he was going only half way to Oxford. He took us as far as he was going and let us off. We started walking again. Soon we saw a car going the other way. It came to a violent halt, did a U-turn and stopped beside us. It was Fred Wright, the brother of one older monk and uncle of three others. He happened to be staying at Saint Benet's and said he would go to look for us. It was certainly an answer to prayer; we could so easily still have been in the other car; and on Fred's part was a wonderful act of both kindness and faith. He capped it by buying us a drink at a pub on the way back.

At the end of that summer of 1950, and before school started again, the four of us who were left from a novitiate of ten, were due for our Solemn Profession of vows. This is the ceremony at which one becomes fully a monk, and for ever. It normally occurs at the end of one's fourth year as a monk. The vows, for a Benedictine, are not the three standard vows of poverty, chastity and obedience, though these are included. Our wording is Stability, *Conversatio Morum*, and Obedience. Stability means staying put in the monastic community and in its customs. *Conversatio* is hard to translate but means roughly striving to behave as a monk should. Obedience is to the Gospels, the Canon Law of the church, the Rule of Saint Benedict, the Constitutions of the English Benedictine Congregation, the abbot, who is believed to hold the place of Christ in the monastery, the other monks, and to the customs of the particular monastery. Chastity and poverty can be placed under any of our three vows; in fact, each of the three vows seems to present the whole of monastic life, but seen by each from a different angle.

This Solemn Profession committed me to being a monk for life. It also meant that I, the last male of the family, would be unable, by marrying, to carry on the family name. So a family, which first came to prominence through its contact with the Benedictines, when 'Little Jack Horner' became steward of Glastonbury Abbey, and in due course acquired from the abbey the Manor of Mells, came, as it were, full circle and terminated with my Solemn Profession in the Benedictine Abbey of Ampleforth.

One characteristic of the life is distinctive and should be noted here: the Benedictine unit is the abbey. A Benedictine monk belongs to one particular abbey. It is quite exceptional for him to live and work anywhere other than in his abbey or one of its dependent houses. If an abbey makes a foundation, the new house is juridically part of the abbey, but if the new house, in due course, thrives and becomes independent, each of its monks who came from the founding abbey has a fully free choice (unusual for a monk) whether to return to the founding abbey or to transfer his stability to the new house.

This characteristic has a variety of consequences. The position of the abbot is considerably enhanced. Subject to the documents already mentioned, the rules for the house are made on the spot, and so are flexible; they can be readily adapted to a monastery in USA or to one in Africa; they are not 'one size fits all'. But it also means that an abbey must find all its officials from within itself. For a small abbey, this can be a problem. It further means that clashes of personality cannot be solved by sending one of the personalities to another house.

The following school year, I returned to Saint Benet's, this time for a year's Theology with the Dominicans at Blackfriars, a few doors down the street. Brother Hugh and I started at Blackfriars together. I loved it and he did not. He was sent back for a second year and I was not. We were taught Dogmatic Theology by Father Victor White, who was also a student of Jungian psychology, and Moral Theology by Father Antoninus Finili, a gentle man who loved cricket, which endeared him to me. We also studied the prophet Jeremiah, for whom I have ever since had much affection. I enjoyed having time to think at length about all the material, which was not possible at Ampleforth. Of course I loved being at Oxford again, but even apart from that, these were two good years.

When the next school year, 1951, started at Ampleforth, I resumed my theological studies there with the three remaining monks of my year, and also started some regular teaching in the school. This was to be in Latin and Greek, but a little after the term had started I was told that I would also be teaching Greek History. This was a pleasant prospect, but the timing gave me no chance to prepare in advance. As the Oxford system of attending lectures in various topics of Greek history does not quickly translate into a consecutive course in the subject, preparation for that one course absorbed a disproportionate amount of time. Later, I had one year teaching English, and several teaching Religious Instruction, and later yet, became Associate Head of Classics. I continued working in the monastic library, which I had begun as a novice.

I was also coaching in our three major sports, rugby football, athletics (track), and cricket. Cricket was the most enjoyable. I was Father Brendan's assistant with the Colts, that is, the best cricketers under 16. They are rewarding to coach both because they have natural talent and because progress is most rapid at that age. As Father Brendan was a batsman (batter) and wicket-keeper (catcher) and I was a bowler (pitcher), we meshed well.

He took the Colts to play at another school. He came back, after an hour's bus ride, still furious. The last thing their coach had said to him was, 'Oh, there's our Irish Sergeant Major, he's a Catholic; dishonest of course.' It was not clear whether he was disparaging Irish Catholics, or all the Irish, or all Catholics, or all of them, but that kind of view was a not uncommon at the time.

There was also a move to reorganize the cricket. It seemed to me to threaten the Colts, and when the headmaster called a meeting of coaches and house-masters to discuss it, I spoke out rather firmly against it. Later, feeling that I had perhaps been too firm, I went to the headmaster to apologize. He gave me good advice, saying that someone in my position at a meeting like that should state his case as cogently as he could, and so should all the others. It was then the headmaster's business to decide, but he could not make a good decision unless he had heard the various points of view vigorously presented. I bore that in mind, especially when I became a headmaster, and, later, a pastor.

I also learnt something unexpected from coaching hurdles. We had a monk who had been a near-Olympic hurdler. He was giving a demonstration. His form was excellent, but he was a little out of practice and let his toe drop as he went over the hurdle. He fell on the cinder track and cut his face badly.

But rugby was the most eventful. I was given a house (dormitory) junior team to coach through the house matches. That house had an unusually strong first team, and consequently an above average junior team, with powerful running backs, who kept fumbling the ball. We spent most of our practice time on that, and when they thought they were good, I dipped the ball in a muddy stream that ran by the practice area and went on until they could hold on to that slippery object. In the second round with very little time left we were two points behind. At this crucial moment, the captain of our team exhorted his team thus: 'Continue to display a spirit of quiet efficiency, Saint Oswald's.' After that they deserved to win, and did. They went on to win the cup. Because I knew so much less about rugby than about cricket, I spent much more time and thought studying rugby, so much so that the players thought I was much keener on rugby than on cricket, but just the opposite was true.

Our timetable now was that we rose at 5 a.m. for Matins, now called Vigils, (in Latin vigiliae, watch) and Lauds (*laudes*, praises) in church at 5:20; then Prime (*prima*, first), breakfast, Conventual Mass with Terce (*tertia*, third) before and Sext (*sexta*, sixth) after it. None (*nona*, ninth) the last of the 'little hours', was said before lunch and Vespers (*vesperae*, evening) before supper. These 'little hours' were prayers named after the hours of the Roman day, first, third, sixth and ninth, or roughly 7 and 9 a.m., noon and 3 p.m.[9] Compline (*completorium*, completion) the church's night prayer was at 9:00 p.m. followed by the *summum silentium* (total silence), which was punctiliously observed until after Lauds next morning.. Any essential communication during it was done in writing. Lights had to be out by 10:15. All the singing in

---

9. *The Romans divided the hours of daylight into 12 horae (hours). Therefore the length of one hora varied with the time of year.*

church was the Gregorian chant, or plainchant, in Latin. There were usually at least forty monks in choir, several of whom had outstanding voices. On special feasts we had Pontifical High Mass and Pontifical Vespers. The celebrants wore our special cloth of gold vestments. These and the singing had made a great impression on me when I was in the school, and still did when I was a monk.

In the school, classes, normally of 45 minutes, started at 8:45 a.m. with a half-hour break at 11:00, and two more classes from 11:30 until 1:00 p.m. After a short visit to the Blessed Sacrament in church, came lunch, followed by compulsory sports for all from 2:30 to about 3.40. There was one class at 4:15, then tea at 5:00, then three more classes from 5:15 to 7:30. After a second short visit to the Blessed Sacrament came supper, and at 9:00 p.m. night prayers, and so to bed. It was a busy day, whose saddest aspect was that those monks with a full schedule in the school could not also attend all the monastic offices in choir. They said these on their own.

School vacations were about five weeks at Christmas, about three at Easter or thereabouts, and about eight in the summer, usually from near the end of July until the latter part of September. Priests had a month of vacation on their own, usually with their family. Junior monks had their holiday together for about ten days and often in the Lake District. This involved a bicycle ride of just over a hundred miles, and over the Pennine Hills. This was hardest in the year after the novitiate, when we had not been on a bicycle for at least two years. One of these holidays nearly started in disaster: soon after leaving the monastery we came to Sutton Bank, a steep, almost precipitous descent. The first part was steep but straight; the second had some bends and was in places steeper. Early in the second part, my handlebars started to rotate, and ended parallel with the wheels, bringing my hands one in front of the other. I was going too fast to brake safely, and whizzed down the rest of the descent in a curiously twisted position. I could not stop until I reached the bottom of the hill. One of us had a spanner (wrench) and we cured the problem.

The chief attraction of the Lake District is its scenery of lakes and mountains, and the chief activities, walking and climbing. The chief snag was that from our hotel, almost every walk started with an exhausting climb up Dungeon Ghyll (ravine). One year our stay coincided with the feast of our Lady of the Snows, commemorating a miraculous snowfall in Rome one August. A Catholic climbing club held an annual Mass at 6 a.m. on that feast on Sca Fell Pike, the highest peak in the Lake District at just over 3200 feet. It was about a three-hour climb, which started with Dungeon Ghyll. We had decided that we were on holiday and would not attend, but on the way back from our walk on the previous day, two of us ganged up on a third, rather serious, junior saying that we did not see how he could conscientiously stay in bed when others were toiling up the mountain to honor Our Lady. We went on for a while, and eventually persuaded him to go. We could then hardly stay in bed ourselves. We set out before 3 a.m., fasting, and reached our goal a little before 6. We were the only people in sight. It was light by then, but cold and windy with a damp mist swirling around us. We were hot from the climb and cold from the mist. In due course, but well after 6 a.m., the real mountaineers appeared, and we had our Mass, after which we raced back down the mountain to a late breakfast and snooze.

The main job of a monk, qua monk, is his life of prayer and contemplation, but we are not mendicants, and so must also earn a living. In our case there were two principal choices: work in the school or work on our parishes. This reflects our historical background, which we mentioned above and elaborate here. The exact date of the foundation of our community at Westminster, which was then a little outside the city of London, is uncertain, but we know of its restoration by Saint Dunstan some time between 957 and 970. It became the royal abbey of Westminster and saw the coronation of the Kings of England until its dissolution by Henry VIII in 1540. There was a brief restoration of the abbey under Mary Tudor, and then final suppression under Elizabeth I in 1559, when the land and buildings were taken over by the new Church of England. The monks scattered, and Englishmen who wanted to be Benedictines had to go abroad.

In 1608, some of these formed a new monastery at Dieulouard in Eastern France. Two of them had been clothed as monks by the last survivor of Westminster, thus barely preserving the continuity from Westminster to Dieulouard, and so to Ampleforth. The monks ministered to the Catholics near Dieulouard, but also promised to cross the English Channel to minister, at the risk of their lives, to Catholics in England. They were expelled from France in 1793 at the French Revolution, and returned to England, where the penal laws were by then a dead letter. They tried, with little success, to start a school. In due course, many of the places where they ministered became parishes staffed by our monks. After some years of wandering, the monks from Dieulouard settled at Ampleforth in, traditionally, 1802. Here they successfully established a boys' school. Hence, today, the two principal choices of practical work are still teaching in the school or working on a parish. In view of my preparation, it seemed likely that the choice made for me would be the school, and that was how I saw my future. I was quite content. And so, for several years, it turned out. Virtually all Ampleforth monks at that time became priests, so I pursued the course of Theology for the priesthood, did my teaching of Greek, Latin and Ancient History in the school, helped enthusiastically in the monastic library, and coached the various sports at a lowly level except for cricket. I also collected some of the odd-jobs around the monastery: kitchen liaison, a thankless task as an intermediary between the monks and the kitchen, relaying complaints in both directions, but without power to do anything about them. A change was made from hot milk with coffee at breakfast to cold milk. There came bitter complaints, 'Why can't we have hot milk?' A year or two later this was reversed, and again there were bitter complaints, 'Why can't we have cold milk?' I was also in charge, for a while, of the 'Dive', a monastic mini-store supplying mostly toiletries but also the source of cigarettes and tobacco. There was a ration for smokers, but some wanted to exceed it. I was told to try to get them to keep to the ration, but was very unpopular when I did so. I was told, 'I've been a monk much longer than you,' which was almost always true.

About this time, we decided to produce a book to celebrate the sesquicentenary of our arrival at Ampleforth in 1802. It came to be called *Ampleforth and its Origins*. I had a small hand in it: I wrote a chapter on Saint Alban Roe, the only canonized saint of our community, procured the illustrations, and contributed the title.

I was also a member, with several other monks, of the abbey's fire brigade. We were tested one day when the roof of one of our houses (dormitories) caught fire. Although the hose in the house proved inadequate, we put the fire out with relays of buckets of water. The housemaster was seen rescuing his two most valuable possessions: the four volumes of his Breviary (prayer book) and his fishing rod. The engine of the small fire-pump failed to start. Kit, one of our maintenance men, had been cursing it for some time, when Father Abbot came by. We asked him to bless the machine. He replied, 'It sounds as if Kit has blessed it quite sufficiently.' We later discovered the reason the machine would not start: one of the monks had borrowed the machine's rotor arm for the beagle hunt's car, and had forgotten to return it.

On 19 July 1953, I was ordained to the priesthood by the Bishop of Middlesborough. This memorable day was made all the more memorable for me in that all four of the officers of the Artillery Headquarters of 7th Indian Division, of whom only two were Catholic, attended. They spent the previous night in the Station Hotel in York. The question arose of how to greet the Abbot. Lionel (Bulgy) Leach, who had been to school at Ampleforth, explained that it was correct to genuflect, kiss the ring on the abbot's right hand, and address him as Father Abbot. Bulgy then conducted a rehearsal in this famous and rather formal hotel. He took the part of the abbot, sat in an armchair in the venerable foyer while the others knelt to him and kissed his hand. No photographs survive.

A few days later Abbot Herbert gave me my first assignment away from the abbey: I was to go to serve as chaplain for a week to Jimmy and Anne Price and their family. Jimmy and I had overlapped in the school, but he was older than I. They lived at Jedburgh, just north of the border with Scotland. My first Mass for them was, appropriately on the feast of Saint Anne. My duties were varied, and included driving to market a double-decker lorry (truck) full of sheep. Our sheep were put in a pen at the end of the line of pens, and moved up by stages towards the door into the ring. When we were fairly close, Jimmy had to leave us, but promised to be back before we entered the ring. He was not, and to my horror the door opened and we were herded into the ring, facing a bank of knowledgeable and critical border farmers. They asked me questions, some of which I could answer, and some not. We were about to be dismissed in ignominy, when Jimmy rushed in. We sold no sheep. That evening the Prices had a piper in, and after dinner he played his pipes and we danced highland reels. I did a bit better at that. All in all, it was a delightful week, and led to many more such.

One summer, Bulgy Leach took me to the opera at Glyndebourne for Mozart's *Magic Flute*. Glyndebourne is in Sussex near Lewes. Many people drive there and park in a large field. The interval is a long one, so they bring a picnic supper, which they have at their tailgates. The field is also a long one, and at the very far end of it was a herd of cows. We made some comment on this to one of the staff, who replied that the cows usually came down to look at the visitors, but they did not like Mozart and never came near when the opera was by him.

This was not the only intrusion of my past into my present. General Messervy, who commanded our division for most of our time in Burma, sent his two sons to Ampleforth, and Brigadier Dyer, who commanded an

Armored Brigade, sent one. General Evans, who had taken over in Burma from General Messervy, became GOC-in-C of Northern Command, and was stationed at York. He inspected our OTC (ROTC) and also, being a keen cricketer, came to watch some of our cricket matches. As a young subaltern he had opened the batting for the Warwickshire Regiment with Lieutenant (later Field Marshal) Montgomery as his partner. I saw him several times, and his warm greeting raised my monastic stock considerably. When I was sent to USA, I went to see him in York to tell him. His ADC, understandably, tried to brush off this young cleric, but General Evans heard my voice, came out of his office, and invited me to lunch.

In the summer of 1953, my father and stepmother took me to Holland and Denmark. There were still fierce restrictions on how much money you could take out of England, so as much booking as possible had to be done before departure. We started with a night flight from London to Amsterdam. From the air, both cities, but especially Amsterdam, looked amazingly beautiful in the dark. In Holland we saw acres of tulips, and the strange sight of masts and sails moving through the landscape with no hull in sight as they passed along the countless canals. We visited many art galleries, from which I remember Rembrandt's *The Night Watch* (1642), a special exhibition of Van Gogh with many of his earliest paintings of Potato Eaters and others, and charming Vermeers at Delft, where my father was the millionth visitor and received a box of chocolates.

Each morning I got up early, walked to the Cathedral and said Mass in Latin with a small Dutch boy serving. The prayers at the end were in the vernacular. I said my bit and the boy replied 'Bet voor ons' (Pray for us). I thought he said 'wait for us'. So I waited. I said my part again. So did he. Then I remembered my German, and we went on.

We then went by night train to Denmark. In our compartment were two or three Lutherans, one of whom was a young woman who was returning to Copenhagen to be ordained Deaconess. We had a long conversation about women and the priesthood, which she thought was inevitable and I, then, thought was preposterous. The journey passed quickly. In Denmark we visited the main Museum, where I found the editor of the text of the Parian Marble, a Greek chronological list which, as I was teaching Greek History, was of great interest to me. I was not enchanted by the Mermaid, but I did love the Tivoli Gardens. We went to the northern tip of Denmark, visited Hamlet's Elsinore, and looked across at Sweden, which is as close as I have ever been to Scandinavia.

Back at Ampleforth, I was settling into the routine and learning how to mesh my duties in the school into my monastic life. I was teaching between 28 and 32 periods a week – this is easier in a boarding school than in a day school, but not much. I went on coaching the Colts for cricket and was promoted to do the same for rugby. In each case I was the assistant coach. I also coached young boys for the 120 yards high hurdles. I could tell them what to do, and demonstrate the exercises but not the hurdling. I had one plump and very unathletic boy who refused at the first hurdle. He tried again and refused again. I said he could do it if he tried, to which he replied seriously, 'Do you really think so?' I said I did, but I was wrong. I took off all the bars, leaving an obstacle perhaps a foot high. He ran up again, jumped, landed on the hurdle, and smashed it. We agreed that he should try something else. I was also appointed school librarian. My only qualifications were that I had been an assistant to the monastery's librarian, and that I liked books.

Once ordained priest, I was given charge of a tiny parish in the small village of Oswaldkirk, two miles east of the abbey. I had about fifty parishioners in all. We celebrated Mass in the village hall, and collected money, mostly by annual jumble sales, to build a church. I bought a tiny motorcycle (98 cc), which was an ideal runabout, and even took me across the moors to Scarborough.

I had the idea of visiting everyone in the village, Catholic or otherwise. After a few calls I reached the house of a delightful, middle-aged lady, who said, "Coom in and 'ave a coop o' tea, luv". I explained what I was doing and we chatted for a while. When I asked her if she had any questions or comments, she had indeed. She listed several families with four, six, or in one case ten children, and ended with, 'You know what I think, it's not natural'. I replied that you could say many things about that, but you had to admit that it was natural.

I was also asked to take over the OTC. The previous commandant had done it for many years and certainly deserved a rest, but I was overburdened already, and anyway had been quite content to leave the army behind. Hesitantly I went to the Prior and said that I did not think I could manage it, or at least could not give it the time it deserved. He agreed.

Seventeen

A CHANGE OF CONTINENT

Ampleforth lies on one side of a green and peaceful valley, and my life, though busy, seemed peaceful and regular. At the end of the summer of 1954, however, Prior Aelred Graham, a monk of Ampleforth who had been lent to Portsmouth Priory (now Abbey) in Rhode Island, USA, came to England with a proposal for a foundation in Saint Louis, Missouri. Providentially, he came at a time when Ampleforth was looking to make a foundation somewhere, but had not found the right place.

From here on much of my story has already been told in *In Good Soil*, our history of Saint Louis Priory 1954-1973,[10] dealing with the founding of our monastery and school in Saint Louis, Missouri. I am intending here to write a personal memoir, but, if it is to be intelligible, I cannot avoid some repetition here of what I wrote there.

Prior Aelred told us that a group of men in Saint Louis, a city about which few of us knew anything, wanted to establish a college-preparatory school and were looking for a group to staff it. Prior Aelred presented the proposal persuasively to the monks, so the Abbot's Council of Seniors decided that the idea was worth taking seriously. Abbot Herbert Byrne then invited the group in Saint Louis to send a delegation to Ampleforth to tell us more. They arrived in November and laid their case before the Abbot's Council, which recommended that the abbot put the proposal to the solemnly professed monks of the community, and, in preparation, send a reconnaissance party to Saint Louis. Accordingly, two senior and respected monks visited Saint Louis and came back with a very favorable report. In January 1955, the solemnly professed monks assembled for an Extraordinary Conventual Chapter and accepted the proposal by the surprising margin of four to one. The original plan was to send nine monks, but that had to be reduced to three, which had dire consequences.

Next came the selection of the team. It was to start with a Prior, a Procurator (Business Manager), and a Headmaster. I felt secure that I would not be any of

10. *In Good Soil by Timothy Horner, OSB, Saint Louis (Saint Louis Abbey Press) 2001.*

those three, and so, when one of my Oswaldkirk parishioners told me she had heard that I was going to Saint Louis, I shrugged it off with 'Oh no: I'm sure the abbot would tell me before it was known in the parish'. Nonetheless, on Good Friday, the abbot sent for me and started with 'Father, I think you had better sit down'. Then I knew. He confirmed it with the words, 'Father dear, I am going to uproot you'.

The other two members of the team were Father Columba Cary-Elwes, then Prior of the abbey, and Father Luke Rigby, who was teaching English in the school and had been a pupil of C.S.Lewis at Oxford. For the rest of the school year we three were too busy to do much planning, but we did have a few meetings, often to answer questions from Saint Louis. We went through the arduous process of obtaining visas – as I was born in what was by 1955 Pakistan, the US Consulate wanted to put me in the very small Pakistani quota – but with the powerful help of the group in Saint Louis and their congressmen we eventually received all the necessary papers. Father Columba and I then went to Oxford for a short course on American ways. It was a useful overview, but the two best pieces of advice that I received came from elsewhere. Sir Herbert Read, whose wife was a parishioner in Oswaldkirk, said that those who had made a fortune were much admired, but those who had inherited a fortune had still to prove themselves. My uncle David told me that, tot for tot, liquor in America was stronger than liquor in England. As we were going to be dealing with many of the affluent, and as public relations and alcohol were closely related, those were relevant pieces of advice.

Then there was an interlude in the literal sense. The Old Amplefordian Cricket Club, alumni of the school, played several matches during our summer term, and then had a tour in August, to which any monks who were Old Amplefordians and cricketers, might be invited. I was so invited, joined the tour, and had the pleasure of playing in Hove on the county ground of Sussex, my county, and contributed a jumping slips catch, which was both spectacular and lucky.

After that we were nearly ready to go, but first came a delightful surprise. Sir Ernest Barker, who had married my aunt Olivia, had sent me an invitation to take his son Nicolas on a trip to Greece, for which he would pay. He addressed it to Ampleforth College, Near York and the Post Office sent it to New York, whence it was returned to me a couple of months later. Having, of course, had no reply from me, he telephoned and asked why I had ignored his invitation. I was as puzzled as he was angry, but we got it sorted out, the abbot gave his permission, and off we flew.

The name *Horner* looks very like *Homer*, and I was admitted to Greece by the Greek Customs officials as MR. HOMER, but never received any further recognition as 'Founder's Kin'. Sir Ernest was a friend of the Canadian Ambassador, who arranged for us to be met and installed in a hotel far beyond our means. He entertained us knowledgeably later.

We traveled occasionally by train or by sea, but most the time by bus or on foot. By bus was the most exciting. The buses were military vehicles left over from World War II. There was little doubt that on a journey of any length over the hilly terrain they would break down. Every seat was always taken and camp stools were then set out in the central gangway. Baggage, chickens and pets went on top and were held in place by an enormous tarpaulin. The little girl sitting next to me on one occasion held a brown paper bag. As the bus moved off, the bag began to wriggle and a long, brown ear emerged. The driver stopped and demanded that the pet rabbit be put on top. The girl wept, we pleaded, and eventually I said something in my limited greek – it may have been *Kyrie, Eleison* (Lord, have mercy) – which made them all laugh, and the driver relented. On another occasion, Nicolas and I managed to sit together at the back of the bus. We were coming to Akro-Korinth towards evening, and there was a full moon. We both wanted to climb the mountain, but there was no way to reach the driver nor to attract his attention. We had been eating grapes from a bag, so we made the bag into a ball and threw it at the driver, who braked hard and asked indignantly who did that. I said 'Ego' and explained in stumbling Greek that we wanted to get off and climb the mountain. Everyone was on our side, and he kindly agreed to stop. We climbed the mountain and had a wonderful view over the plain of Argos by full moon.

Father Barnabas had warned me at Ampleforth that the harbor, Piraeus, was so crowded that when one ship weighed anchor, several other anchors would come with it. I was skeptical, but when Nicolas and I boarded our ship for Crete (deck class), and she pulled up her anchor, at least one other anchor came with it. It took an hour or two to disentangle them. We then made our big mistake. It was hot by day, but quite cold at night and at sea. All the experienced travelers made for the engine room, but we went up on deck. At bedtime we went down to the engine room, but there was not an inch of floor space vacant. We went back on deck. Two Cretan soldiers noticed our plight and had a spare blanket each, which they lent us. After a while, I started to itch and scratch. I looked over at Nicolas, and he was scratching too. We were not the only living things in the blankets. But, better itch than freeze, and in the morning we

(L to R) Father Luke, Father Columba, myself and Father Ian study a letter from St. Louis.

returned the blankets with profuse thanks. When the soldiers, who were Greek Orthodox, saw me saying my Breviary, they wanted to see it, and showed me in return their own beautiful prayer books.

We visited the Archaeological Museum in Herakleion, the world's best for things Minoan, then Knossos, where there are *in situ* copies of the famous frescoes, the originals being in the museum in Herakleion. Finally we went to Phaistos on the South shore. The bus-ride over the spine of Crete was exciting. After Phaistos, Nicolas and I decided to walk from there to Ayia Triadha. It was hot, we were thirsty; we saw an olive tree and sampled the olives. They were unripe and bitterly astringent, and made us thirstier still, but Agia Triadha was worth it. We went cabin-class on the ship back to Athens.

Our other sea-voyage was to Mount Athos at the north-western corner of the Aegean Sea. We were entertained at one of the monasteries by the monks with ouzo (aniseed) and loukoumi (Turkish delight). We were shown some of the monks' cells, and met an old monk who had lived for many years in Chicago. He said it was common for Greek men like him to emigrate, make money, set up their family, and then return to Greece and join a monastery. After a while, Nicolas and I asked if we might see the library. They told us to go on upstairs until we came to it. There were, as we half expected, priceless treasures – books and illuminated manuscripts – on the open shelves. We became absorbed, and the next thing we knew was the ship's siren summoning stragglers. We raced downstairs. As we passed the calefactory where we had been entertained, we saw the novices wolfing the remains of our ouzo and loukoumi. *Plus ça change* . . .

It was a wonderful introduction to Greece. In 1955 one could walk all over the Acropolis and its temples, while school children picnicked on the hallowed marble of the Parthenon. At Mycenae there was one sleepy guard and few visitors; and in the less known sites, we were often the only visitors. The same was true in Crete. I also learnt that the classical wonders of Greece were far from being its only wonders. I knew something of pre-classical Mycenae, but nothing of the medieval mosaics at Daphne and Hosios Loukas. I also tested on the spot some of the optical refinements of the

A last farewell to the homeland.

Parthenon: if you put an object at one end of the platform on which the columns stand, and walk to the other end, you cannot, when you bend down, see the object. The platform rises a few inches to the center and drops again to the far end. That gives a liveliness, which would not be there except for that rise. And there are many other such refinements. I have been back to Greece several times, but no time was quite like the first.

Eighteen

WE CROSS THE ATLANTIC

Back at Ampleforth, as the day of our departure for America drew near, we re-read very carefully the excellent report of our two senior monks; we studied air photographs; we discussed what to take and what to leave; then, on October 3, 1955 we left Ampleforth, and on October 7, 1955 left Southampton on the *Queen Elizabeth*.

We were three very different people: Father Columba Cary-Elwes was interested in and had written about monastic spirituality, and especially what it had to offer to boys. He taught Religion and modern languages and was a housemaster (in charge of a dormitory) in the school, and then Prior in the monastery. He was fifty-one. His uncle had been a Jesuit missionary in China, and Father Columba had thought of following him.

Father Luke Rigby was thirty-two, had been a priest for five years and had a parish at Kirkby Moorside, near Ampleforth. He taught Religion and English in the school. He was also interested in calligraphy and golf.

I was thirty-five, interested in the classics and classical archaeology, travel (owing to the Army), cricket, squash racquets, tennis and golf, riding a horse and sailing a boat, photography and working on a wood-lathe. I had been a priest for two years, and had a tiny parish at Oswaldkirk, very near the abbey. I taught Classics, Religious Instruction, and one year of English.

At our first dinner on board the *Queen Elizabeth* we found a bottle of champagne on the table. At first we thought this was part of queenly hospitality, but soon were told that it came from Mr. Fred Wright, a dedicated Old Amplefordian, brother or uncle of several monks. He was the one who rescued us at Oxford after the tandem collapsed. We drank his health, and our own. The voyage was uneventful: we sat with two learned Jesuits, who were returning from a conference on Patristics; we met enough unevenness for the Queen to put out her stabilisers once or twice; we were invited to the Captain's table; we visited the engine room; we never won the competition to guess the mileage covered in the day.

In due course Father Columba, who had made the voyage before, gathered us on deck to see the Manhattan skyline, so familiar to us from the movies. 'There it is', he said, but it turned out to be a set of storage units for natural gas, called in England 'gasometers'. Right then he lost his status as local expert. The skyline was magnificent when it did appear, surreal had it not been real.

We were very well entertained in New York by Mr. and Mrs. Robert L. Hoguet, friends of Portsmouth Priory. They showed us around. We visited the United Nations Building, Wall Street, and the Frick Museum. At the Frick, the guards wore side-arms. We had earlier seen a sign 'No parking on the pavement'. Pavement to us meant sidewalk. Mentally putting the 'pavement' and the side-arms together, (did they really need to be told not to park on the sidewalk? Did attendants in a museum really need side-arms?) we wondered what we were getting into. That evening, Mr. Hoguet stated that every lively organization 'lived in the red', and his daughter inveighed against corporal punishment.

We were to meet two quite unforeseen difficulties: language problems and sense of humor. Words like *pavement* or *rubber* had quite different meanings, and many other words like *urchin* or *old* had quite different connotations in UK and USA. But beyond that, many words or phrases or even tones of voice were interpreted differently. We have already noticed *pavement*. We soon met *rubber*, which to us meant *eraser*. Harder were occasions such as this: I was invited to a barbecue by some prospective parents. They asked me what I would like to drink. I said, flippantly, that I never drank anything except champagne. No English hostess would have taken that seriously from a monk. Two weeks later I had forgotten all about it and turned up for the barbecue. We had a cocktail, went to the barbecue pit for our steak and fixings, and then to the table, where there was a bottle of excellent champagne. I said, 'Hurray, what are we celebrating?' My host said, 'But, Father, you said you never drank anything except champagne.' I felt most embarrassed and said I really was not being serious. His wife saved the day by rounding on her husband with 'There you are, dear, I told you he was joking.'

Or again, when Archbishop Fulton Sheen, a distinguished orator, came to talk to the priests of our Archdiocese about a mission to South America, he started with three unrelated jokes, then delivered the first half of his speech. When heads began to nod, he told three more jokes, and then the second half. An English orator of that caliber might have told no jokes, but would have had a vein of humor running through the whole speech. Both techniques are effective, but I felt a little uneasy with Archbishop Sheen's.

I felt much more uneasy when, after his address, there was a reception at the Chase-Park Plaza Hotel. I was one of several who had the job of shepherding the distinguished guests up to the right floor. Thinking I was being very much acclimated (acclimatized), I turned to one of the priests in my first batch and said 'Father, I'm Father Timothy, a Benedictine, may I ask your name?' The answer was Archbishop X. I did the same on the next trip; the answer was Archabbot Y. Twice bitten, I was more cautious and on the third trip asked 'Father, are you an Archbishop or an Archabbot?' The reply was 'No, I'm an Archimandrite' (superior abbot in the Greek Orthodox Church). After that, we traveled in British silence.

A third example occurred several years later. At first we sent over to Ampleforth for their novitiate young men who wanted to be monks with us. I visited them there and asked them how they liked the English monks. 'Oh, they're fine, they're good, prayerful, observant, and so on, but they have no sense of humor'. I then asked some of the English monks how they liked our American novices. 'Oh, they're fine, they're good, prayerful, observant, and so on, but they have no sense of humor.' If a common sense of humor depends on making the same assumptions about what is normal, that showed how often the English and the Americans do not make the same assumptions. As we found out, that could lead to a variety of difficulties.

None of those three early novices, who were all good candidates, and all graduates of our school, persevered. This discouraged other boys of our school. It was one of the sad results of changing from the original plan of sending nine monks to Saint Louis to sending only three. Had there been nine, one would certainly have been made Novice Master, and there would have been no need to send novices to England. We would also have had other monastic officials such as Guest Master and Director of Vocations; the work load for each of us would have been much lighter; it might have eased relationships within the community. A group of three so easily becomes two and one. This change of numbers, though inevitable because of a change in the situation at Ampleforth, was, at least from our point of view, the most serious mistake made.

A different form of the problem of language became apparent only gradually. The various bodies that accredit schools make periodical visits to the schools, just as do the inspectors of schools in England. The visiting committe forms sub-committees to look at various aspects of the school. At one school, I was on the 'Philosophy and Objectives' sub-committee. We made our visits and met to discuss and collect our impressions. I was then asked to write our report, which I did in longhand, and handed it in to be typed. Next morning when I arrived, they were reading a report. They asked me what I thought. I replied that I thought the bits that I could understand sounded quite sensible. They laughed and said that I should think so, since I had written it. This I denied hotly. 'Oh well,' they said, 'of course we had to translate it into educational jargon, otherwise no one would have paid any attention to it.' I was reminded of this when I visited our doctor and showed him a patch on my forearm to make sure it was not a melanoma. He said it was desiccated, epiphytic, dermatitis. I replied, 'You mean it's just a dry spot on my skin'. He agreed.

I dislike jargon, and yet, had he told me it was a dry spot on my skin, I might well have retorted that I could have told him that. I can imagine myself or others saying 'Guess what: I have desiccated epiphytic dermatitis' but never 'guess what: I have a dry spot on my skin'; the latter would be neither news-worthy nor conversation-worthy. So there is a place and a need for technical language, but then there is danger of misunderstanding, as when the Vatican spoke of 'objectively disordered acts' as a technical, theological description, and the media thought the Vatican was simply being offensive.

We also missed hearing English spoken as we knew it. A guest stayed with us who was very English. When he left we were surprised how much we had all enjoyed simply listening to him speak.

Nineteen

ARRIVAL IN SAINT LOUIS

ur next stop on our way to Saint Louis was at Saint Anselm Priory (now Abbey) in Washington, DC. This was one of the two Benedictine monasteries of the English Congregation then in US: the other was Portsmouth Priory (now Abbey). We were to be the third. We were shown around Washington, and met our senators, but the most important event was a meeting of the three of us, at which we found that we all agreed that the monastery had priority over the school, and that our daily timetable ought to make it possible for the monks both to do their work in the school and to attend all the monastic prayers and other exercises. This had not been possible at Ampleforth. We also agreed in our conviction that this whole project really was God's will for us, a conviction that helped to carry us through the difficulties that lay ahead, and one that surely proved to be correct.

As we drew nearer to our new home, we were slightly uneasy about Saint Louis being a stronghold of Jesuit education. In the North of England there are two prominent Catholic boarding schools: Ampleforth, which is Benedictine, and Stonyhurst, which is Jesuit. As has been shown above, (p. 48) they were a little wary of one another. We were also apprehensive that the Jesuits of Saint Louis might, not without reason, be less than delighted at the arrival of an educational competitor, as they owned both Saint Louis University and Saint Louis University High School. But they took the line that there were plenty of boys to go round, and were unfailingly friendly, hospitable, and helpful. Later they founded De Smet High School, not far from us, showing that, at least then, there were indeed plenty of boys to go round. At that time we considered that continental-European Jesuits were more intellectual and less hospitable than American. English Jesuits, we thought, were in the middle on both counts, which was probably about as true as most generalizations.

We continued by train via Covington, Kentucky to Saint Louis on (then) rather wobbly track. The Mississippi was disappointingly low and muddy, anything but a mighty river. We were met at the platform in Saint Louis by Mr.

Frederick M. Switzer, President of Catholic Preparatory School for Boys, Incorporated, (INC) and a large group of our supporters. The temperature was in the 80s, we were wearing thick, English, woolen suits and topcoats, and we wanted nothing more than to get to our new home and have a shower. Instead we were whisked off to a reception, where we felt, and were, on display. I was introduced to Monsignor Mullaly. He had served in Burma, and it was hoped that we might have much in common, but Burma is a large country, in which he had been in the North and we in the centre and South, so there was no overlap.

Towards evening we were driven out to the Stannard (now Switzer) house, our home-to-be. On the way, Fred Switzer said he hoped we would not be disappointed that the house was an old house. We thought quickly that it could hardly have been built before the 1800s, so it could not be that old. He added that it was built in 1937, so it was eighteen years old. We soon came to accept that our 'old' was likely to be much older than theirs, and their 'big' much bigger than ours.

Mason Road ran down one side of a small valley, and there on the other side, two or three hundred yards away, was the main house on the property. All its lights were lit, and as it was by then almost dark, it seemed to be floating on air, an enchanted palace. Our doubts and fears started to melt away. The assembled guests were waiting for dinner, but Father Columba rightly insisted that we must say Vespers and Compline first, which put into immediate effect what we had decided in Washington.

Dinner followed and the guests departed, but not before the Treasurer of INC, had thrust into Father Luke's hand an envelope, which he said should be of some help. It contained a check for $10,000, which was far more money than any of us had ever held in hand. It would be worth nearer $150,000 in 2011. For many years, INC, as they had promised, took financial care of us, and very generously too. This included organizing the fund-raising. I especially was grateful for this, as it meant that I did not have to, and heads of colleges and schools often did have to. In fact, some have been called great educators, meaning that they raised much money.

The enchanted palace, which was to be our home for the next three years, was sturdy and comfortable, but had one curious inconvenience: you could not put your head out of any window because of double glazing in winter and mosquito screens in summer. None of us had known how often the English like to put their heads out of the window. We were taken by surprise also by the temperature at which houses were kept. If we observed English norms, visitors would keep on their warm, outdoor clothing. On the other hand, we had arrived at a season of gorgeous sunsets. The house faced west, and we could sit and watch those beautiful glows. Also, for a few nights, we could see the *aurora borealis*, mainly green, to my surprise. We have never seen it again.

The first property INC had acquired was of about 50 acres. Ampleforth had several thousand acres, but the story that Abbot Herbert Byrne, when informed of the 50 acres, exclaimed 'Do you expect us to run a school on a pocket handkerchief?' is probably apocryphal. INC quickly acquired the Stannard House and its 38 acres, and we were soon enabled by INC to add to that. We reached 175 acres, but some of that was given us as an investment. We sold it and now have about 150 acres of pleasant terrain. Wildlife, too. finds the terrain pleasant. In our time here we have seen deer and squirrels in abundance, even superabundance, tracks in the snow of a mountain lion, a badger (once), jackals, foxes, opossums, raccoons, skunks, weasels, wild cats, chipmunks, groundhogs, rabbits, moles and voles and small rodents, a pileated woodpecker (once), great blue herons, eagles, turkey buzzards, wild turkeys, tame peacocks, hawks of various species, swans, owls, geese in gaggles, ducks including three great northern ducks, blue jays, cardinals, orioles, blue-birds, humming birds, and all sorts of common birds, luna moths, monarch butterflies and chrysalises, and other moths and butterflies, (much rarer now than when we first came) black widow spiders (one on our flagpole), and brown recluses (some in my carpentry shop, and some living in the drain of my shower, but now extinct). In the early days we had dogs dropped off on our property but none stayed for long. Of all these my most vivid memory is of a cardinal that sat on the top of a tree, facing the morning sun with his scarlet breast brilliant against the blue sky, and singing fortissimo.

Twenty

OUR PREPARATIONS

We arrived on October 19, 1955, and school was to open early in September, 1956. We had ten and a half months in which to procure students, faculty and staff, buildings and supplies. But above all we needed information. And all that was just for the school. There were also monastic needs, of which perhaps the most urgent was to get the members of INC to absorb, and not give merely notional assent to, the ideas that we had come to found not a school, but a monastery that would run a school, and that monks lived a much simpler and more regulated life than they. The first cook they recommended to us had been used to having footmen to do the dirty work, and the first grocery store they recommended was very attractive but very expensive. 'It's cheaper in the long run' they said, without specifying the length of the run. We brought with us a keen sense of frugality, sharpened by the plain fact that since the members of INC were paying our expenses, we should in justice be careful with their money.

We saw this as applying not only to our own living, but also to the buildings and equipment that we needed for monastery and school. In the school we tried to steer between shoddiness and extravagance, which led us to form a lay building committee to scrutinize the specifications for our buildings. We were both pleased and a little alarmed to find that they were able by their expertise to save us thousands of dollars without lessening the quality of the building. INC was grateful.

But first of all we had to get driving licenses. We had been given an elderly Cadillac, which someone described by saying, 'Anything longer would be a bus.' We took this out for a trial run by daylight. The three of us then set out for a police station recommended by INC as being friendly to Catholic priests. Father Luke and I had driven frequently and far, but Father Columba obtained his license in England in 1921, when you simply went to a Post Office, paid your fee, and received your license. He had not driven since. At our test he went first, and was asked to switch on the lights, which he had not practiced. The

Cadillac had a row of knobs, so he pulled the first and the hood shot up; the next, and the windshield-wipers came on; the third produced a squirt of detergent. The police officer then intervened. But we all passed, which confirmed INC's recommendation.

At the same time I had to start to organize a school office. When the monks' choir moved down to the ground floor, I was able to take over as the headmaster's office the master bedroom at the south end of the Stannard House. It was also my cell, and I had my bed and a chest of drawers behind the bookcase. It had a pleasant view, with windows all round, but this meant that it had three outside walls and a roof. As the heating and air-conditioning were rudimentary and at the other end of the house, the office was usually too hot in summer and

Fred Switzer addresses a meeting on our lawn of Catholic Preparatory School for Boys Incorporated (INC).

too cold in winter. It was flanked by 'his' and 'her' dressing rooms, both in two parts. 'His' became mine, but 'hers' became the secretary's office, with her office in the dressing room and the files and machinery in the bathroom.

Then we hired a secretary, Christine Little, who was able to organize the files and much of the routine. She stayed for three years, which we found later was double her usual stay. The office furniture was this: telephone, type-writer, Ditto machine (a purple duplicator), and a file-cabinet, plus desk, table, and chair. A Gestetner, (a black ink duplicator), came later. There was no copying machine, and, of course, no fax and no computers. Our phones had no capacity for voice mail, and none for a recorded reply. This meant, as we were to learn to our cost, that if school had to be cancelled for snow, we could not record a message that there was no school, but I had to sit by the phone from 5 a.m. answering queries. I had to do the same if there was doubt about school opening. The usual query was 'Is there school today?' so I would answer simply 'Yes'. One ingenious boy asked instead 'Is school cancelled today?' and to his delight heard 'Yes'. But I recognized his voice and called him back.

For projection in the classroom we acquired a massive machine called an epidiascope, which was later superseded by overhead projectors. Classroom blackboards were still black and the chalk mostly white, but some colors were available. In the monastery we had one black and white TV.

We spent much time visiting local schools, with a view, mainly, to clarifying our architectural ideas and choosing an architect; there were endless meetings among ourselves, with INC, with prospective supporters or parents, diocesan clergy, educators, possible architects, and others.

The meetings with prospective supporters were usually at dinner-time and at a country club. These were both friend- and fund-raising affairs. The program was nearly two hours of happy hour, followed by dinner and speeches. The drinks were usually hard liquor – little wine was drunk then – but at the dinner itself, there was coffee or water, and no wine. Sometimes there was not much intelligible conversation either. The speakers were the three monks, who dealt with the business side, the school, the monastery and the spiritual side. Then Fred Switzer dealt with the fund-raising. The three monks got to know one another's speeches fairly well, and sometimes poached. None of the monks was a great orator, but we could usually be clear, sometimes funny, and on occasion seemed brilliant, as when Father Columba said that some action would really set the cat among the pigeons, a cliché to English ears but hailed here as a gleaming new metaphor. He could also preach splendid, five-minute ferverinos, and is remembered for his fund-raising exhortation, based on the children's game, 'Think of a number: double it.'

We soon found that there was little point in saying to a new audience anything serious for the first minute or two, until they became somewhat used to what they called our English brogue. I therefore used to start with a joke. At some outside meeting I was planning to start with a story of three men in a railway carriage traveling to Wigan. As the train slowed down, the first man said to the second, 'C-C-Can you T-T-Tell me if this is W-W-W-Wigan?' The second man said nothing, so the first repeated his question. Again the second man made no reply, so the third man said it was Wigan. When the train moved on, the third man rebuked the second, who retorted, Y-Y-YES, I know, but D-D-Do you think I W-W-Wanted a B-B-Bloody N-N-Nose? Then to my horror the man who was to introduce me started, 'We are V-V-Very P-P-P-leased to have Father T-T-Timothy to T-T-Talk to us T-T-Tonight'.

The whole set-up with our supporters was very different from the English habit of a glass of sherry before the meal, and wine and conversation with the meal. It was also tiring, but we got to know many people, and sometimes the results were tangible. Later on, after I had given a report on the school, the millionaire sitting next to me said, 'That was a splendid report, Father; I'll give you another $10,000.' We did need to make ourselves known both so as to raise money and so as to attract students to the school.

We were busy, but there were lighter moments too. The Bridlespur Hunt held a meet at Priory. We gave them a stirrup cup and sent them off. In mid-afternoon they straggled back. I met one of them and asked if they had had a good hunt. 'Oh yes'. 'Did you kill?' 'Yes'. 'Was it a good run?' At this point he looked at his feet and fidgeted a bit before saying, 'Well, not exactly.' 'What happened?' 'Well, er, one of the horses trod on the fox.' The fox had gone to ground in a culvert which took a tiny stream under a lane. When the fox thought the coast was clear, it emerged, but at the same moment a horse was crossing the stream, trod on the fox, and broke its back.

On another occasion, when, for the sake of PR, we were still accepting dinner invitations, the three of us were going to a house whose location I knew only roughly. I got out of the car and rang the doorbell of a house in the right area. I was in clerical dress, and when the owner came to the door, her lower jaw dropped. She directed us to the other side of the street, where we found our friend's house, and I thought no more of it. It became the talk of that neighborhood, because in the first house they were having a meeting of Planned Parenthood, and the hostess thought the Archdiocese had sent three priests to protest.

We needed a general educational plan. When in the army I learnt sound bites like 'No good plan without good information', 'sweat saves blood, brains save sweat and blood', 'Never underestimate the enemy', 'Time spent in reconnaissance is seldom wasted', and 'order, counter-order, disorder', I little expected to apply them as headmaster or pastor, but they were often extremely applicable, especially the last.[11] This time it was the first and fourth that were

11. See also page 77.

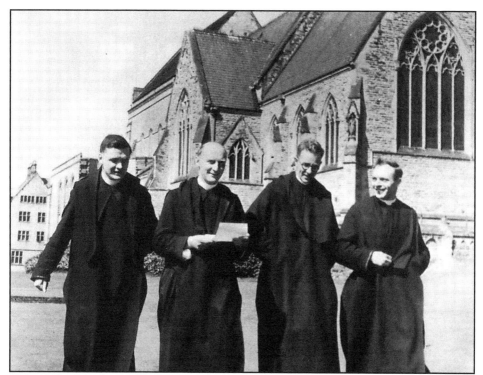

Fathers Luke, Columba, myself and Ian consider their future. Ampleforth's old church is in the background.

Fred Switzer greets the three founders on our arrival at Union Station, Saint Louis.

Here I am greeting guests à la Lord Louis Mountbatten.

Abbot Herbert Byrne blesses the foundation stone of the monastery with Cardinal Ritter, Prior Tunink of Pevely, Father Clarke, pastor of Saint Monica, Creve Coeur, Prior Columba and myself, November 4, 1957.

The honor Students of this first class meet Archbishop Ritter.

151

Our church (Architect: Hellmuth, Obata & Kassabaum; Contractor: McCarthy Brothers) was consecrated on September 7, 1962. The material is thin-shell concrete.

Speech-making

Teaching

Fundraising

Relaxing

Counseling

Celebration of Silver Jubilee of Priesthood. Top: In church; Bottom: Elsewhere.

Selling my book, In Good Soil, the Founding of Saint Louis Priory and School.

Speaking at the opening of the first extension of the school gym.

Andy Busch and I at the annual alumni picnic at Grant's Farm.

155

My portrait, painted by Father Columba's cousin, Simon Elwes, who also painted Father Columba. Both were shown at the Royal Academy's summer show, but in different years.

helpful. My main reconnaissance to acquire good information was an extensive trip by car to the East Coast, and especially to New England. This was the home of many of the best college-preparatory schools, whose aims seemed closest to ours, and likewise the home of many of the colleges to which we hoped to send students.

This trip of about five thousand miles by car, a six cylinder Chevrolet, was an experience. Gas (petrol) was cheap, normally around 23 cents a gallon, but dropping as low as 15 cents during gas wars. In general, we noted that in US things were cheaper, but labor much more expensive than in England. I slept several nights in a sleeping bag in the car, including one night in the mountains of West Virginia, where it was so cold that a bottle of medicine burst during the night and the steering wheel was too cold to hold for long the next morning.

The trip was in two parts, before and after Christmas. For them I was on my own, but for Christmas itself Fathers Columba, Luke, and I had agreed to meet at Portsmouth Priory in Rhode Island. While we were there, Father Luke and I drove into Providence. There we were looking at the map, and rolled slowly through a red light at a crossroads. Police on all four corners blew their whistles, and the nearest one descended on us with a face of fury. We instinctively unbuttoned out topcoats and showed our clerical collars. The face of fury changed to a broad grin. The officer said, 'I'm so sorry, Father, can I help you find your way'. It was more humiliating than a ticket.

The American network of interstate highways made the whole trip much easier, and sometimes more interesting. There are billboards near the highways, of which two caught my eye: 'BETHLEHEM INN – FAMILY RATES'; did they sense the incongruity? And 'STAY AT OUR MOTEL: IT IS LITERALLY OUT OF THIS WORLD'; did they notice the impossibility? To avert somnolence the highways avoid long straight stretches. They also enable one's top speed and one's average speed to be almost the same, and the mileage covered to be huge. I once started from Saint Louis for New York in the small hours of the morning, and covered over one thousand miles by evening. At 65 mph that is about fifteen and a half hours. On the next day, a Sunday, at about 7 a.m., I drove up Fifth Avenue in New York at the top allowable speed, with hardly a car in sight.

The schools and colleges I visited were uniformly hospitable and generous with time and information, and often put me up for the night. The trip was successful and reassuring. I visited Harvard, Yale, Princeton, M.I.T., Brown, Cornell, Wesleyan CT, West Point, and other colleges; and Lawrenceville, Groton, Exeter, Andover,

Canterbury, Portsmouth, Hotchkiss, Choate, Millbrook, Saint Paul's, and other schools. I talked to Deans of Admissions and Headmasters, and learnt that in their schools the curriculum, and in their colleges the expectations, were well within what we were qualified to offer. I also got the impression, later confirmed by practice teaching at the Benedictine schools in Portsmouth, Rhode Island and Washington, DC, that American boys were similar to English boys, and that there should not be significant differences in discipline. What I failed to see was that our initial group of ninth-graders with no Seniors, Juniors, and Sophomores above them, and no established traditions to follow, might well be very different from ninth-graders in a complete and established school. In September, 1956, we soon discovered my mistake.

We were lucky to coincide with a period when eastern colleges were very eager to show that they were not just East Coast, WASP (White, Anglo-Saxon, Protestant) enclaves. It was said that their perfect candidate would be an American-Indian girl from North Dakota. A Catholic boy from the Mid-West could not have quite the same rarity value, but was a step in the right direction. Later, I spent part of most summers visiting colleges and introducing our school to them.

For some years the information acquired on this first trip provided the outline for our educational discussions, and the majority of our graduates went to colleges that I had visited, and which then visited us. The trip was the first, but not the longest, of many similar trips. After the first few years, I visited colleges around the country, mostly by car, and so set wheel in all the forty-eight contiguous states, plus a few in Canada. In this way I made known the name of our Priory School, disseminated information about it, gathered information about, and a first-hand impression of, the colleges, and solved one of our problems as exiles: that of having no family at hand to welcome us for our summer vacation.

We then set about collecting a ninth grade. We already had a faculty, as the monks were to do almost all the teaching. Three of us were here, and Father Ian Petit joined us just before school started. For the boys we held an entrance examination and interviews. We still could not believe that boys of thirteen or fourteen would really not know any foreign languages, nor any mathematics beyond arithmetic, so we set required papers in English and Math, and I composed optional papers in Algebra, Geometry, Latin, Greek, French, German, and Italian, and Father Columba one in Spanish. We also required a standard IQ test. We were skeptical of IQ tests, but came to see them as blunt instruments best used in conjunction with the interview, the boy's transcript from his Grade School, and other information. On the day of the examination, two boys took the optional French, and that was it, which made correction easy. From the evidence provided by our tests in English and Arithmetic, the IQ test, and the interview, we chose a class of thirty from the sixty-six applicants.

I attached much importance to the interview, and thought it important to have more than one interviewer. It is good to be able not only to judge a boy's response to oneself but also to observe his response to others. We did occasionally change our verdict on a boy either way because of the interview. Reading a passage aloud was also a helpful diagnostic. The interview was also usually a chance to meet the parents. Although it was my firm policy not to hold the parents against the boy, it was helpful to know something about them, for the good of the boy. Should the family be dysfunctional, this is often reflected in the boy and his behavior, and although this makes our life more difficult, we should not hold that against the boy. We are here for his good, not for our own comfort.

One providential result of the examination was this: we had been saying at all our meetings that we would not take in boys whose only claim was wealthy parents. Many were skeptical. Come the examination, we did turn down one such boy. This sad event turned out to be a brilliant, but totally unplanned, stroke of Public Relations. People commented, 'These monks really mean what they say.'

Choosing a style of architecture and an architect, and planning what to build and where, took much longer. We knew we were beginners, and were anxious not to build buildings of a style or in a place that we would later regret. Our travels – for I was by no means the only traveler – also helped us to form some ideas of what style of architecture we wanted, and what kind of architect. Many of the school buildings we saw were in neo-colonial or neo-classical styles, and many of our supporters wanted us to follow suit. That would have been safe, could have been elegant, but also seemed unadventurous. At the other end of the scale I saw, for example at the Massachusetts Institute of Technology, some striking examples of thoroughly modern buildings, which were certainly adventurous but seemed too harsh for Saint Louis. One architect from Mexico, when asked about the structural engineering of his exciting buildings, replied that he simply designed and built the buildings, and if they stayed up, he knew that their engineering was sound; if not, not. That was too adventurous for us. But here again we were pleased by the generosity of the architects with their time and ideas.

East façade of our headquarters, the Stannard, now Switzer House.

The Stannard, now Switzer House (above) was the sturdiest building on the property, and seemed to be a natural center. Abbot Herbert and Prior Columba, on their previous visit, had decided that it should be our temporary monastery. Our first step, a false one, was to ask its architect to produce a plan for buildings to carry the school through the first few years. He gave us a drawing, which linked the Stannard House to the barn north of it, incorporated this barn, a shed and archway building, and added some new buildings to fill in the gaps. It looked attractive and 'specs' were sent out for bids. His initial estimate had been $60,000 but the lowest bid was nearly $174,000. We had to start again. We decided to remodel the buildings we had, turn the barn into classrooms, and survive with that for two years. There was hardly time to do more before the start of the school year. By the start of the third year we hoped to have completed a new monastery, the ground floor of which would be used for the school. In March, 1956, we chose the Saint Louis firm of Hellmuth, Obata, and Kassabaum, hereafter HOK, as our architects, but put the immediate remodeling into the experienced hands of the contractor, John O'Brien.

Twenty-One

MONASTIC LIFE, USA

While all this was going on we had also to establish our own monastic routine. The first item was the timetable, which was as follows:

4:40 a.m.	Rise
5:00 a.m.	*Matins* and *Lauds*
	Two rounds of Masses
	(Each priest said his own private Mass)
	Meditation
	Prime and *Terce*
	Breakfast
8:45 a.m.	*Sext*, Conventual Mass
12:30 p.m.	Lunch, followed by *None*
	(which rhymes with tone)
6:00 p.m.	*Vespers*
6:30 p.m.	Supper
8:30 p.m.	*Compline*
9:40 p.m.	Lights out

The words italicized are, as stated on page 123, the names of the 'hours' of prayer said by the monks together in the chapel. Each monk had also to fit in a half-hour of what was then called Spiritual Reading and has now become, *Lectio Divina* (Divine Reading). We also had to establish a number of practical customs or rules (where to leave the car key, times and places of silence, where to get toothpaste, etc.) such as every family has. This happened piecemeal until we had enough customs to need a written *Customary*, for ourselves, for those joining our community, and for guests.

We spent a good deal of our time talking: to INC, to our architects, to other schools, to our prospective parents and their children, to supporters, and to one another. INC, and later the parents, were, as we soon recognized, close to us in a way that no outside body could have been to Ampleforth. INC's members, and the boys' parents, were geographically close, and equipped with a telephone system that encouraged contact rather than, as at Ampleforth then, discouraging it; also we were dependent on INC not only for financial support but also for local knowledge. They knew the best shops, doctors, and dentists, and could guide us to the most friendly police. In countless ways we relied on their support and guidance. As the telephone brought INC close to us, so it brought everyone else. In one Telephone Book *Saint Louis Priory School* was listed immediately after *Saint Louis Obedience Training School for Dogs*. Occasionally I received such calls as 'Do you teach obedience?' or 'Do you charge kennel fees?' I found that I had to ask 'Does your candidate have two legs or four?'

We were quite inexperienced shoppers. I was taken into an expensive department store, where my guides said I would be shocked by the prices. As we walked in I saw a rack of what seemed to me to be rather flimsy, cotton dresses. I asked how much they were and the clerk said 'seven fifty'. Translating that as $7.50, I thought that was about right, but the clerk went on to say that I could get two for $1400; and that was over fifty years ago.

In business matters Father Luke, searching again for frugality, was led by Mother Hellmuth, RSCJ, his counterpart at a Sacred Heart girls' school, to places such as Railway Salvage stores, second-hand furniture shops, Government Surplus depots, and the like.

But our close relationship with INC was a matter not simply of expedience, but also of policy and justice, and, in due course, of friendship.. We all wanted the laity to have not just a token, but a real, share in our activities and in our decision making, but at the same time to maintain our ultimate control. This sharing was uncommon at that time, but we meant it. How it worked out was that we listened very carefully to INC's advice and usually followed it. They for their part came to recognize that it worked best if the final decision rested with us. This was all the more remarkable in that they could so easily have felt that he who pays the piper calls the tune. This happy outcome was largely the result of one of Father Columba's greatest achievements: establishing and maintaining a very firm relationship of trust, respect, and friendship with Mr. Fred Switzer, the chairman of INC. They were quite different men. Fred was serious, practical, well-organized, with good judgment and plenty of commonsense. Father Columba was more spiritual, visionary, intellectual, and could be playful. Each had a strong will and abundant drive.

We also spent long hours talking with our architects, which meant mostly with Mr. Gyo Obata, their designer of genius. The first topic was the remodeling of existing buildings, which was on a small scale and simple. Next came the overall plan, and then the church. Discussion of the church was the showpiece of our discussions. Gyo was not Catholic, and we had never before planned a church, so we had first to think out and agree on what we wanted and why, and then explain it to Gyo. He had to listen carefully and then outline ways of meeting our needs, at which point we had to listen carefully. These discussions consumed much time, which sometimes felt like too much time, but their very length, and the pauses for reflection between discussions, enabled all parties to clarify their ideas. So it came about that in the end all, or almost all, parties were pleased with the results.

We asked that the church be the dominant architectural feature on the campus, be tall enough to be dignified, have the altar as close to and as visible to the people as possible, encourage participation rather than spectatorship, be as boy-proof as possible, and be of stone. When the cost of stone was shown to be far beyond our budget, we let the architects recommend the material, and they chose thin-shell concrete. Next they produced two models: one was an octagonal glass wall with a frilly concrete roof, the other, also octagonal, looked more like a pinecone or artichoke. Of the four monks present two voted for the glass wall and two, of whom I was one, for the artichoke. Gyo's casting vote was for the artichoke. In due course the octagon, with help from Pier Nervi, evolved into a circle, and the triangular windows into parabolas. Nervi was the Italian engineer/architect in concrete who designed Italy's stadium for the Olympic Games in Rome in 1960. The final result was a round church with the altar in the middle, the monks' choir east of it, and the people all around the altar. All this took place early in 1957, but then, as the family that promised to finance the church could not yet find the money, we put the plans into cold storage until August, 1960, when construction began.[12]

When we visited other local schools and talked to them, our focus was mainly on architecture and layout, but it was also informative for us just to see other schools in action. I was taken to a football game and encountered cheerleaders for the first time. I asked one of them if she liked football and received the reply, 'Oh no! I just come to watch the boys'. It was all very different from a

12. For more details on the church, see In Good Soil, page 226.

rugby match at Ampleforth. There were hazards too. At one game, Father Ian was standing next to the mother of one of the players. When her son scored a touchdown, she threw her arms round Father Ian.

As architectural ideas began to form in our minds, our talks with HOK moved on from the church to the whole campus. The church was to be central physically, aesthetically, and spiritually. The monastery, into which we moved in 1958 before the church was built, was south of the church with the high school eventually east of the church. Initially the monastery had the school's classrooms on the ground floor and the monks' cells on the floor above. In 1970 the high school moved out into its new building, and the monks took over the whole of the monastery, and stayed there until the new monastic quadrangle was finished in 2001. The Junior School started in a small house south-east of the Stannard House and moved in 1968 to its present building closer to, and south of, the High School.

By now I had had time to form some general impressions. The first was of the amazing warmth and generosity of our friends and of all those we met. This showed itself not only in cordiality, hospitality, and financial support, but also in continued hard work on our behalf. The next two impressions, as has already been mentioned, were prompted by 'pavement' and 'side-arms. When Bernard Shaw called England and America two countries separated by a common language, he was closer to the truth than we had imagined. Words with different meanings were not the main problem: one simply had to learn that a car's engine is normally under a hood, not a bonnet. More dangerous were words with different nuances. In a report I described a boy as a little urchin. An English parent would have smiled and said, 'Yes, he has always been a bit scruffy'. The American parent was incensed. We were also taken aback by the number of people who commented on our accent. We thought then that it was they who had the accent. André Maurois mentions an English gentlewoman in France who expostulates, 'But *I'm* not the foreigner; *you* are the foreigners'. At the time of our arrival we were a bit like her, but we soon learnt.

We also soon found that the reaction to us simply as English was often either unearned admiration or unearned hostility. We once went out to dinner, and our good Catholic host asked Father Columba to say grace after the meal as well as before. As Father Columba concluded, 'and may the souls of the faithful departed through the mercy of God rest in peace', our host chimed in, 'and God rest the Irish who rotted in English jails.' And this was only partly jest.

Another reaction to us was simply giggles. We were talking with a group of college co-eds. Every now and then they would turn away from us and their shoulders would shake. One of them, when she turned back said, 'Do go on talking; it does not matter what you say, just go on talking.' As she and her speech were from the deep South, we found her comment paradoxical.

As to side-arms, most English people at that time took pride in their police carrying only a truncheon (night-stick). All three of us were startled at seeing the guards at the Frick Museum armed. We did not immediately infer that we had come to a culture of violence, but we did wonder, if this was needed in New York, what it would be like farther west.

Meals were different too. We were used to four, smaller meals a day, afternoon tea being the fourth. Unlike T.S. Eliot's Bostonians, few, if any, Saint Louisans tinkled their tea-cups and we soon abandoned tea. Many in Saint Louis had no breakfast, or only coffee or orange juice, but we did keep that important meal. If we were taken to a restaurant, the helpings, especially of meat, seemed to us enormous.

Very early on we planned what is a very common English way of getting to know people: a tea-party, at which we planned to serve tea, sandwiches, cakes, and so on, but no alcohol. As we began to recognize the role of alcohol in American friend-raising, we started to get cold feet. Fortunately the affair was a great success, and we felt we had perhaps shown that entertaining did not have to include alcohol. Several weeks later we discovered that our guests too had had cold feet, and had gathered ahead of time at a well-known bar to prepare themselves.

We also found that Americans hold and use their knife and fork differently from the English, so we had to be cautious, when having lunch with the boys, about suggesting that their way of holding and using the cutlery was déclassé.

We also sensed early on, though it was only later that we articulated it, that the typical American mind is instinctively *a priori*, and the English instinctively *a posteriori*: that is, that the former likes to lay down a principle and deduce ideas and actions from it, but the latter prefers to examine the data and, if necessary, work out a principle from the data. This may be why US has a written constitution and UK does not. We met this instinct first in an unfamiliar use of the word 'philosophy': 'What is your philosophy of lathe-work?', and were baffled. Both instincts work, however, and when combined can be complementary and effective.

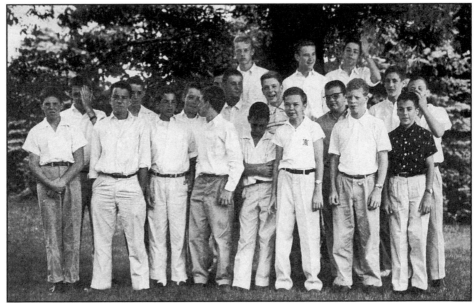

Before the school opened, we held a summer school for the incoming ninth graders.

Having acquired a full class of boys, we thought both they and we would benefit from a summer school. We did not expect to teach them very much, but at least they and we should get to know and understand one another, and that was how it turned out. They sat at tables and chairs, as the desks had not yet arrived. They were rowdier than we expected, a warning of what might come. We took a photo of them, which remains one of my favorite photos of our first class.

Fathers Columba, Luke and I celebrated July 4 with the British Consul, who lived within walking distance. He introduced us to the mint Julep. We had one, which seemed easy to drink, and then another. Then we realized that they were more powerful than we thought, and I remembered my Uncle David's advice. The path home was narrow, and we had to walk with care.

Twenty-Two

THE DRIVE TO THE WEST COAST

We had already accepted the bigness of the United States. Salisbury Plain is large for England but would fit over 3,000 times into the Great Plains area of the United States. In the summer of 1956, Father Columba and I experienced this bigness by driving to the West Coast and back. After nearly 700 miles, mostly across the plains of Kansas, we stayed at Cheyenne Wells with the Catholic pastor. As a young priest, when they still had occasional Indian raids, he staged a debate with the Protestant minister. He was warned that he might have to flee for his life, but it was his opponent who had to flee.

We approached the Rocky Mountains. I was expecting something bigger and rockier, as the last big mountains I had seen were the Himalaya range, and Mount Everest is almost twice as high as Pike's Peak. But the colors at dawn and dusk were beautiful. We followed the Trail Ridge Road, over 12,000 feet, the longest stretch of high road in the country. We approached the descent to Estes Park almost out of gas, and I had to coast down, using the engine as little as I could. Next day we approached the Tetons from the east. We came over the last ridge, and there was Jackson Lake in the foreground and then the Tetons, snow-capped and rocky. What a sight!

Our car was a Ford station wagon with a thunderbird engine, of which Father Columba said 'This car just wants to go 80'. We had taken out the back seat and laid down a mattress, so that he could sleep in the back. I slept across the front seat. In Yellowstone Park we found a little side road with street lamps, and small plots for parking and sleeping. After supper, I was standing under a lamp finishing my prayers, when out of the forest padded a grown bear. I thought 'If I run, it will run faster', so I walked back to the car as nonchalantly as I could. The bear went round to the back, where Father Columba was half asleep with the tailgate down and his toes protruding. I warned him that a bear was sniffing at his toes. He said I was pulling his leg. I said I was not, but the bear might, so he half raised himself, saw the bear's snout and gave a great yelp. For the bear one sniff and the yelp were enough, and it ambled off. Next morning we saw an elk mother with her calf, which I rank with a baby hippo as the ugliest infant animals I have seen.

At Salt Lake City we stayed with the Catholic bishop. He showed us the Mormon Tabernacle, 250' x 150', built in 1864-67 without interior columns and without nail or screw. Its acoustics are remarkable. We drove to the Bonneville Salt Flats, where Captain G.E.T. Eyston was racing. I had been in school with his nephew. A side road led us to a gate, where a man was coming out. We asked him if he knew where we could find Eyston: he replied, 'I am he'. We talked for a bit, and he invited us to lunch in Salt Lake City, but we faced a long drive in the opposite direction.

San Francisco was the first American city that really appealed to us. Its Presidio was founded in 1776, so it was closer to our 'old'. It had a past and was proud of it. We were shown the sights by the brother-in-law of a friend in Saint Louis, and then started back home. We were duly amazed by some giant Redwoods, and then made a brief descent into Death Valley, where we walked hardly twenty yards, which was enough. We took a tour of the Hoover Dam where, when a man fell into the concrete, they had to stop work and dig out his body because it less strong than the concrete. The dam's construction cost one hundred lives. In Las Vegas the temperature was 116°. We drove down the Strip and looked in on a game of black jack and a set of slot machines. No one appeared to be enjoying it. There is one of America's highest concentrations of religious women there. The gamblers must ask for their prayers and offer a tithe in gratitude if they are heard.

We stopped next at the Canyons. We had been advised to start with the Little Colorado Canyon, where the drop of 600 feet is sheer and more dramatic. I parked facing the canyon, against a railroad tie, which was all there was to prevent me driving over the top. When we were ready to leave, Father Columba took the wheel, put us into second gear and said, 'This is reverse, isn't it?' I shrieked, 'NO' and was able to knock the stick shift into neutral. At the Grand Canyon, the first sight is always so much more than one expects. The size, the variety of colors, the strata, the changes with the time of day, leave you at a loss for reaction. We also met two alumni from our school in England.

After these wonders our attitude to the Painted Desert, the Petrified Forest, and other such was almost blasé, but one sight got to us. We reached Holbrook, Arizona, found the Catholic church in the town square, and were told that the pastor was at the carnival, also in the town square. On a platform was an ample man in a T-shirt announcing winners in the beauty competition. Father Columba commented that the pastor must be most disturbed by this hubbub at his front door, and I replied in jest that the man on the platform probably was the pastor. I was right.

Somewhere near here we stopped for coffee. A group of seedy-looking men looked in. When we drove off, we heard an ominous noise and found a long screw in the tire.

After Santa Fe we headed north-east under the Sangre de Cristo mountains. There it started to hail. The road was soon covered with golf-ball size hailstones. It was like driving over shingle several inches deep. We reached Holy Cross Abbey in Canyon City, where we saw government surplus in action. The Abbey school had a magnificently equipped metal-working shop, whose machinery and equipment came from a chain of military bases in Colorado, which sold their machinery at the end of each year at low cost, and bought new ones; otherwise their budget would have been reduced. Holy Cross gave us many duplicates from their library. Being in the back of the car they raised the beam of our headlights and by dusk caused annoyance to oncoming drivers.

Our last stop was in Topeka, Kansas, where the Catholic priest had to sing a Mass for the Dead every day even if there were no congregation. We reduced his total by two.

This trip too was of about 5,000 miles and we really felt the size of the United States. We had seen it on the map, and yet we were surprised on our second day to reach the Rocky Mountains so soon, because we thought we would cross them, and there would be the Pacific. But the mountains went on for hundreds of miles, and there were two deserts and more mountains before the Pacific. In England, if you drive for fifty miles, you will be in countryside quite different from what you started in. Here we drove for hundreds of miles and it was just the same. We experienced desert, heat, and a violent hailstorm. We visited several of the country's major attractions. We met people of wide variety and saw people living and acting in many different ways. Apart from the seedy men, all were most friendly and hospitable. In a word, we experienced size, diversity and hospitality.

Twenty-Three

SCHOOL OPENS

We returned on August 24, and school was due to open on September 6. On September 4, a little man from the County Building Authority accosted me outside the Barn and asked where the rest rooms were. I pointed proudly to the converted equipment shed. 'And is there a covered way to them?' 'Not yet.' 'What will the boys do if it rains?' 'Get a little wet.' He then threatened to close the school unless we gave them cover. I told Father Luke, who told our contractor, who had once employed the little man; our contractor took care of him. But we did, as we had always planned, install a covered way, which later became a home for bumble bees, but no one was ever stung.

After anguished discussion, we set the tuition at $750, which today seems unbelievably low. Then, it was more than the other Catholic schools, but less than the other independent schools.

We now had a student body, a faculty, textbooks, and classrooms; we had all we needed except desks. These had been ordered months ahead of time. Each time Father Luke enquired he was told next month, next week, a few days, tomorrow. Eighty cartons eventually arrived the evening before school was due to open. We had them put in the Barn classrooms and planned to set them out after supper.

To our horror, when we opened the cartons, the desks were 'knocked down', that is, assembly was required. Fortunately they had the holes already drilled; unfortunately they were drilled in the wrong places. We had no electric drill, so it looked as if we would have to make all the holes with a hand brace and bit, but a parent came by and was able to lend us an electric drill. He stayed to help, and so did two alumni of our school in England, who happened to be visiting us. Many holes were needed for each of the thirty desks, and we were there until midnight. It was worth it. In the middle of proceedings, out of one the cartons there jumped a huge and hungry tropical tarantula with black, vivid blue, red, green, and perhaps other colors on its large body. With legs outstretched it would have covered a large plate. Father Columba yelled, 'Kill it, Timothy', but instead I put the gorgeous creature on a desk top and shoveled it, kindly but not wisely, out into the night. It would have been bad publicity if it had bitten someone on our opening day. For us, it was a welcome distraction at a rather tense time. As we crept off to bed, Father Ian Petit, quoted Stanley Holloway, the English comedian, 'Let battle commence'. He was a prophet.

After all those excitements, opening day itself was an anti-climax. The school bus arrived so early that the official photographer was not yet there, nor was anyone else with a camera, so there is no picture of that historic moment. Our first event was Mass, then an assembly and a tour, issue of textbooks, lunch, a visit to the Blessed Sacrament, issue of sports equipment, a short sports practice, and the bus home. Next day we really started. The subjects were Religious Instruction, Latin, French or Spanish, Math, English, and History. Greek was an option, during which the greekless had a study hall. A little more than half the class started Greek. There was a period each for Art, Music, General Knowledge, and choir. There were three periods of homework a night. The bus arrived at 8.40 a.m. and left at 5 p.m. Each day there were seven class periods of 45 minutes, plus lunch and sports.

Initially our teaching and organizing were inevitably based on our experience at Ampleforth, but we soon found that not all of it was valid for these very different circumstances. A small example: at Ampleforth when the lake froze over and the ice was deemed able to bear the weight of many boys, a holiday was declared, and we all migrated to the lake to skate. Such days were rare. So, when our first winter here came and our much smaller pond froze, we declared a holiday, took a long rope and a ladder, and went down to skate. We soon saw that if we did this every time the pond froze, we would have very little school in the winter.

We also very soon recognized that a Midwest ninth grade with no upperclassmen above them and no school 'traditions of civility' was indeed very different from the freshmen Father Luke and I had taught at Portsmouth and Washington. We also identified a core group who had been at the same grade school and were used to a rowdy break in a confined playground in the city. We provided a much larger area in which to rush around, and rush they did, to such an extent that Father Columba called it 'mass hysteria'. I was not so appalled by it as the others, partly perhaps because of experience in the army. But also, there are two ways of establishing order: one is to start very strict and then gradually relax, the other is to start rather lax, observe the ringleaders and then pounce. Although the second is harder work, I think it is better in the long run, because it is easier to identify and neutralize the troublemakers. In our case the ringleader was the boy favored by INC, whom I did not want to accept into the school. After a few weeks I was under strong pressure from our faculty to let him go, which I was content to do. This episode had the further good effect that INC never again interfered with my judgment.

We found that priests commanded great respect then, and were told that teachers as such did not, which we later found to be true. We were surprised again that hardly any grade schools taught algebra, geometry, or a foreign language. Learning by heart, which we did not despise and which is inevitable in the early stages of those subjects, comes more easily and less tediously to a bright, young boy, and is his principal mental capacity. We also noted that of this first class all except two had seen a sheep and only two, the sea. Ten years later, it was the opposite.

To much of what surprised us we had given notional, but not real, assent. The nearness of INC and of the parents, for example, was obvious, and yet the reality of it came as a surprise. At Ampleforth in 1955 to receive a phone call from a parent was extremely rare. It was a major operation both for the parent, owing to the difficulty of making long-distance calls, and for the monastic exchange operator, and for the monks, owing to their distance from the telephone, about 100 yards in my case. The Stannard House, having belonged to the president of South-Western Bell Telephone, had an extension phone in almost every room. (Eighteen months after we moved in, Bell discovered this, came and removed them, and tried, without success, to get Father Luke to pay rent.) Not only were the parents closer, but they also expected much more communication with the school than we were accustomed to.

Nor were phone calls to us only from Saint Louis. Long-distance calls within the country went through almost instantaneously. Accustomed to English ways, I dialed a number in Washington, DC and sat back to collect my thoughts. In seconds I was talking, with uncollected thoughts, to the man I had called. Another evening the phone rang and a man wanted to sell me a plot of land near Cape Canaveral. He started badly by telling me his name and saying 'How about you call me Sol and I call you Tim?' I did not agree. Many times I told him I was not in the market but he persisted. After forty-five minutes I finally said there was something he needed to know: I was a monk, I took a vow of poverty, and I had $120 a year of freely disposable money on my vacation. His response was immediate: 'Oh well, goodnight, Father.' Why did I not think of that sooner?

Transatlantic calls to Ampleforth were still very slow, and cablegrams were often unsatisfactory. This could hamper our capacity to plan. Mail might take a week each way, and if the abbot in England needed to consult his Council,

I was moderator of the Mother's Club, but Father Luke was also involved.

that body met only once a month. Normally we could accommodate that, but when a prompt and complex decision was needed, then there was real difficulty. For example, we were invited to take over a summer camp, and the owners needed to know quickly. We could not give them an answer quickly.

One by-product of the closeness of the parents was the formation of a Mothers' Club. I was hesitant. There was no such thing at Ampleforth, and so we had no experience of it. But also, on my eastern tour, I had been advised several times to be cautious about Parent Teacher Associations, and our scouts from Ampleforth in 1954 had been similarly advised, so my hesitation was not, as was often suspected, due to misogynism. Also we had not yet fully taken in that education was the province of the mother rather than of the father. The Mothers' Club Minutes book, providentially lost, is said to have started, 'On April 26, 1957, Father Timothy reluctantly acquiesced in the formation of a Mothers' Club'.

This club has turned out to be one of the main pillars of our support, and to it I devoted much time and effort. In a day school especially, it is invaluable to have a margin of good will with the parents. The Mothers provided that. They did, with their various activities, make a most valuable financial contribution, but they also built up many strong friendships with the monks and lay faculty, and among themselves. Their first projects were House Tours. I was astonished that people would pay to go and see one another's houses, but they did. The mothers also hosted book reviews, travelogues, and panel discussions. Then they made a quantum leap and became the first school in Saint Louis to hold an auction. It was called *Xanadu*, though we have not built a pleasure dome with the proceeds. Financially this was a huge success: in their first year they made $10,000, having never before with any project made more than $4,500. Now they are making hundreds of thousands of dollars a year. It is an immense amount of work. Besides making money directly, they also brought my mother over for a visit, and when I retired from headmaster, enabled me to take her on a tour of Ireland. When I stopped being headmaster, I shed, sadly, my direct connection with the Mothers' Club.

Meanwhile things were beginning to take shape. In the barn classrooms there was little or no interference by noise from next door, and they seemed to be a great success. But not quite everyone thought so. One of the occasional dogs on campus was a large Airedale. He was able to rest his paws on the window ledge and look in. He did so one day when I was teaching, listened for a minute or two, gave a huge yawn and moved on. Another dog, a basset, who lived across the road, always knew when we had a cross-country meet. He joined in and usually came in first, but he ran only the last quarter mile.

As no science was taught in the first year, there was no need for labs, but that did become a problem in our second year, when Father Thomas Loughlin joined us from Ampleforth to teach science. His first lab was a converted kitchen. Fortunately, he was inventive. We introduced weekly faculty meetings, which meant initially the monks. The rudiments of a disciplinary system emerged.

There also emerged an embryonic sports program, using, by their kindness, other people's gyms for basketball. This included the gyms of two public schools. We brought with us the belief that sports should be for all the boys, and we soon recognized the importance of football for the morale of the school. In our first year we had a few contests with other schools and won two games of football, one against a Lutheran school, whose jerseys had GRACE printed on them. Inevitably some theological wit commented, 'They had grace, but we gave them the works.' Our other victory was over a new public school, won by a two-point conversion in the last seconds. Our footballers, being few, often had to play both offense and defense, and so were often doing well until the fourth quarter, by when they were exhausted.

We did better at sports with smaller teams, such as basketball and tennis, and individuals could shine in swimming and wrestling. One wrestler, who had hurt his wrist, ingeniously put the bandage on the other wrist and successfully bamboozled his opponent, who attacked the good wrist. For our first year, we hired a lay Athletic Director, Mr. Ervin T. Leimer, who did most of the coaching, with the monks filling in where they could. Nearly fifty years later Erv's wife died, and I sent him a note. He replied that he still followed in the newspaper Priory's sports results. I coached hurdles, which I had done before, and shot put and the discus, of which I knew nothing. I had to study a book to find out from what part of the hand the discus was intended to emerge. To my and everyone else's surprise, one of our discoboli won the event at our first inter-scholastic track meet. The same boy, when we rashly played a soccer power house, scored our only goal (they scored 10) by unorthodoxly taking the ball from the kick-off, dribbling straight up the field, and shooting.

Then we ran into a wholly unexpected obstacle. When we arrived we started playing other schools at various sports, and only after a year or two discovered that we needed the permission of the Missouri State High School Activities Association (MSHSAA) to do so. No such permission is required in England, and the idea that in this land of the free we needed permission to play other schools never entered the head of any of us. We apologized, became members, and when we started competitive rugby, dutifully asked for their permission. They replied that they did not recognize the game, and did not mind what we did.

There were also other, far more distant worries. The Suez Canal crisis was developing. It did not, of course, affect us directly, but I remember thinking, and I expect the other monks did too, that we were witnessing at least a symbol of the decline, if not the end, of the British Empire, presaged by the fall of Singapore in World War II.

Twenty-Four

THOUGHTS ON EDUCATION

I have commented on the unfamiliar use of the word 'philosophy': We were often asked to explain our philosophy of education. What follows is based on our early attempts to do so, and on what I wrote in *In Good Soil.*

Basic was the primacy of the monastery and the consequent precedence of the monastic schedule over that of the school. School activities were not scheduled at the same time as the monks' prayer, and so in the early years here it was possible for all of us to attend all the Divine Office in choir. That was impossible at Ampleforth, and this impossibility was another reason for our never becoming a boarding, or partly boarding school. There were, of course, exceptions to our universal attendance in choir, but it was our norm. We desired this schedule for our own sake, but also hoped that fidelity to it would be an example to the boys, and reinforce what they learnt in religion classes and from their own experience of daily Mass. Monastic influence was also dominant in the classroom as the solid subjects were all taught by monks except the B set of History.

To understand the principles on which the school was established one must go far back into history. In the beginning there were no schools, and bringing up children was the natural corollary of generating them. The two formed a continuum and were, both equally, seen as the right and duty of parents. So strong was this view that in civilizations where Wisdom Literature existed – Egypt, Mesopotamia and Israel, for example – the life-molding words of wisdom were often cast in the form of a father's instruction to his child, "Listen, my son . . ." When, much later, Christian monasticism started in the Egyptian and other deserts, the venerated elder who could produce the words to set others on the right path was called abba (father) or amma (mother). The former accounts for our use of the title 'abbot'. But as the knowledge and skills needed for civilized life became more specialized, parents found they had neither the time nor the ability to impart these skills to their children, and hired others to do so. Thus, gradually, schools were born.

From this it is clear that the phrase *in loco parentis* (in the place of a parent), though rightly unpopular when invoked in defense of paternalism, contains much truth. Parents are the natural educators of their children and schoolmasters are their delegates. This idea, in which is contained the concept of the 'Priory Family' (now Abbey Family), was the basis of our relationship with our students and with their families, and this too led us away from the idea of a boarding school, since many of the parents of boarders would be too far away to be meaningfully 'family'. After graduation we try to make a reality the idea that graduates, though no longer 'children' of the family, are still part of the family, as are their parents, as well as the friends and benefactors of the monastery and school.

It is also clear that although schools provide a service to parents and although they are staffed by teachers and staff, what they are about is the boys (or girls)[13]. Parents are needed, obviously; teachers are useful because without them there would be no teaching, though there could be other means of instruction; but the students are the purpose and consequently the focus of the school. The school is primarily for their good. This does not mean that they always know what is good for them. If teachers, as professionals, do not, as a rule, know better than the boys what is good for the boys, they probably should not be teaching. It is the same with doctors, lawyers and other professionals.

The point is important. Many people: parents, grandparents, teachers, coaches, architects, manufacturers, suppliers, salesmen and others, may benefit from the existence of schools, but schools are run for the sake of the students and not for the sake of anyone else. If one takes simply and solely this educational point of view, the reason for consulting the interests of the faculty is that a good and stable faculty is a benefit to the boys. Similarly the educational reason for trying to establish a good relationship with the boys' families is that harmony between the home and the school is a help to the boys, especially if anything goes wrong. Fortunately there are many other reasons, Christian, humanitarian, professional, social and even economic, for being nice to faculty and parents, but the basic concern is always the good of the students.

The good of the boy comes into admissions too. From the beginning we aimed to judge the boy on his own merits. We were quite clear that we should not accept a boy just because his parents had been or might be generous donors. There was also general agreement with my view that we should not hold the

13. *From here on I speak only of boys.*

parents' shortcomings against the boy. We would all like to have classrooms full of bright, well-behaved boys from bright, well-behaved families. Our lives would then be much easier, but that is not the criterion. The criterion must be the good of the boy; and the difficult boy is often the one who most needs the school. But what about exemplary parents? I felt the same as with parents with shortcomings, but I did also feel that, *other things being equal*, the likelihood of strong support from the home could be counted as a plus for the boy.

Our aim in the school was to lay simple, solid, and strong foundations, half-expecting, or perhaps less than half, that in five to ten years, as Abbot Herbert and others had suggested, eager young Americans would become monks and snatch the school out of our hands. We therefore offered what seemed to us the obvious subjects: Religion, English, Math, Latin, French or Spanish, and History, with Greek as an elective. We intended to add Science for the last three years, and did so. Later it spread to all grades. We hoped that the boys would reach in all these subjects at least the level below which we thought one could not be regarded as having had a good education. We also had one period a week of general knowledge and one of musical appreciation. When we added grades 7 and 8, Father Ian had one period called 'Ology', a name borrowed from Ampleforth, in which he talked of anything that caught his interest, like the dance of the bees.

When the school was small, field trips were easy. A few station wagons, and off we went. I remember one to the Art Museum. A docent took us round and ended in the room of the Impressionists. After a minute or two she asked them what they saw. A ninth grader, who was far from the top of the class, answered, 'Color and light'. Could you describe the Impressionists better in three words? We also took them to hear the Symphony, which gave special concerts for schools, and even came and played a short program for us in our gym.

We were suspicious of bandwagons: so often today's craze became tomorrow's bust. So when Language Labs were being vigorously touted, we stood back and waited. We also stayed away from 'undifferentiated space' for classrooms. On the other hand when computers appeared, we were among the first schools, and possibly the first, to make use of them in the classroom. We have not, however, jumped on the 'every boy his own laptop' bandwagon. In 2011, differentiated instruction appeared. It is being discussed.

We were also suspicious of polysyllabic jargon. I applied for an educational grant and submitted the request in normal English. It was rejected for lack of 'proper' form. Again, quite recently I was reading a report by an NGO in Africa. They thought that success with malnourished children under six was more likely if, besides giving them food, they also provided emotional and social support to them and to their mothers. It took them fifty pages, with many graphs and tables to show 'scientifically' what commonsense would have accepted at once. The considered judgment of an experienced professional seemed to carry slight weight unless it were supported by an abundance of measurable facts. We found that alarming.

Mr. Reynolds Medart with the students of Mechanical Drawing. We were blessed indeed to have him donate so much time to this and to carpentry and photography.

We did also recognize that the human brain can be more dependable than technology. The first two examples that come to mind are both medical: one of our boys, a keen footballer, started at summer camp to bleed from his ear. His doctor, after all due tests, told him not to play that season. After the end of the season, he was in the office of a wise old doctor and told him the story. The doctor called for an otoscope and looked in the boy's ear. He then asked for a pair of tweezers and pulled out an earwig, harmless except that it had bitten the boy's ear and caused the bleeding. The boy could, without danger, have played all season. The old doctor knew this because, before air-conditioning, many people slept out in Forest Park and were bitten by earwigs.

The other example concerned the same doctor. I developed acute pain in a joint of my ring finger. The slightest touch was torture. X-rays and tests showed no cause. The old doctor happened to come by, heard the details, and said that I had gout. He gave me a little red pill to take, and said the pain would go away in a few minutes. I did not believe any of it, but I took the pill, and in a few minutes the pain vanished.

Academics are not the whole of school life, so we started a variety of activities in a rudimentary way: music, art, carpentry, mechanical drawing, and later drama and photography. Kevin Kline, had his introduction to acting

Kevin Kline, his brother Chris, and I enjoy a reflection on Kevin's workshop.

on the lawn behind the Stannard (Switzer) House. In 1997, when we named our new theater *The Kevin Kline Theater,* Kevin came back and gave us an enthralling workshop for teachers, students and the Abbey Family in which he commented on , and then acted out, Shakespearian plays, including *Henry V* and *Richard III.*

180

The school was to be in the English tradition but was for American boys and in an American setting. If there were parents who expected from us little Lord Fauntleroys, they were to be disappointed. Therefore, although our first reaction to football and baseball was disappointment, and although each of us in his heart preferred rugby and cricket, we opted for the standard American sports, and likewise activities.

In other words, there was nothing especially startling about what we planned to do, but we did hope to do it well, to challenge even the brightest boys, and to teach them to think. That last expression, 'to teach them to think', occurred frequently in our early publicity, but you cannot do it in a vacuum. You have to provide something to think about by teaching a subject in a thought-provoking way. Memory is essential, especially for younger boys and in the earlier stages of a subject, but is not where education takes place. If a boy memorized what the teacher had said and regurgitated it, he was to be given a bare pass (60%). He could hardly be failed for repeating the teacher's undoubted truths, but he could hardly be praised for doing no thinking of his own. Along the same lines and to encourage independent research, we were keen to collect a good library and to encourage the boys to use it. Of course much of this was modified as we went along.

Twenty-Five

NON-SCHOLASTIC ACTIVITIES

The school was not the only thing keeping me busy. In the monastery we had our own monastic schedule of prayer and monastic duties, which took up three hours or more of the day, mostly in the early morning. We also had spiritual demands from outside. Other religious men and women, and some lay organizations asked us to preach Days of Recollection, or Retreats. Then, that could mean eighteen or more conferences.

My first Retreat was at a Maryknoll convent a mile or two from Sing Sing, the maximum security prison. Usually when you see heads begin to nod, you know it is past time to stop. In this case, there was a sister in her nineties. They wheeled her in and at once she dozed off. When she started to wake up, I learnt it was time to stop.

I had mentioned in a conference that it was a good thing to keep in practice any talent you might have, and gave as a trivial example that my nanny had taught me how to make a cord out of a piece of string. Later a young sister knocked on my door. Perhaps most young retreat-givers dream of transforming someone's spiritual life. After some chit-chat, I asked her if I could help her. 'Oh yes, Father' she said, 'I have a piece of string; could you show me how to make a cord from it?' She taught me more than I taught her.

Another Retreat was in Saint Louis, and happened to coincide with a professional golf tournament at a local Country Club. I had a free afternoon and a ticket to one of the practice rounds. I sneaked away, was standing under a fine, autumnal tree watching Jack Nicklaus' approach shot when, unknown to me, a Post-Dispatch photographer took a picture, which was published in the evening paper. When I returned to the convent, they asked me if I had had a good afternoon, and I said I had. 'Where did you go?' I came clean. At that point they showed me the picture.

At a later retreat in Alabama, we woke one morning to see fiery crosses from the Ku Klux Klan burning on the lawn. At the other end of the Fahrenheit scale, I gave a Retreat in Kentucky in the winter at about 0 degrees F. I did not notice until I was in bed and just getting warm that the window in my room was slightly open. I did not want to get up and get cold again, but the wind was whistling through the gap and I could not sleep. At last I got up and found that the window was jammed. I returned to bed knowing that I could do nothing about it, and at once fell fast asleep.

There were many other Retreats and Days of Recollection to priests, to men and women religious, and to laity.

We also took part with enthusiasm in an archdiocesan program about vocations to priesthood and religious life. Before we left England, INC had told us that Saint Louis, being then 40% Catholic, was a fertile source of vocations to priesthood and religious life, so we went eagerly to various grade schools and told them what monks do. At the end we distributed forms, which they could mail to us if they wanted more information. After one of my visits, a hundred requests came in. The Sister must have told them that all the boys should express interest. I was amused, but Father Columba, who had to answer them, was not.

Our schedule during the school year gradually took shape, but that still left the summer. We had a summer school every year at the beginning of the summer, and our monastic eight-day Retreat at the end of it, but that left about a month in the middle for needed relaxation. For our Retreat we normally brought in a Retreat-giver, usually a Benedictine, but on two occasions we gave the conferences ourselves.

I never, after the first summer, taught in our summer school, but I did for several years teach a summer course at Saint Louis University. The first was a horror: a review of four years of high school Latin in six weeks. It met for three hours a day, six days a week. The Jesuit who was due to teach it wisely died in April and I was asked to take his place. One of the students was a nun of thirty-five, who had done two years of high school Latin and since then had been happily teaching English. I asked her to translate some easy Latin and she did not do very well. I asked her how long she had spent on her homework. To my horror her answer was ten hours. She then told me that at the end of the school year, her superior had sent for her and said, 'Sister, you will be teaching Latin next year; you had better go and learn some.' I lost my cool and wrote a fierce letter to her superior. There was no reply, but some time in September I received a nice letter from the Sister saying that she was not teaching Latin, but happily back in English.

Next year I was teaching the Roman poet, Lucan. In the first two-hour class we struggled through some twenty lines. Lucan is hard, but these were graduate students. After class, one brother asked if we were going to go at that speed for the whole course. I certainly hoped not, but he went on, 'No, I mean that fast.' I suggested a change of course, and he ageed.

Another way of spending the summer was this: in 1957, Fred Switzer invited me to take his son anywhere in the world. Though I did not know this at the time, his son, Fred Junior, was trying to decide between monasticism and marriage. We went to Mexico, Peru and Panama; then, for whatever reasons, Fred chose marriage. In Mexico we attended a bullfight. I admired the skill and the pageantry, but was indignant that even if the bull won, he did not survive. I have never seen another. We visited the pre-Columbian ruins at Teotihuacan, marveled at their pyramids and learnt of their human sacrifices. We also visited the silver city of Taxco and heard of the meso-American ball game.

In Peru I had a friend, Hugh Parks, who had been at Ampleforth with me. He had then returned to Peru and married a daughter of the President. He arranged a wonderful schedule for us: we visited Lima, Arequipa, Cuzco, Machu Picchu, Iquitos, and many other places. At Machu Picchu we climbed Huayna Picchu and, at the top, left a message in a bottle, thinking we would not see that again for a while. To our chagrin, we had it given back next evening.

We then flew over the Andes – part of Peru is east of the Andes – to Iquitos on the Amazon. While we were there we had two excitements, neither of which were we aware of at the time. We went in a motorboat for a tourists' ride on the Amazon and a tributary. At one point our guide left us in the boat with a native of the mountains, with whom we tried to converse. When the guide came back, he asked us if all was well. We said yes, and he was relieved, because the native was a headhunter who practiced his trade during the winter and came down to civilization during the summer.

Next day, we rented a dugout canoe and paddled our way down the Amazon and up a tributary, found a spot shaded by overhanging boughs, and had our lunch and a snooze. I was woken by a strange chuffing sound, looked around, and thought I saw a dolphin. I woke Fred, who saw the same: there they were, several dolphins a thousand miles or more from the mouth of the Amazon. When we got back the locals confirmed that these were indeed fresh-water dolphins, and added that we had been very lucky, since anacondas often lay on the overhanging boughs, waiting for their unwary prey.

In Panama we saw the Canal and some of its locks and marveled at the size of the ships they could take; we visited one of the small Caribbean islands, where there were huge and beautiful shells, and then finally returned to Saint Louis.

The monastery had by now instituted a four-year rotation for monks' vacations in England. These generally included a visit to Ampleforth, as well as to family and friends, and for these our Priory paid the fare. I sometimes combined these with family weddings. I had one at Saint Etheldreda, Ely Place, the oldest, functioning Catholic church in England, and another at Farm Street, the Jesuit stronghold, where, as someone else has said, I felt like a lion going into a den of Daniels. On other visits, I was able to go sailing in the English Channel or near Aldeburgh. with my friends, the Jonasons.

For vacations in US, we received a holiday allowance, and if we needed to spend more, we had to earn it by giving retreats or serving on a parish while the pastor took his vacation, and so on. The summer was a problem for the English monks, who did not have their family nearby, with whom they could stay. Our American friends, however, were most generous with their hospitality. The Mudds, for example, had a place on the shore of Lake Walloon in Michigan, just east of Lake Michigan, where monks were always welcome, and where there was swimming, sailing, golf, etc. And there were many other generous friends.

Part of the purpose was to get away from the hot and humid summer in Saint Louis, but that meant traveling quite a long way. We soon discovered various cheap forms of travel: Greyhound bus with a clergy discount, similar discounts on the railroads, even Auto-Driveaway. Often wealthy Saint Louisans wanted to have their car with them on vacation but did not want the chore of driving it there themselves. Auto-Driveaway found a reliable driver who would drive the car for them. The driver received an allowance for gas and had free transportation. The difficulty was to find a car going close to where we were going. One year I was to fly from Boston back to England by TWA. Someone wanted his car brought from Saint Louis to as near as possible to the TWA terminal in Boston. I had to walk a few yards from the monastery to the car, and a few yards at the far end. Otherwise I was on four-lane highways all the way. But such luck was rare.

My good luck continued on the plane. I was traveling on July 4, hoping that all good Americans would stay at home celebrating Independence Day. The British Airways plane had 130 seats but only 13 passengers. Dinner's main course was filet mignon. When I had finished, the steward asked if I would like another, and after that, would I like still another, but two were enough. After dinner I noticed that the man in front of me had finished reading his *London Times*. I asked if I might borrow it. He turned, gave me an icy stare, and turned back to his front. I went sadly to sleep, but next morning I tried again, saying, 'There is a Test Match on between England and Australia; I wonder if I might see the latest score.' He asked me if I was English, and when I agreed, said most graciously, 'My dear chap, I'm so sorry; I'd have talked to you last night if I'd known,'

One year, when I went to Heathrow, having confirmed my flight back to Saint Louis, I was told that the flight was overbooked and there was no seat. That was not a good start, and it did not help that the supervisor was wearing a yachting cap, blue blazer and white flannels, which seemed to me quite out of place at an air terminal. He was also slightly supercilious, so when he came back to say that he had found me a seat on another airline, I was not so gracious as I should have been, and when he said it was a seat in first class, I said I could not pay for that. 'That would not be necessary'. Instead of thanking him as I should, I explained my monastic status, and my vow of poverty, and my scruples about traveling in such luxury. He almost bent his white-clad knee to beg me to accept. I accepted of course. I was soon repaid. We went through customs at Dulles airport in Washington, DC, and then re-boarded the plane. A few minutes after take-off I looked out of the window and seemed to recognize the landscape. We were heading back to Dulles: we passengers had re-boarded, but our baggage had not. It may have been on this same trip that I had further repayment when I reached Saint Louis airport. I had only two quarters on me, and used one of them to call the Abbey. Brother Anthony, who was somewhat deaf, answered. 'This is Father Timothy. Could you get someone to pick me up.' You can't talk to him' was the reply, he's out of town 'But this is Father Timothy.' 'No, you can't talk to him, he's out of town.' The exchange took various forms, and at last I hung up and tried to think how to spend my last quarter. I tried again with 'Brother Anthony, there is a man at the airport who needs a ride back to the Abbey.' 'Oh, who is that?' 'It's Father Timothy.' I half expected the same reply. Instead I heard 'Oh, that's funny; there was a call for him a minute or two ago'.

On another visit to England, I started by going to stay with the Price family in Jedburgh on the Scottish border. I was planning to go on to France to spend some money we had been given for the school library, and Henry Hughes said he would try to arrange for me to meet Baron Rothschild to ask him to make

186

a donation to our library. I had hardly reached the Prices when the phone rang. The call was from Henry in Saint Louis, saying that Baron Rothschild was expecting me to lunch tomorrow. I observed that I had, before I left Saint Louis, told him my dates in France, that it would be very difficult to re-arrange my program, and anyway that would be intolerably rude to my hosts; could he make it later? He could not, so I missed my only chance to have lunch with the Baron.

A week later I did get to France by train from London to Lympne, by air across the channel, and by train to Paris. I planned to stay at a hostel for priests. It was late at night and pouring with rain. I took a taxi and we found the street but could not find #32. I got out and pressed the bell on what seemed to be #32 and a door opened. I found myself in a courtyard with a stairway leading up to the rooms. There was no sign of *Fraternité Sacerdotale*, I was tired, wet, frustrated, and sleepy and sat down on the stairway. I must have dozed, but I soon woke up and decided to knock on some door for guidance.

A friendly Parisienne opened the door, and I started my apologies. She seemed surprisingly pleased to see me, and invited me in. I declined. She said this was #34, and although she did not know the hostel, it must be one door to the left. I departed and did as she said, pressed the doorbell, and received a mild electric shock. I used my suitcase to press it again, and a man in uniform came to the door with his gun pointed at me. It was a gendarmerie, not the hostel. I tried to explain, and in the end he escorted me to the hostel. By now it was after 11 p.m., and they were not pleased to see me so late, but they did in the end find me a room. Next day, I went to the Baron's address, but could get no answer; instead, I visited bookshops in the Boulevard Raspail, and did some sightseeing.

We were punctilious about wearing clerical dress when traveling. This made us a conspicuous target for con artists and others. Once on a long-distance bus I had found a lonely seat at the back, but just before we moved off, a lady came and sat by me. We started to talk, and she asked me if she looked normal. What could I say? She said she was glad: she had just been released from a homicidal reformatory. 'Oh!' I said lamely, 'how interesting! Tell me more.' She did, and fortunately got off at the next stop, leaving me alone and alive.

Members of INC, especially in the early days, were most generous. In 1958, the Pepers, who were going to pick up a new Mercedes in Zurich, invited me to join them there, drive the car over the Alps, stay with them in Rome, and then travel back to Brussels to meet my mother at the 'Expo'. They staggered me by suggesting that I could fly with them from Rome to Istanbul in the morning, spend the afternoon there, and then fly back to Rome that evening, and still get to Brussels in time. I declined, but it was certainly generous.

Once our boys had reached the stage of thinking about admission to college, I embarked on a regular program of visits to colleges and Universities. I was convinced from my first tour of the Universities on the East Coast that this really made a difference to their attitude towards the school. For example, after my visit to Harvard, when we had our first Juniors, the Dean of Admissions at Harvard visited us and interviewed some boys. I was often able to arrange these college visits in areas where we had friends, which both gave me a vacation, and reduced the expense.

From about 1959 through 1974, when I stopped being headmaster, I spent part of most summers in this way. The visits also gave me a good feel for the country and its diversity. In the early days, many, or even perhaps most, of our seniors went to colleges that I had visited, and could report on. Besides collecting catalogues from the colleges, I gave the colleges a profile and history of our school, and invited them to visit us, which they often did. One difficulty was that no sooner had I made personal contact with a dean than he moved on, and I had to start over. The best way of making these visits was by a priory car, a lent car, or on one occasion through a banker friend, a foreclosed car.

In New Orleans I visited Tulane and Loyola Universities during the working day, and Basin Street afterwards, combining business and vacation. I stayed with friends near the Quarter. I was driving back after this visit, and stopped for gas. I was wearing an open-neck shirt, with my Benedictine medal plainly showing. A hippie walked over and said out of the blue, 'Hey man, cool medal.' He was surprised when I told him what it was.

In the course of visiting colleges in Colorado, I attended an information session at one, in which the Catholic chaplain was speaking. He referred to the Benedictines, who sometimes helped him out, as 'gentlemen priests'. A little later he said that he presided over the Newman Chaplaincy, and would we please stop calling it the Newman Club. At the end he asked for questions or comments. At a pause, I said I would be happy to stop calling it the Newman Club, if he would stop calling the Benedictines gentlemen priests.

I also visited friends in Estes Park. On my first day we went riding over lovely trails. Next day I wanted more but no one else did, so I set out alone. At the entrance I was stopped and told I could go riding only with a guide. I saw a lone horseman, and asked how come? He was a guide. I asked how one became a guide and found that you had to pay a dollar fee. I did so, became a guide, and had my ride. I also drove up Pike's Peak (14,115 feet). On the way down the police stopped all cars and felt their brakes. We were told to wait and let them cool. There was a souvenir shop right by the check point.

Twenty-Six

THE SCHOOL DEVELOPS

For the second school year, we added a new ninth grade, thus filling all four classrooms in the barn, and added a few lay teachers, mostly part-time. Two notable events occurred. A heavy snowfall started one lunchtime, and it was soon clear that the problem was to get the boys home. The school bus could not make it. A few parents did. We marched the rest of the school down to highway 40, where there was a bridge for shelter. The road sloped up to the bridge from both directions, which slowed the cars. We tried to stop each car, and almost all did stop. We asked them where they were going, and would they mind taking a boy or two going that way. Again they almost all agreed, and all the boys got home in the end. No one would dream of doing that today. Did people trust one another more then? Were people more trustworthy? They were certainly less litigious.

The other notable event was a visit from Father Columba's friend, Professor Arnold Toynbee, who had had a son at Ampleforth. He abandoned the classics for Chatham House and current world affairs. He was to talk to the school, and although I was cool to the idea, I set aside time for him. He was not a great lecturer, but was a great conversationalist, and at his best in question and answer. Our fourteen- and fifteen-year olds asked him questions to which he listened with great respect and replied mostly from personal experience. Q: What can you tell us about agriculture in Afghanistan? A: Well, when I was there last summer . . . Q: I hear they are afraid of a Tsunami hitting New Zealand. A: Well, I was talking to their prime minister the year before last, and . . . He held the boys' interest for three class periods. It was rather like talking to a mixture of the Encyclopedia Britannica and the National Geographic Magazine.

Next year, September 1958, we took in, besides the new ninth grade, small seventh and eighth grades. There have been occasional thoughts since then of going down to the fifth grade, but we have never done so. The two lower grades went into the Singer House, but the monastery building, in which were to be the extra classrooms for the high school, was not ready until mid-November, so we had two and a half months with teaching in every nook and cranny of the existing buildings: the year of the sardine.

I was still doing some teaching, and did so until I became pastor in 1981. I thought the headmaster should do so, if only to remind himself of the difficulties. My courses at Oxford were in the Classics, so I taught them. I added a course in Religious Instruction to the seniors, and at various times, when a teacher was sick, taught a class or two in most of the subjects. This included teaching a class in Spanish, which I did not know, but got by on my knowledge of Latin and French. I was pleased to hear, as I left the classroom, one boy murmur to another, 'I didn't know Father Timothy knew Spanish'. We have always had a high percentage of monks teaching in the school. For as long as I was headmaster, it was over a half. As I write (2010) it is still nearly one quarter. That may not sound like very much, but I believe there is only one other Catholic school in Saint Louis with a comparable percentage, and it is staffed by religious Sisters.

I also thought that, provided that they were young enough, coaches should play their game from time to time, to remind themselves of the effort involved. I likewise believed that all the boys should play sports and learn to go on playing for the good of the team when tired or even hurt, depending on the kind of hurt. As a side effect, in a day school they return to their parents with at least some of their surplus energy released. I noticed from the early photos of our football players a great difference of 'philosophy'. English boys playing a game were encouraged to conserve effort and even to try to make it look easy and graceful. An English writer on cricket described sports as 'physical fine arts'. Here, our football players wanted their photos to show them making maximum effort, contorted faces and all. Grace usually goes with skill, certainly conserves energy and leads to longer endurance (more important in games where there is no substitution), and probably reduces injuries. Are not the sports sections of our newspapers filled both with comments on the players' effort or lack of it, and with reports on injuries?

I watched almost all of our Varsity football games both home and away. Each year for one of the away games, two parents took Father Paul and me on a picnic. They chose some beauty spot; we set out early, had our picnic, and arrived in time for the kick-off. Once we had a puncture. To Father Paul's and my surprise, they lamented that we were some way from any house, and so could not call the AAA. We asked if they had a spare wheel and a jack, and when they did, we offered to change the wheel. "Do you really know how to do that?" they asked in amazement. They were so impressed that they photographed us on the job, enlarged the photo, turned it into a jigsaw puzzle, and sent it to us for Christmas. Another time, the mother got locked into the visitors' rest room and missed the first half. A third year, we missed the intended beauty spot and ate our picnic overlooking a railroad goods yard.

I also did some coaching in soccer and track, and occasionally pitched batting practice for our Varsity baseball when our next opponents were to start a southpaw. I started to referee some of the club rugby in Saint Louis, and that led to my being asked to coach a team drawn from Saint Louis Univerisity, Washington U., Southern Illinois U., and other Universities. The game caught on, and the season ended with Saint Louis U. fielding two teams of fifteen players all from Saint Louis University. We were invited to play a demonstration game against the Ramblers, one of the other club teams, before a football game of the Saint Louis Cardinals' professional team at Sportsman's Park. After our game, I watched part of the pro game from the sidelines. It was against Pittsburgh, and I greeted their giant, Big Daddy Lipscomb. In all his armor he looked like Goliath.

I introduced rugby to the school when Mr. Harry Langenberg, a local rugby enthusiast who went on playing himself for countless years, offered a cup for Missouri high schools. We had quite a number of players, but it was hard at first to find any opposition. We defeated a team of boys from several schools, won the cup, and so became State Champions. We successfully defended the cup twice during the next seventeen years, thus remaining State Champions. The sad irony was that when a monk joined us who knew far more about rugby than I, and I gleefully handed him the whistle, they lost their first game. So it is true that I am the only Priory coach whose teams have never been defeated, and also the only one whose teams have been State Champions for seventeen straight years; true, but wholly misleading.

I was taken to watch various games at various levels, starting with football. My first impression was, as recorded in a letter to Ampleforth, of a 'slow, poor game played in full armor'. I complained to a friend, Tom Tobin, that, compared with rugby, just as it was becoming exciting, it stopped. He helped me greatly by saying I should think of it as animated chess. I came to enjoy it very much, especially, with Tom's help, at the pro level, because the pros were so skillful, and at the grade school level, because they were hardly strong enough to hurt one another. After one grade school game a fifth- or sixth-grader, probably a bench-warmer, came running, or waddling, to greet his mother with, all the time, a grin from ear to ear, 'Hey, Mom, guess what.' 'What?' 'We lost. 'What was the score?' '50-0.' The grin never faded. He must have been put in to play towards the end. I hoped that all his life he would be so cheerful in adversity. Basketball I never really enjoyed at any level, except Magic Johnson.

Baseball was my favorite. Like cricket, it is a bat and ball game and the defense starts with the ball, but otherwise they are quite unlike. At our first Cardinals' game we were trailing by one run with one out in the bottom of the ninth and the batter hit what looked to my cricketer's eye like a sizzling off drive which should score a run or two. The man next to me snorted 'routine double play', and left. The fielding and throwing were superb, but of course they wore gloves, which cricketers, except the wicket-keeper (catcher) never do. The pitching was skillful but from my point of view limited by being all in the air. In cricket the ball hits the turf before reaching the batsman, so it can both curve in the air and spin off the turf, which gives the bowler more options. A fast bowler can reach about the same speed as a pitcher (in the 90s) and in both games 100 mph has been recorded, but the average speed is higher in baseball. In cricket, the batting area is in the middle of the field and you may hit the ball in any direction with a great variety of strokes. Baseball was, to our eyes, constricted by the 90° angle into which the batter had to hit the ball, and the strokes were limited to a swing and a bunt. We did recognize, though, that to hit a pitched ball with a round bat demanded a much better eye than to hit a bowled ball with the flat surface of a cricket bat.

I like baseball mostly because it is a game of bat and ball, but partly also because of a banner that used to be unfurled at the games. It read 'See John 3:16'. I was impressed by their assumption that we would all know what that said, namely 'God loved the world so much that he gave his only Son, so that everyone who believes in him may not be lost but have eternal life.' I have not seen it for a while: perhaps the banner-bearers died. There have been other, much greater changes too. The umpire's decision used to be final, with no argument; complete games by a pitcher were commoner – think of Bob Gibson; players were much more likely to belong to the area, or even the city, in which they were playing; and so on. But most of all, money now plays a far larger part. Around 1960, Stan Musial, already a super-star, made the headlines for getting a salary in six figures: $100,000. Also, I could get into the ballpark for 50¢, and then go up to the Red Bird Roost, to which Mr. Busch, the owner of the Cardinals, some of whose sons were in our school, gave me a pass, and where I could, in our early days, get free beer, hot dogs, etc.

Mention of Bob Gibson reminds me that he and his family spent two summers on our property in the house of Brian Barry, our faculty member, and his family, who were away. Mr. Gibson was finding it difficult to find a summer home and we were glad to help. I was driving past the house one day, and his two very young daughters were playing outside. I stopped and talked, and they asked if they could come for a ride in the car. I agreed readily, but then thought they ought to get their mother's permission. They went in to do so and, sadly, I never saw them again.

In the late 1950s I took a monk newly arrived from England to see a game at Sportsman's Park. I told him all I knew about the game. That did not take long, but just as I saying that sometimes the ball is hit up into the crowd, someone catches it, and is given a 'contract', right on cue a high fly ball came to where we sitting and, with little competition, I stood up and caught it. I have a contract with the Cardinals as an 'honorary, off-the-field outfielder, never to trade my loyalty to another club'. It is signed by Mr. Busch. Two of our boys were sitting nearby, and came over. They both asked if I had caught that ball. The first pounded his fist and said, 'That's not fair; I've been coming to the games all my life and never had a ball come to me. This is almost your first game. It's not right.' I assumed he was putting it on, but he was genuinely angry. The other asked if I had my glove with me. 'No'. Then, in shocked tones, 'You caught it with your bare hands?' At another game soon after, the batter had a good swing resulting in a foul tip. The ball was coming at high speed straight to me, and it would have been an exciting catch. It hit one of the hawsers supporting the backstop and dropped several rows away. Had I caught that with my bare hands, I would have earned a contract.

In the early days, Father Luke and I played cricket in Forest Park with a club side. Some of the players were first class, others were competent, and others novices. We played on matting, and it was occasionally hard to find the ball in the outfield. Father Luke and I had to stop because it took too much time, but not before he played for Chicago against Saint Louis and I for Saint Louis against Chicago. Later there was an international Match between the United States and Canada. I wish we had kept playing, and could then call ourselves Test Match cricketers. While we watched, an elderly car pulled up and disgorged

Here I am showing the press my hook shot in cricket.

a quantity of college students. They stood behind us, heard our comments, and asked us to explain the game. We did our best, and one of the girls asked me how I would compare cricket with baseball. Father Luke says I replied, 'My dear girl, cricket is infinitely superior.' I may have thought so, but I doubt if I said so. Later I met in London a member of the Marylebone Cricket Club (MCC), which at that time ruled cricket in England and the world. Our club was the Missouri Cricket Association (MCA), but I could not resist telling him that I had been playing for the MCC in Saint Louis. 'Oh, I didn't know we had sent a team out there.' I told him it was The Missouri Cricket Club and he nearly had apoplexy. He recovered, I apologized and told him the truth.

I also played a little tennis, a little golf, and as much squash as I could. After I had hip surgery, our school built a squash court, just as Ampleforth had done soon after I came to US. Only at Oxford did I belong to an establishment that had its own courts. For the first few years we had an Allcomers soccer match (faculty vs. boys) and Fathers and Sons softball, in which I played.

I stayed reasonably fit owing largely to a chance encounter in Montreal. I invited a priest to walk up the Mont Réal. He was older than I, but it was I who was saying, 'Let's pause for a moment to admire the view.' I commented on his fitness and asked him how he did it. He told me about the 5BX plan, a series of graduated exercises designed for the Canadian Air Force in World War II. I bought the book and did the exercises from the beginning, After six weeks of puffing and panting I looked at the chart: I was at the level of a healthy 12 year old. I did eventually reach my proper level and maintained it. The exercises took eleven minutes. I did them last thing at night in my office, while watching TV. I saw eleven minutes of countless movies, kept fit, and slept well.

Twenty-Seven

ACCLIMATION (ACCLIMATIZATION)

By the end of the second school year we were beginning to articulate what we felt were the similarities and differences between American and English boys. The similarities were greater than the differences. This would probably be true of all boys in the old and new worlds, and perhaps in the whole world. They are shrewd judges of some aspects of character, especially of the phony. English boys show more respect for the teacher qua teacher, are more tolerant of eccentricities and may even enjoy them. I have never heard one say to a teacher anything like 'my father could buy several of you' as I heard here, once only. American boys have more social self-confidence, but, to our surprise, seem more likely, when rebuked, to say 'Father X does not like me' than 'I'll show him what I can really do'. I had expected more 'frontier spirit' and ruggedness.

They also seemed more prone to coughs and colds. We noticed that they would drop a cracker (biscuit) on the floor and throw it away. An English boy would blow most of the germs off it and eat it and them. I wondered whether, in doing so, he inoculated himself against the germs. I mentioned this once to a doctor, who, to my surprise, thought there might be something in it. This may be far from the mark, but one thing is certainly true: although there was little to choose in innate ability, by the time they reach the ninth grade American boys in general have learnt, because they have been exposed to, less than English boys, just as English boys in general have learnt less than continental European boys. By high school, at age 13, I had had six years of Latin and French, a little Greek, and two years of Algebra and Geometry.

We were also becoming acclimated, rather than acclimatized, to the American scene. We gradually learnt that we could be quite economical with our own monastic needs but that it was unwise to be so with school buildings and classroom furniture. But many items could be bought at Government surplus or even railway salvage, and there were many forms of discount available, especially for charitable organizations. Some public libraries were glad to find a good home for their duplicates, which were invaluable to our library that

197

Distributing the mail at our family style lunch was a chance to relate to the boys. One of the faculty was at each table; the food was served in large dishes from which the boys helped themselves.

was starting from scratch. But there were also areas where quality was the most economical policy.

One of Ampleforth's characteristics was a tradition of hard work. We brought that across the Atlantic with us, and we had expected to be very busy at the start. But the busyness showed no sign of decreasing. The special initial effort showed signs of becoming standard procedure. We have not yet fully solved the problem, but we have survived it. An upbringing on team sports, playing tired and so on for the sake of the team, does have some carry-over into adult life. I certainly met in the army and elsewhere adults who had not played team sports in their youth and had not much stamina in later life.

Regardless, we did give considerable thought to planning relaxation. Here are some examples: Saint Louis has an excellent zoo with an amazing range of animals, birds and 'herps'.[14] I was in a clerical suit and standing at the back of a group watching a Myna bird, which saw me and said 'The Lord be with you'. Embarrassed, I replied softly (before Vatican II) 'and with your spirit' and

14. *'Herps' (or sometimes 'herptiles' or 'herpetofauna') are snakes, frogs, tortoises, lizards, crocodiles, and such, but exclude fish.*

198

moved quickly away. At another time there was a baby hippo, very ugly, and later there was a baby male elephant, to which 'baby' scarcely applied.

It was a mixed relaxation when a friend of a friend was opening a restaurant in Taylorville, Illinois. My friend and I were invited, but when we got there, the new owner was in a panic. The guests were to arrive at any minute, and the bartender had not turned up. In his panic he turned to me and asked if I would mind standing in for a few minutes. He was embarrassed to ask any of his local guests. So I did. The real bartender never came. I knew a little about drinks but less about quantities, so the evening was a roaring success. Unfortunately, the bar-tender's failure was an omen; waiters and even sometimes chefs failed to turn up, and the restaurant failed. But at least it had a memorable start.

We had a friend, Bo Naunheim, who owned a small airplane. I flew with him to Chicago to see an exhibition at the Field Museum. The weather was poor, and we made an instrumental landing. I was curious and a little anxious, but when we emerged from the clouds at about 200 feet, our line was only a foot or two off the center of the runway. Going back we had to fly through a cloud with sleet, and were afraid of icing up, but again all was well. On another trip, he asked me if I would like to take the stick. I found it surprisingly hard to maintain both height and direction. When I concentrated on one, the other wavered.

Other friends were willing to trust us to stay, unsupervised, in their homes or farms in the country. Late one evening I was driving to one such on a quiet country road with a wide grass verge. On the verge was feeding a herd of deer. Startled by the car, they started one after another to jump over the fence into the field by the roadside. Silver in the headlights and graceful they were, a sight I still remember vividly. At another home in the country, I was sitting quietly at the fireside saying Compline, the church's night prayer, when I heard a rustling and saw a snake emerging through a hole in the plaster. I fetched an ax and cut off its head. The snake was four feet long. I reported this when I came back to Saint Louis and was told that it was a harmless, and indeed beneficial, grass snake On my next visit there, as I walked in at the door, there was a small, vividly green snake coiled on a chair. The last snake I had seen of this color was a Russell's viper in Burma.[15] one of the world's most poisonous snakes. I was about to look for the ax, when I noticed that it was not breathing. This was not surprising as it was made of plastic.

15. I was told the Burma snake was a Russell's Viper. It was bright green, but in google's pictures of the viper, it is brown.

Twenty-Eight

THE ROUGH AND THE SMOOTH

The tale of our school's growth has been told elsewhere, so I shall try to limit this account to what concerns me directly. We have always enjoyed a good relationship with all the Archbishops of Saint Louis since we have been here. We also realized the importance of good relations with the clergy, but that has not precluded the occasional disagreement. One such was over the Archdiocesan Synod of 1960. These Synods used to occur about every ten years. Their statutes laid down general rules for the organization of the Archdiocese. They did not change much, and one would refer to them rather than read them straight through.

When the draft statutes of the Synod were sent to us, I was about to put them on the shelf for reference. Then, fortunately, I looked at the section on education to make sure that all was well. It was not. The previous statutes had placed 'Catholic parish and diocesan schools' under the supervision of the School Office of the Archdiocese. The new statutes omitted the words 'parish and diocesan' thus appearing to place all Catholic schools in the Archdiocese under the new Archdiocesan Superintendent of Schools. This supervision would have included selection of teachers, choice of textbooks, school calendar, and much more, so it was a matter of major concern to us, and also to the Jesuits, Sacred Heart Religious, and other congregations that had schools in the Archdiocese. We alerted them.

I did extensive research, we consulted a Benedictine Canon lawyer, and Father Columba wrote a masterly letter making our points irenically but firmly. It was a good example of his and my diverse but complementary strengths cooperating harmoniously. The statutes were revised and we were left autonomous, but we recognized our need to work with the Archdiocese, especially as we were eager not even to seem as though we had come to US to show the Archdiocese how to run a boys' school. As with the parents, so with the Archdiocese: we were not used to such closeness. It was not so at Ampleforth, and I was slow to recognize the difference.

200

The complementary strengths of Father Columba and me did not always prevail over our conflicting temperaments. This had been true at Ampleforth before we came here, and when I commented on it to Abbot Herbert Byrne, he agreed. 'Yes, you don't overlap much,' he said, 'but if you can complement one another, think how much of the spectrum you will cover'. We tried, and made some headway, but not enough, and so in June 1959, a letter was sent out to our parents and others announcing my return to England. That led to several letters of dismay from here to Abbot Herbert at Ampleforth. To clarify the situation, Father Columba made a transatlantic call to Abbot Herbert, at a time when such calls were a major undertaking, and the connection was often poor. Father Columba understood, or rather misunderstood, that the monk being sent out instead of me was to be the headmaster. His experience did not seem to be suitable for that, and in fact he was not intended to be headmaster. Father Columba asked for me to be left for another year, when a fresh decision would be made. Abbot Herbert agreed, but said later that important decisions must never again be made over the transatlantic telephone. In 1960, Father (later Abbot) Patrick Barry and Father (later Abbot and then Cardinal) Basil Hume were sent out to evaluate the situation. As a result I was kept on as headmaster.

At the beginning of each school year, the Archdiocese held in Kiel Auditorium a Convention for all its teachers, which in those days meant several thousand religious sisters, a hundred or so priests and a few lay teachers. All the monks attended. At my first such gathering I was twice discomfited: I was talking to a formidable Sister and explained who I was and what I did. She asked me what I had my doctorate in. I said I had none, and would have explained the English practice in such matters, but she turned and walked away. The second time I returned after one of the breaks, but not to my original seat. I was reading the program, when I felt a presence looming over me. I sprang up and, using a common English expression, said, 'Oh! I'm sorry, Sister; did I pinch your seat?' Only when she blushed, did I realize how she was taking it.

At the corresponding Convention a year or two later, I was asked to introduce ex-Mayor Aloys P. Kaufmann, who was to introduce the Governor of Missouri, Warren E. Hearnes, who was to address the Convention. All went well until Mayor Kaufmann rose to thank the Governor for his inspiring message, and ended with, 'And now I hand the microphone back to my good friend Father er, Father er . . .' I had to hasten to his side and murmur 'Timothy'. We had never met before.

We had many meetings with INC at which I had to survive the happy hour and then report on the school. One of these meetings was quite different. We had a number of slides of the school taken with a camera with a special lens, such that the slides could be shown on the wide screen that had come into use for movies. The slides were to be projected on the screen of the Tivoli Theatre before the première of the movie, *South Pacific*. We were discussing with Fred Switzer of INC who should narrate the slides. Father Columba said that as they were mostly of the school, the obvious person was Father Timothy. There was a long pause, and then Fred replied, 'Yes, I'm sure he would do it very well, but I'm afraid he might make some jokes – and we are talking about money.' There was a gale of monastic laughter, which showed the difference of the monks' point of view.

I was asked to preside at a meeting of the supporters of the Saint Louis Symphony who wanted to complain to the management about the content of the programs – not enough old favorites. It was a lively meeting. Another was with the art school of Washington University about an exhibition of abstract painting. Some other groups were: the Daughters of Saint Francis of Sales, the Alumnae of Villa Duchesne (a Sacred Heart school for girls), the Wednesday Club, and the American Association of University Women, to whom I used, like Lewis Carroll's Walrus,

> *To talk of many things*
> *Of shoes, and ships, and sealing wax,*
> *Of cabbages and kings*

or of Russian icons, or trips to Iran. The Wednesday Club asked me to a tea-time meeting to talk about The *Lost Treasures of the Middle Ages*. I asked for the lights to be turned out and said nothing for about a minute. There really was a little 'tinkling among the teacups' so I asked for lights to be turned on, and said that this was all we really knew about the lost treasures; and now I would show them some slides. The Italian Club of Saint Louis asked me to talk also about lost treasures, this time those of Monte Cassino. This was easier, since much of the loss was in World War II, and many of the treasures had been recovered. A friend produced some slides, one of which was of a manuscript page of Gregorian chant. I asked if they would like me to sing it. When I did so, to my surprise and delight, they applauded. Being applauded by Italians for my singing made me feel like a diva at La Scala.

One invitation led to unexpected action, but I did not have to say a word. Saint John's Mercy Hospital moved from downtown Saint Louis to a site close to us. We were invited to the cutting of the ribbon at their opening. I was standing near the ribbon and waiting for the ceremony to begin. Suddenly one of the Sisters thrust a large pair of scissors into my hand and asked if I would cut one of the ribbons. I asked if I had to say anything or read a blessing, and was assured that I had nothing to do except cut. Someone must have failed to turn up, so with the others I made my cut and the hospital opened.

I had other meetings too, often with the Saint Louis Classical Club. I was also invited to address other schools on a variety of topics ranging from Saint George, (thank God for the *Legenda Aurea*) to 'Zen and the Art of Motorcycle Maintenance'. Some addresses were at graduations. One of these was at a girls' school just across the road from Webster College. I drove to Webster College, crossed the road, found what was obviously an educational institution and asked the first man I saw to direct me to the library, where I was to meet Sister X. He looked at me oddly and asked if I was sure I was in the right place. It was a United Church of Christ Seminary and this was before ecumenism was vigorous.

My most successful talk was to a graduation at another girls' school. I was invited at about one week's notice (someone had canceled). It was outside on a sunny day and rather hot, so I had two excuses for being brief. I quoted the first stanza of Housman's poem:

> *Loveliest of trees, the cherry now*
> *is hung with bloom along the bough . . .*

and compared the seniors and their talents to the cherry trees. If all the blooms were allowed to become cherries, their weight would break the branches. So too, if the seniors tried to develop all their talents, they would break themselves.

Our own seniors heard before we did of the tradition of the senior prank. Practical jokes are one of the hardest forms of humor to carry off successfully. At Christ Church, after a rowing victory, the eight captured a swan, put a black bow tie round its neck and left it in the small pond of the Mercury fountain in Tom Quad. When we came down next morning, there it was swimming in the pond looking most decorative in its evening dress in the morning sunshine. This was original, courageous, and elegant. A year or two later, other oarsmen stole some of the Steward's ducks and did the same to them. This was neither original, nor courageous, nor elegant.

A group of our seniors, before they were allowed to drive to school, did drive to school and parked down by the gym, about a third of a mile from my office. Father Luke and I heard of this and removed the rotor arms from the cars to immobilize them, and put each rotor arm in an envelope with the engine number. When the seniors could not start their cars, they heard that Father Luke and I had been seen in that area and trudged up to my office to see if I knew why their cars would not start. I explained, and added that it was important to get the proper rotor arm back into each car, for which I would need the engine number, which is on the cylinder block That meant for them a trudge back to the gym, then back up to my office, and then back to their car, more than a mile in all. One boy was still angry when he reached home and expostulated to his parents that the trouble with those monks was that they had no sense of humor. He was surprised at his parents' reaction.

It is only fair to record also one that was a success for the seniors. A noted Girls' school, Villa Duchesne, was seeking a new head of school. Our seniors sent out a letter to our parents announcing the merger of Villa and Priory under Father Timothy. When the first call came to my office, I was on my way to a meeting of Villa's Search Committee, so I told my secretary that far from being the new headmaster of Villa, I was merely a member of the search committee. My secretary then had to deal with dozens of phone calls.

Our own graduations for several years were outside on the lawn behind the Stannard House. The weather was warm and sometimes hot, but four Dutch elms provided shade. We started with Mass outdoors and the rest of the ceremony as usual. We always prayed earnestly for good weather, and usually got it. One year, it was a lovely day with a cool breeze to mitigate the heat. To my amazement the mothers complained. When I asked why, they said the wind would upset their hairdos. After a while, the elms succumbed to the Dutch elm disease, and the church was completed, so we moved inside

As the school grew, so did our lay faculty. At Ampleforth when I was there, all the top positions were held by monks, even though many of the lay faculty were highly competent; and there was a separate Laymasters' Common Room, where monks could enter but not linger. I wanted it to be clear from the beginning that we were one faculty with one faculty room, where both monks and laity would have desks. We gradually included women on the faculty, but, as with African Americans, there were initially few women who were both willing and qualified, and those few were eagerly snapped up. We now in 2011

204

have had for some years a layman as Second Master, for some years a laywoman, succeeding a laywoman, as head of the Junior School, and of the nine Heads of Academic Departments, six are laymen, two laywomen and one a monk.

Twenty-Nine

WE START TO MAKE OURSELVES KNOWN

The next big event was the building of our circular church. We had already completed the plans.[16] The Mudd family, who were giving us the church, were ready, the 'specs' went out, and the bids came back. Quite unusually, the low bid, by McCarthy Brothers, was about 20% lower than the next lowest. When the head of their firm saw the specs, he threw them into the trash can, but his nephews pulled them out, saw that they were interesting, and asked permission to prepare a bid on them. 'Yes, but not on company time' was the response. The arches are all thin-shell parabolas. All the other contractors were planning to use double forms for the concrete, which would be

16. *Our church (Architects; Hellmuth, Obata and Kassabaum; Contractor; McCarthy Brothers) was consecrated on September 7, 1962. The material is thin-shelled concrete. See page 159*

poured into the space between the two forms. McCarthy planned to use a single form, shoot the concrete on with a gun, and smooth it all by hand. This was done, and it was then given several coats of paint of different colors, each looking magnificent until painted over. The concrete was all shot on, and then smoothed, by hand; the painting of the outside was all done by hand; the lath and plaster on the inside was all done by hand and finished by hand with a bath sponge. The floor tiles, too, were all laid by hand. Huge telephone poles supported the inside during construction, and when, on completion of the structure, the poles were removed, the structure sank imperceptibly, if at all.

My room in the monastery faced the church, so, when I was in my room, which was seldom, I had a grandstand view of this fascinating operation. It had its critics at the time, 'it looks like a wedding cake'; but it is now generally recognized as a masterpiece. The only serious problem has been, and still is, acoustics. They favor singing and instrumental music, but make speech hard to hear, unless the church is full.

My only fear was that with all twenty arches being exactly the same, we might, as the years passed, become bored with it, but with the light coming in differently at different times of day and at different seasons of the year, that has not happened. It was intended to be the architectural jewel of the campus, and it is.

The church was consecrated on September 7, 1962. In 1965 the Archdiocese held their priestly Ordinations in it. We crammed in nearly two thousand people and a tower for TV cameras.

During our time we have had a surprising number of visitors seeking to discuss education with us. Some were expatriates like ourselves: we told them of our experiences and they told us of theirs. Such were Hungarian Benedictines from California and Hungarian Cistercians from Texas. The Mother General of the Ursulines came, and so did Father John Main from the Benedictine Abbey of Ealing, in London, who was to be the headmaster of Saint Anselm School in Washington, DC. We learnt from them and, we hoped, they from us. Sometimes I had to travel to the meetings. One was in Chicago in midwinter. I went by train and on arrival saw a Citizen's Advice Bureau and asked the way to Lawndale. They asked North or South. I did not know, so we settled on South. I should take a streetcar (tram) to Pulaski, go south on Pulaski to 3400, and then go four blocks east to Lawndale. I did this, but unfortunately found myself in the middle of a long bridge over railroad tracks and yards, so there were no streets running east. I was carrying a suitcase, had no gloves and the temperature was 15° F below zero, with a bitter wind. I had to walk what seemed like a mile to the end of the bridge, then four blocks east, and a mile back up Lawndale. It must have been a bad neighborhood, for when I knocked on a door and asked to use the phone, they would not let me in. After three attempts, a kind woman did let me in and I called a cab. The meeting was at North Lawndale. That was my introduction to Chicago, the windy city, and I was in no hurry to go back.

I was also invited to be a member of the Higher Education Coordinating Council of Metropolitan Saint Louis, (HECC, now HEC, dropping Coordinating) which had a member or two from secondary schools but was otherwise a distinguished group of College Presidents. Most of the business impinged but little on secondary schools, but the acceptance or non-acceptance by colleges of the results of the Advanced Placement (AP) examinations was of great concern. My contribution here was, from experience, that the better the college, the more generous it was in acceptance. Harvard was most generous. It was often the lesser colleges that claimed that there was no course like their freshman chemistry course. I was able to add that when our boys were choosing their college, they took into account the college's attitude towards AP results. As we were enthusiastic supporters of the AP tests, we naturally favored generous colleges. So did our parents, because it saved them money if their sons graduated sooner. For our seniors it meant either that they graduated from college sooner, or that they were excused some required courses and had a greater choice of electives. I was a member of HECC from 1963 to 1977, and was secretary for the latter part of that time. As a result of this, when the College Board held in Saint Louis a workshop on their Advanced Placement program, I was asked to preside at one of the sessions. This led to my becoming a member of the College Board's Advanced Placement Committee. This was for three years, and entailed an annual meeting in New York, and an occasional appearance at regional meetings.

I drove to one of these annual meetings, and planned to visit Bucknell University in Lewisburg, Pennsylvania, on the way. Although the meeting was in June, I encountered heavy flooding in the East and much of Interstate highway 80 was closed. I had to make a detour on country lanes, and on one hill met a two-foot wave coming down the hill. I spluttered and splashed along and eventually reached Lewisburg, where there was martial law, with police and soldiers at the main corners. Again I had to make a detour to avoid them. The Admissions staff assumed I would not be coming, but someone was there, and we exchanged some information and I drove on. I was a little late for the meeting in New York, and parked in the hotel garage. In my haste I left my beautiful, brand-new sleeping bag visible in the car. I saw it no more. My only consolation was that there was also on the floor a slide projector, over which I had hastily thrown my windcheater. The thief did not see that.

College admissions brought into focus for us the question of accreditation. I had met the question on my original tour of New England, but the situation was different there. On the whole the independent schools were there before the public schools, and had great prestige. Also there were many of them.

In the Midwest we did not feel comfortable with our agency, and anyway, the English monks had no education credits. That kind of preparation for teaching hardly existed then in England, and no Ampleforth monks had such credits, nor did the teachers at most English independent schools.

Here it was state universities that were the problem. Some had a flat rule of taking no one from the lower half of the senior class. But we had a boy who failed academically with us, transferred to a public school and was on the Dean's List there. Another senior was turned down by an out-of-state University for their Veterinary program because he was in the lower half of the class. I asked if they would let him come and take an exam with them. They agreed, and on the results not only accepted him but gave him a full Semester of credit. We eventually joined the Independent Schools Association of the Central States (ISACS) and are accredited by them. Colleges accept this.

There was also accreditation of a different kind in Athletics. We wanted to join the ABC League, which consisted of schools similar to ours, where sports are important but where academics come first. We applied, and were turned down because we were Catholic. This was in the early 1960s, and we were blackballed by the head of the governing body of one of the member schools. When this became known, he was the subject of such constant ribbing, and per-haps more than ribbing, that he agreed to let their headmaster come over and 'vet' me. That must have been embarrassing for their headmaster, but he was English, had played rugby for Cambridge and England, and had an outlook similar to my own. I could not match his athletic talent, but I had played cricket for the Authentics Cricket Club at Oxford, so I passed his scrutiny, and we were admitted.

College visits occupied most of my summers. I counted them as vacation since I was often able to combine visits to colleges with visits to friends. The core of every College visit was the time I spent with their Admissions Officers, mostly with the Dean of Admissions. I handed over a dossier on our school and came away with an up-to-date Catalogue from the college. I am mildly allergic to campus tours, but I usually walked around a little on my own, and was surprised how much of an impression I could get just from that. It was often enough for me to feel confident in saying to our seniors, 'I think this college is, or is not, worth your visit'. I have written elsewhere on the serious side of these visits. There was often a lighter side too.

On almost my first visit I had an appointment with the Dean of Admissions of Saint Norbert's College in De Pere, Wisconsin. I was late, and when I reached the main building, a man was walking out. I thought this might be the Dean of Admissions and asked him if he was. He drew himself up and replied that he was Vince Lombardi. That meant nothing to me in my newness, so I said I was Timothy Horner and walked on. Later I learnt that the Green Bay Packers were having their summer camp there, that I had just met one of the most famous football coaches ever, and that I was one of a tiny minority of men in US who did not recognize the name.

Another summer I stayed with friends near Atlanta; my first excursion was north-east as far as Richmond. I was driving in a small Opel along the Blue Ridge Parkway admiring the view in the early morning with a slight mist still lingering. I rounded a bend, and there standing in the middle of the road was a majestic bald eagle about as tall as the car. I drove back by way of Nashville, where, after visiting Vanderbilt and then the full scale model of the Parthenon, I thought to visit Fisk University. We may already have had African American students, and certainly planned to have more. I entered the Administration Building and walked around looking for the Admissions Office but could find no one. I tried various offices, which were open but empty. I had the eerie feeling that there were people around, but no one was visible. So I left, wondering whether, although I was wearing a clerical suit, they thought that I was from the Ku Klux Klan. This was in about 1960.

The second excursion was with my hostess and her mother. I planned to visit Spring Hill in Mobile on the way, and then colleges in New Orleans. We stopped for a shrimp lunch at Biloxi, which, before the oil spill, claimed to be the Sea Food Capital of the World. We found a café at the end of a dilapidated wooden pier, between the boards of which we could see the waves. For $1.75 they gave us a large plate piled high with cooked shrimps, and a bottle of ketchup dumped on the table. It was not elegant, but the shrimps, which we had to shell, were delicious. On the way back, we noticed on the other side of the road a Heritage House. There we were elegantly served, with tablecloths, silver and so on, and each of us was given a plate with a circle in the middle for some catsup and twelve small compartments round the side, in each of which was one shelled shrimp. The price was $1.75. In New Orleans we had dinner at one of the famous restaurants. The dining area was an open patio with slim pillars. Vines were using them for support: so was a huge tarantula. We asked the waiter to remove it; he did so without surprise. The food was good.

Another summer I drove via Colorado to the North-West. I asked friends in Colorado what they would like me to bring back for them, They asked for a salmon. I visited a number of colleges in Oregon and Washington, including Bing Crosby's Gonzaga University, and then went on to Vancouver and visited the University of British Columbia. Some photographs that I took of their beautiful campus later persuaded a rather dreamy visitor to the Priory to go to study there.

Then I headed to the harbor and met a salmon-fishing boat just docking. I chose a good salmon and asked them to pack it for me. They gave me three packs of dry ice and told me to put in a deep freeze each evening. After staying a few days at the Benedictine Abbey of Westminster in Mission, British Columbia, I drove on up the Fraser Canyon to a campsite at Kicking Horse Creek. There, for 50¢, I was admitted to the site and found a loop in the creek just big enough for the car. I slept in the car, lulled to sleep by the waters of the creek. In the morning I woke to see 10,000-foot mountains around me, had a hot shower, found an outlet for my electric razor, and then walked to the camp store down one side of the creek, accompanied down the other side by a bear and her two cubs.

In Banff the only deep freeze I could find for the salmon was at a hospital. I asked if there was anywhere I could set my sleeping bag. They said there was roller bed in a disused operating theatre. But in the middle of the night some men came in and I woke to find myself in motion on the way to surgery. I persuaded them I was not their victim. Thence I drove on up the Icefield Highway and paused at the Columbia ice field and its glacier. I met moose, elk, deer, and other fauna on the way to Jasper, where I slept in the car at a campground for another 50¢, while others were sleeping in Jasper Lodge for $160 a night. I doubt if they were 320 times more comfortable.

There I picked up a priest who was heading back to Chicago, and had his company until we parted somewhere in South Dakota. The worst night for the salmon was in a small town somewhere north of Yellowstone. All the deep freezes in the cafés were full. Eventually a kind owner said she had room in her deep freeze at home. I explained that we would be leaving very early in the morning, and she replied that there was an outside stair down to the basement; she would leave the door unlocked and we could go in and retrieve the fish. Next morning we did that, and I was half way to the freezer, when a man's voice asked, very reasonably, who I was and what I was doing. I said that I had come for my salmon. 'What salmon?' 'The one in the deep freeze'. This was her husband, a salesman, who finished his rounds up north earlier than expected, had come home in the middle of the night, and did not want to disturb his wife. He had come down the outside stair and was sleeping on the couch. We got things sorted out, but I'm sure neither of us wanted to start the day like that. The story had a happy ending. My friends in Colorado cooked the salmon and it was delicious, well worth all the trouble.

My aunt, Norah Morawski, lived in Toronto, with her husband, John, a forester. She was the magnet that drew me to Eastern Canada to visit the University of Toronto, McGill, and Laval University in Québec. She weighed under a hundred pounds and was a motorcycle test driver, which was how she met and married my uncle Maurice, who died during World War II. She then married John Morawski, a Pole, who looked so much like General Eisenhower that when John and the general were together at a Reception in London during that war, guests kept coming to the General saying, 'We know your other brothers, but who is this one?'

Another magnet was an Old Amplefordian, who was a doctor in Kingston, Ontario, whom I visited *en route*. This tour was not one of my most productive, but we did send a senior or two to Toronto and McGill, and others have applied. In Québec, I visited the Plains of Abraham, the scene of the crucial battle between the British and the French in 1759. There were many plaques recording valiant French deeds of arms, but I could find none stating that General Wolfe won the battle, captured Québec, but died in doing so.

Most of these visits were during the summer, but I was able also to get away occasionally during the spring break or at other times of the school year. One year I went to the South-West during the baseball World Series. Our Cardinals, to whom I was contracted to pay undying allegiance,[17] were playing Detroit. When, in Houston, I went in to visit the Dean of Admissions at Rice, Detroit was batting. When I came out, 45 minutes later, Detroit was still batting in the same inning. They scored 13 runs.[18]

In Dallas I visited the site of President Kennedy's assassination, and then Southern Methodist University, who were not thrilled at seeing a Catholic priest, and Texas Christian College, who were. I got as far as the University of Texas, but there had been a murder on campus that day, and I was unable to see anyone.

One tour was in the middle of winter. I wanted to fit into the schedule a visit to an alumnus, Peter Igoe, who was in the navy, but stationed in a remote part of upper New York State, far from any sea. I arrived late and he was just leaving for duty. He entrusted me to his landlady, who gave me dinner. I was settling down to watch some game on TV, when, slightly to my surprise, she asked if she could join me. Unwarily I agreed. We were sitting on a sofa. She seemed to be getting closer, so I inched away, but this happened more than once, and eventually I ran out of inches. She then expressed her intentions not only in deeds but also in words. I explained that although I was in holiday garb I was really a monk, which she refused to believe. I had noticed as I drove up that there were trotting races that evening in Saratoga Springs, so I sprang up, saying that I had to go to the races. I found trotting a skillful but eviscerated form of racing, which I am glad to have seen once. I stayed out late, crept in quietly, and was greeted next morning at breakfast with 'Oh, how disappointing! I thought you had left'.

Cornell was also on my list, and I was due to stay at the Catholic chaplaincy. I pressed the electric doorbell there, and the lights went out all over Cornell. I must have been the last straw, and the power cut lasted for the rest of my visit. There was a priest visiting who was a chaplain to the New York waterfront. He had fascinating stories to tell of his ministry on the docks, and told them well. Next morning, I was driving on ice most of the way, and there was no sun to guide me. To my chagrin, after an hour I found that I was on the right road but in the wrong direction. In all my visits, that was the only major map-reading blunder. I had to retrace my steps and lost two precious hours. But that was

17. See page 185.
18. That will not sound like much to a cricketer, but is equivalent to a stand of perhaps 200 in a Test Match.

better than losing my life would have been, and which might have been when, a few hours later on an interstate, I had to pass big truck in a heavy snowstorm. The snow was bad enough, but the truck with its spray was a traveling blizzard, into which it was an act of faith, and perhaps folly, to plunge, but I was already two hours late.

One other visit deserves mention, and that was to Dartmouth College in New Hampshire for a workshop on Admissions. They told us a true story about computers, which has been a comfort to me and to others. A Math professor spent some years working out all the equations that needed to be solved in order to answer his problem. He took his lengthy program to the computer. This was a circular, time-sharing monster with many stations. It worked a little at your problem, then moved on to the next station. He was told to come back the same time tomorrow. He did, and was given an envelope, which he tore open and, to his chagrin, found a blank sheet of paper. 'Send for the supervisor.' The supervisor asked to see his program, read it through, and started to laugh. 'Why are you laughing? 'Look at your last command to the computer. How does it read?' 'Solve these equations.' 'Yes' said the supervisor, 'and you did not add "and print out the answers" ' Few secretaries could have solved the equations, but every secretary would have known that the professor wanted the answers printed out. The computer needed to be told to do so.

Thirty

EXPANSION

The early sixties were a time of consolidation in the school; in the mid-sixties we absorbed the impact of the Second Vatican Council; in the late sixties we were ready to expand. This meant further building, starting in 1967 with the Junior School and followed two years later by the High School. We planned the new buildings and were fortunate to have them ready in time. We had an educational consultant to help with the planning. For the high school, he spent a morning advocating undifferentiated space instead of regular classrooms. He was eloquent and persuasive, and when we went to lunch, many of the faculty seemed to be in favor. I had visited a local school that had tried it, and I was not impressed. We stayed with regular classrooms. The Junior School building seemed enormous after the very cramped quarters in which the boys had survived before, but by 2009 it had to be expanded. The High School, likewise, seemed ample at the time, but has since been expanded. It is a split-level building having one story on the west and two on the east, to match the slope of the ground.

As everything else expanded, so did our examinations both for the school and for entry into the school. We held them in the gym, and that meant transporting desks down there. Each boy carried one desk. One year we had about 180 candidates, or maybe more, for entry, so the whole process, correcting the papers and interviewing the candidates took much longer. I met an African American mother and her daughter at the door. I assumed she was looking for her son, but no! She wanted her daughter to take the tests. I said there was little point in that as this was a boys' school and did not take in girls. She said I was being racist, and nothing I could say persuaded her otherwise. Eventually I gave in and pointed to a seat for her daughter. At that point the girl herself said she did not want to take the test if she could not be accepted however well she did. Her mother then agreed.

Expansion meant also that the monks had come to terms, sadly, with being unable to attend all the monastic duties in choir, and consequently with saying privately parts of the Divine Office, which the other monks recited in choir.

We also continued to wrestle with the problem of overwork. In the early days, to continue Ampleforth's tradition of hard work tradition was a matter not of virtue but of necessity. There were simply not enough monks to do all the work on a normal schedule, and so we made a special effort. But by 1965 we had eleven monks from Ampleforth, and nine full-time lay teachers. The original monks, however, were not notably good at delegating. Father Luke and I were told that we tended to be entrepreneurial rather than managerial, which cannot have helped. We certainly tended to carry plans in our heads, which gave us flexibility, and Five Year Plans with Mission Statements, Goals and Objectives were unfamiliar. The initial special effort was, therefore, in danger of becoming the norm. The danger was aggravated by a tendency to feel guilty if one was not overworking. It was not as easy as might be imagined to convince oneself that this was folly. I think I am a lazy workaholic: I am quite happy doing nothing, at least for a time, but find it hard not to do what I can see is there to be done, even if it could wait.

After the closure of the Second Vatican Council in 1965 we had first of all an internal change: In 1967, Father Columba was taken back to Ampleforth by the new abbot, Basil Hume, later Cardinal Archbishop of Westminster. In his place Abbot Basil appointed Father Luke as Prior. Although Father Columba had in very many ways given us an excellent start, I found Father Luke much easier to deal with. It was mainly with him that the community implemented the changes called for by Vatican II: Mass and Liturgy in English, concelebration, that is, having one or more priests join the principal celebrant in celebrating the one Mass, consultation with the laity (which we had already been doing), and many more.

We watched a VCR tape entitled *Paradigm*, from which I remember two scenes: in the first a Yuppie bought an expensive sports car and took it out for a run. As he approached a corner a young feminist, as he judged, came round the corner, swerving and somewhat out of control, and yelled at him, 'Pig'! With a quick reaction he yelled back at her, 'Cow', felt pleased with himself, rounded the corner, and there was the pig in the middle of the road. He destroyed the pig and wrecked his car. He had the wrong paradigm. She was not a young feminist.

In the second scene, the Swiss, who had almost a monopoly of the market for watches, were shown a new-fangled, digital watch. They knew that nothing could match the motion of the famous Swiss watches, and paid no heed. A year or two later, the Japanese controlled the market. The Swiss, too, had the wrong paradigm.

It was clear to us that after Vatican II, there was a shift of paradigm, or rather of paradigms. It was also clear that some of us shifted paradigms more easily and more rapidly than others, and that some paradigms should not be shifted. Our liturgy is the vehicle of our prayer, which is central to our life. Liturgical form, which can very easily become an end rather than a means, can also arouse very strong feelings in a monastic community. The Benedictine instinct about change is that it should be organic: the new should grow out of the old. This made us suspicious of those around us who wanted to throw out all the old ways, even with contempt, and so we proceeded cautiously. There were those who appealed to the motto of Monte Cassino, Saint Benedict's monastery, *succisa virescit* (cut down, it grows strong again), but that applies more to cutting down by force from outside than to peaceful change from within.

Not all the changes were connected with Vatican II. For example, the clash between denial of self and self-fulfillment was due more to the spirit of the times. Saint Benedict emphasizes the danger of self-will, wanting one's own way, but incoming novices were seeking self-fulfillment, and so having one's own way. The two can be harmonized, but only with thought and effort. Incoming novices had difficulty also with commitment: 'But, Father, I shall not be the same person in ten years time as I am now.' But one cannot be a whole-hearted monk without that commitment. The same hesitation about commitment was often observable when we counseled engaged or married couples.

In the school I had to wrestle with the problem of daily Mass. Through the late sixties we had Mass for the whole school every day. We were disturbed by being told by parents that their sons were saying on Sundays, 'Look, Mom, I have been to Mass five times this week. Give us a break.' I could not fully agree, but had to concede that the sons had a point. So I appointed a committee who met for, literally, years but could reach no recommendation. Eventually I decided to cancel the daily Mass and to have one Mass on Friday for the whole school, which we still do. We considered that we could count more on the Catholic influence that Catholic families had on their children; and we did not want to reduce Mass to four times a week, and then to three, and so down to one. Nor did we want to reduce the boys' respect for Sunday Mass in their own parish. We did encourage Form Masters to have at least one Mass a week for their Form, and some had more.

May I digress for a moment on this matter of decisions. Soon after we came here, a famous major league baseball umpire retired and was being interviewed on the radio. He was asked how many bad calls he thought he had made in his career, and answered 'none'. When they said that was ridiculous, he replied that he had made every call as he saw it, and so he, at least, thought they were all correct. I was struck by that, even though I did not quite agree. But it did comfort me when I had to make major decisions. I thought about them, sought advice about them and prayed about them. I could not say, with the umpire, that I was confident that they were all correct, but I could say to myself that they were the best I could do at the time.

Another area for decisions was technology. Computers were appearing above the horizon. I knew nothing about computers, and it may have been my visit to Dartmouth College that prompted me to attend a two-week course being given downtown by Texas Instruments. A computer then filled a room or two with itself and all its attendant reels of tape. The course taught us what a computer was, what it could do, how fast it could do it, and how it was programmed. I was suitably impressed, and when I came back, said to Mr. Barry, who was already interested in these things, 'I think computers are here to stay, and I think we had better get into them.' He did so with a vengeance, and we were, as already mentioned, the first school, or one of the first, in Saint Louis to do so.

Part of our program has always been to give the boys a sense of service, so when we received an appeal from a school in Molapowabojang, Botswana, saying that if we could send them $1000, they would be able to build a school, we took it up enthusiastically. The money was needed to buy the concrete blocks, etc., and they would do the constructing. Each class in the school was set a sum to achieve. We soon had $990 plus and sent them their check for $1000. They kept us informed with photographs of their progress, and soon they had their building. Then each time we had a change of pattern in our T-shirts, we sent them the remainder of our stock of the old pattern. In return we were delighted to receive photos of their African pupils running about the Kalahari Desert with PRIORY on their T-shirts. We have had a whole variety of service projects since then.

In 1966, I was invited by Henry Hughes to attend the Kentucky Derby. Before we left, his wife, Marjorie, advised us to go to the paddock and choose a strong-looking horse with a jockey with a determined eye. We drove to Churchill Downs, followed Marjorie's advice and chose Kauai King at 11-2. We secured a good place on the grass, but at the last moment Henry decided there was a better place nearer the finish. No doubt there was, but we were too late, and all we saw of the race was the jockeys' caps bobbing up and down. The horses and the rest of each jockey were hidden by the crowd. Kauai King won, but as all bets were on the Tote, our price had shortened to 9-4. Nonetheless, the school library benefited quite handsomely, and has a number of books inscribed 'presented by K. King'.

There were also spiritual demands being made on our time. Maryville University moved out from downtown to a campus close to us and asked us to provide Mass for the Sisters. I was part of that team, and in the end head of it. Other Convents nearby needed Mass on occasion, and the Visitation Sisters regularly. Others farther afield needed Retreats, mainly during the summer. We were also called on for spiritual direction for individuals, who took an hour or two once or twice a month. Most of us had several individuals, and it soon added up. When, in 1966, Saint Anselm Parish was formed, with a diocesan priest, Monsignor Robert P. Slattery, as pastor, but using our church, the pastor asked for talks by the monks, the hearing of Confessions and celebration of Masses.

I was a member of the Archdiocesan Ecumenical Commission for many years. I wanted to organize a grand ecumenical procession through downtown Saint Louis from the Episcopalian Cathedral to either the New or the Old Catholic Cathedral during Christian Unity Week in January or on the Feast of King Saint Louis IX in August. The weather was judged likely to be too cold for one and too hot for the other, and nothing came of it.

Into the school some of the turmoil of college life trickled down, but gently. No one held me captive in my office, but hair grew longer, and began to cover more of the face, there was greater pressure to drive to school, and so on. The most overt expression of it came at a graduation when the Valedictorian's address was critical of previous generations. Providentially, I had taken a shower just before the ceremony and had dislodged some wax in my ear, and could hardly hear, so my emotions were not aroused. I thanked him for taking his convictions seriously and went to the next item. That was in 1969.

Next year we had an interesting application from a Japanese boy to come into our ninth grade. He and his family were originally Chinese. They moved to Taiwan to escape the Communists, and thence to Japan for reasons of business. That involved changing their name from Yu to Yui, so the boy came to us as Jimi Yui. He had been at a British school in Hong Kong, but that had not worked out well. His mother's brother was a professor at Washington University in Saint Louis, so they approached us, saying that if we could accept Jimi, he could stay with his Uncle, Stanley Spector. We did accept him, and after some catch-up summer work, he fitted in well and graduated very creditably. His family was very grateful and showed it in due course.

Thirty-One

SABBATICAL

By this time we had introduced a program of sabbaticals for the faculty, and so, after we weathered the ruffles of the late sixties, I was given a sabbatical from December 1970 until August 1971, just after we moved into the new building for the high school.

I spent the first three months at Oxford, attending some lectures and reading mostly about Greek History in the library of the Ashmolean Museum and at the Bodleian Library. I was also preparing for a trip I had planned with some English friends, to drive from England to Iran and back. One of the special items on the trip was the Rock of Bisitun, with carvings and a trilingual, cuneiform (with wedge-shaped symbols) inscription placed there by the Persian King Darius late in the sixth century BC. I was in the Ashmolean studying an elephant portfolio of the inscription. Opposite me was an elderly, very learned-looking don, who was reading a similar volume. I asked him if he was an expert in Old Persian, the language of the part of the inscription that I was studying. Sadly he shook his head and replied, 'Babylonian, yes; and Elamite, yes; but Old Persian, no'. Next day I returned to my volume, and a young undergraduate came in. He took out another large volume and started to study it. He asked me if I was an expert in Old Persian. I was strongly tempted to reply, 'Babylonian, yes; . . .' but resisted, just.

My English friends and I set off on April 18, 1971, and were gone for ten weeks. There were four or, for a time, five of us. We had a Volkswagen minibus fitted with bunks just under the roof, a two-ring propane gas cooker, a roof that could be raised so that we could all stand upright inside. We also had a tent for two. My companions were a married couple, Lila and Paul, both of whom were physicians, their daughter, Lydia, and her boyfriend, Peter. Most of the time only one of the doctors was with us, while the other ran the practice. This was, apart from my travels in the army, one of the two great trips of my adult life. We visited many of the standard sites, but I describe only the highlights.

We crossed the English Channel by hovercraft, speedy and smooth, drove to Brussels, where Paul had relatives, and on to Cologne; then up the Rhine Valley with castles and churches on every side, and through the Black Forest on the autobahn to Munich. The autobahns in Germany seem to urge you to accelerate more than interstates in US, and some cars that passed us must have reached 100 mph. In Munich I was specially looking forward to seeing the sculptures from the Temple of Aphaea in Aegina. We found them all under wraps and surrounded by the dust of vigorous restoration. The restorers kindly lifted the wraps, but it was hard to get a good impression. Still, when we visited the temple itself on its island close to Athens, I was glad to have had even a glimpse of them. We camped for the next night near the enchanting Thiersee, a lake amid snowy mountains. It was, apart from the temperature, a Lotusland, where we might well have been beguiled to stay and forget the odyssey that lay ahead.

We crossed the Alps by the Wurzenpass, sped down the length of then Yugoslavia, stopping in Zagreb. There we were having a picnic in the city centre, and had pulled two park benches to make a right angle so that we could converse and pass food. A kind resident said that if we did that we would be arrested, so we un-did it quickly. Later, we tried to photograph some colorfully dressed peasant women who were working in the fields, but they fled. Presumably they were Muslims. Later, in Iran, we did manage to persuade a young woman, apparently walking with her father to her wedding, to allow us to photo her gorgeous bridal outfit. She was more pleased than the father.

We drove via Belgrade to Thessaloniki, whence we headed east along the north shore of the Aegean Sea to Istanbul. There, half a mile from the campground, we knew by the strong smell of marijuana that we were on the hippie trail. We met it several more times. Paul was most interested in the old, large fishing boats moored in the Golden Horn. He went on board and we did not see him for a while.

We celebrated Mass each day on the van's tailgate. I had brought all the necessities except wine, which we planned to buy as we went along, but in Turkey, a mainly Muslim country, wine was surprisingly hard to find. Prayer was no problem while someone else was driving, but reading in the van gave me a headache, so I often substituted the rosary for the breviary.

We crossed the Bosporus and drove to Ankara to visit the world's best collection of Hittite art, (second millennium BC) and then walked up to what we thought must have been the acropolis of ancient Ancyra, home of *monumentum Ancyranum*, the list of the Roman Emperor Augustus' exploits. For the first of only two times I felt a little unsafe. Having admired the Hittite art in the museum, we went to the Hittite capital of Hattusas, now Bogazkale, a vast area, of which we saw only a small part. The Hittite artefacts in the museum were more impressive than the ruined buildings. My only previous contact with the Hittites was Uriah and his wife, Bathsheba, who became King David's wife, and then mother of King Solomon, and so an ancestor of Jesus. We hurried on to Samsun, where we bought provisions. At one stall Lydia bought vegetables, spices, etc. in seven small brown paper bags, of which I inadvertently left one behind. We walked back to the car, half a mile or so, and found a small boy on a bicycle with the missing bag. He would not accept a tip, but eventually we persuaded him to buy some candy for himself. Would that happen in UK or US? The incident also made us aware of how conspicuous we were.

We drove along the South shore of the Black Sea, and stopped for a swim. It was April 28 and warm enough for the cool water to be welcome; and there were no anacondas. From Trabzon we turned inland and climbed steadily towards Erzurum, identifying on the way, at least to our satisfaction, the spot from which Xenophon's soldiers would have first seen the Black Sea and uttered their famous cry, THALASSA, THALASSA (The Sea, The Sea). The night at Erzurum, elevation 6400 feet, was bitterly cold. Next day we saw a small stream by the road, with a sign 'Euphrates'. I said it could not be, as it was flowing NNW and the mouth of the Euphrates was south-east of us. But it was the Euphrates, which we were to see again in majesty at Babylon. We picnicked here, dangled our feet in the stream and had our toes nibbled by minnows.

We had found that the main roads were good, but had two disadvantages: they were used by the big trucks, of which there were amazingly many; they were also infested by small boys throwing stones. The trucks were their primary target, but we were much more vulnerable. We learnt that if we waved at them with fully open hands, they would wave back similarly, and by the time they picked up their stones again we were out of range. We also found that both petrol (gas) and propane gas cylinders were easy to come by, so we had only one long hunt for propane on the whole trip. The maps supplied by the AA in London were excellent with only two exceptions: they showed a road going north from Shiraz, which for much of the way was a pebbly river-bed, and another across a river delta in Southern Turkey. If the road ever existed, it had been washed away by floods.

After passing south of Mount Ararat, we crossed directly into Iran and had plain sailing down to Tehran, except for one long, slight but steady climb against the wind. Our VW had been averaging 60 mph without difficulty, but the combination of gradient and wind was too much, and we dropped our speed. It happened on the day of one of our longest drives, just over 400 miles, so we were late. But we got to Tehran in the end, and there we smelt once more the hippie trail.

The Shah's nephew had been in the school at Ampleforth and it would have been interesting to visit him at the palace, but we had been warned that European visitors might cause difficulties for the royal family and so we stayed away. It was in fact the year when Iran celebrated 2500 consecutive years of kingship, but this kingship came to an end soon after the celebration. Instead we visited the fine museum in Tehran, where I admired Luristan bronzes (1500-700 BC), which I had never seen, and much else.

The next day, on our way south, we stopped for our picnic lunch in a deserted caravanserai in the middle of a desert. Out of nowhere appeared a group of small boys carrying school books and walking home from school. They gathered round to watch us and chattered. Remembering that Urdu, of which I could recall some from my days with the Indian Army, was, like Persian, an Indo-European language, I said to one of the boys, 'May I have a *dekho* (look) at your *kitab*. (book)? '*Kitab, kitab*' he replied excitedly, and showed me his book. We were hardly less excited that we understood him. We made sundry other linguistic contacts including the numerals up to 12, they ate some of our sandwiches, and we went on our way to Isfahan.

Isfahan was a bit of homework that I must have skimped, and partly because I was therefore expecting little, I was stunned. There is a Persian saying, '*Esfahan nesf-e jahan.*' (Isfahan is half the world). The central maidan (city square) by itself would almost earn that description; it is one of the world's largest squares, with mosques that are a blaze of ceramic tiles, with bright blue dominating and enhanced by bright sunlight. There are a palace, mosques, madrasahs (schools), and other buildings in many styles. The ceramic 'stalactites' over many formal entrances were beautiful, technically interesting, and quite new to me. The palace, they told us, was designed by an Italian, and reminded me of Florence. There is also the River Zayendeh with several elegant bridges. The river rises in the desert north of Isfahan and sinks back into the desert to the south.

But amid all this, I was fascinated by a man sitting on the sidewalk in the maidan, and turning wood. His 'lathe' had a more or less recognizable headstock, but his tailstock was the gap between his big toe and the toe next it. His power came from a bow. He wound the bowstring twice round the wood – he was doing all spindle turning – and as he pushed the bow forward, the wood spun in one direction, and as he brought it back spun in the other. One hand worked the bow, the other the chisel. He must have been using fairly soft wood and a well sharpened chisel, and was making quite beautiful small objects. We could have spent much longer there, but the constellation of Pasargadae, Naqsh-i-Rustam and Persepolis, our next stops, were what I had come all this way to see.

We did our duty by, and (in 1971) were able to enter, the Tomb of Cyrus the Great at Pasargadae, saved from destruction by a quick-witted caretaker who convinced the Arab conquerors that the tomb was that not of Cyrus but of the mother of King Solomon. We then briefly visited the tombs and sculptures at Naqsh-i-Rustam.

At Persepolis we lingered. Persepolis under King Darius became the capital of the Persian Empire, and its buildings, started in late sixth century BC, were, like those of New Delhi, designed to impress the subjects of an Empire. Even its ruins are impressive. You climb a long flight of steps onto the platform, which is roughly 1400 feet by 1000 feet, and sometimes as much as fifty feet above the level of the plain below it on the south-west. From the top of the steps you pass through the Gateway of All Nations, a massive entrance gateway with three sets of wooden double-doors about 40 feet high and covered with metal, and a waiting room about 82 feet square. The two exit doors lead either to the Apadana, (Royal Audience hall) 197 feet square with wooden columns 65 feet high, or to the Throne Hall, or Hall of the 1000 columns, which were only 37 feet high, used mostly for subjects of the Persian Empire.

As they left the two exit doors, visitors would have been struck and impressed not only by the buildings, but equally by several stairways and by their low-relief carvings. The main stairway was 23 feet wide with broad treads 14 inches deep and shallow risers of 4 inches, which animals could manage. The stairs are flanked by low reliefs showing the King, Persian and Median dignitaries and soldiers, and delegates from the subject nations bringing their tribute of products from their countries: lions, camels, bulls, and other animals, storage vessels, clothing, food, grain, etc. This parade of the tributaries took place on New Year's Day, which was the day of the vernal equinox, about March 21.

Also on the platform were five palaces, a Treasury, storerooms, harem, barracks, stables, etc. and around at least parts of the perimeter a defensive wall, of which very little remains. The platform ran SSW to NNE. Below it was the plain, and on that plain already when we were there in early May, luxurious tents were being prepared for the dignitaries who would attend the celebration in October. I was reminded of Herodotus' description of the luxurious Persian tents captured by the Greeks after their decisive victory at Plataea in 479 BC, which virtually ended the Persian attempt to conquer Greece.

I remembered also Cyrus' reply to the Persians' suggestion that they should move from their barren country to one of the fertile lands that they had conquered, 'Soft countries breed soft men. It is not the property of any one soil to produce fine fruits and good soldiers too:' an early example of geographical determinism. Having now seen Persepolis, and having previously seen the Athenian Acropolis, I had to ask whether the 'better' side won the Persian Wars. In architecture and sculpture there was little to choose between them; we have too little Persian literature to compare, though it is hard to imagine them prevailing over the Greeks; in terms of humanity the Persian Empire compares favorably with the Delian League and the Athenian Empire; in religion the palm must go to the Persians, but in philosophy to the Greeks. Persian youths, Herodotus tells us, were taught to ride straight, to shoot straight, and to tell the truth, a good foundation. They seem to have taken their religion seriously, to have been genuinely concerned with truth and light, themes that are prominent in the New Testament. But most Westerners would, I imagine, vote for the Greeks, pointing to their sense of the value of the individual, their love of free speech, and their steps towards democracy.

We left Persepolis and made for Shiraz, which is apparently not where the Shiraz (Syrah) grape comes from, and then pursued what the map called a 'main motor road' heading for Ahwaz, a little north of the northern end of the Persian Gulf. The road deteriorated and before long we were bumping along the pebbly bed of a dried stream. It was here that we had our only puncture. Nonetheless we did eventually arrive at Ahwaz, in over 100°F temperature. That day, May 10, was our nadir.

Our next stop of importance was at the Rock of Bisitun (or Behistun). We drove up the long, steady gradient of a desert valley. There were scattered Arab tents well back from the road. When the small boys sighted us, they came running down to the road to beg. On the flat we could easily outdistance them, but on this slope we were crawling hardly faster than they were running. We were a very easy target for a rifle, and I was uneasy until we reached the top of the valley. We paid a quick visit to Susa (Hamadan) and then turned back to Bisitun to study, as far as we could, the tri-lingual, cuneiform inscription of King Darius that I had been studying at Oxford..

The centerpiece is a relief showing the god, Ahura Mazda, and below him, Darius with his conquered foes. The inscription is incised around the relief. The whole is 49 feet high, 82 feet wide, and over 300 feet above the road. A British army officer, Sir Henry Rawlinson, in the 1830s and 1840s made 'squeezes' of most of it himself, but hired 'a wild Kurdish boy' for the most risky part. The boy was let down on a rope from the hilltop above the inscription. It is the Rosetta Stone of cuneiform, and is in remarkably good condition, but has suffered and is still suffering some water damage from a trickling spring. Also, passing soldiers, including some in World War II, have taken shots at the figures. The carvers had to make steps for themselves to reach the place. When they had finished, they cut away the steps. It is still possible, though risky, to reach the ledge below the inscription, and I wanted to do so, but my companions would not let me. I was both disappointed and a bit relieved.

We crossed from Iran into Iraq and made for Baghdad, where we knew of no campground. We asked the British Embassy if we could camp there, but they made it clear that this would hardly be proper, would it? They directed us to a space near the airport. We visited the Museum of Baghdad with its unparalleled collection of Sumerian and other treasures. That made reading of the looting in 2003 especially poignant.

From Baghdad we made an expedition to Babylon. The Ishtar Gate with its blue glazed and embossed tiles, is in the Pergamon Museum in Berlin, but there was on the site a replica of part of it. Luckily we were there before Saddam Hussein installed a huge portrait of himself at the entrance. There was no trace of the Hanging Gardens, but some of the processional way was there, and the Euphrates flowed majestically through the site. We asked if we could camp overnight, and eventually persuaded the guards that we meant no harm. We had our meal but needed a shower. There was no such facility, but we filled a bucket with water, changed into our swimsuits and tipped the bucketfuls over each other. The guards watched in amused amazement. When I started my pipe, they wanted to try my tobacco, and me to try theirs. Saddam built walls to give a better impression, but some say he simply disneyfied the place.

We saw and partly climbed the Ziggurat at Borsippa, and wondered why God, Allah, or any deity always lives 'up there on high' and never 'down here', while people, teams, and countries want to be Number One, although one is so low a number.

We headed next for Mosul and the ruins of Niniveh, viewing on the way the minaret at Samarra, 170 feet high, with a unique spiral stair on the outside, and visiting the well- plundered ruins of Ashur and Nimrud. It was very hot at Niniveh. We did not do the ruins justice, but for our picnic joined Jonah in the sun.

To avoid crossing into and out of Syria, we made for the Turkish border at Zakho, where the Customs took an age to examine the VW and us. They were quite pleasant and we were obviously not hippies, or so we thought. As we were the only vehicle all morning, and as they spent much time just chatting with us, we came to the conclusion that we must be their day's entertainment. But we had one of our longer drives, and arrived at Gaziantep rather late, but still just by daylight.

There was nowhere to camp, but some passersby said we could set up our tent in a vacant lot. We had hardly started to do so when the police came by and thought otherwise. One of them spoke English, so we said piteously that we were their guests, dependent on their hospitality, and what did they suggest? They kindly arranged for us to park on the apron of a garage, which we did. We prepared our meal, while they stood around and watched, and shared some of it. They too wanted to smoke some of my tobacco and have me smoke some of theirs. Then we prepared to go to bed and they wanted to watch that too. We persuaded them to say goodnight and to come back in the morning. They did so, shared our breakfast and saw us off. We said they had been very kind and solicitous. Only then did they tell us that a month earlier a party of Germans had done much as we had done, and that a band of wild hillsmen had come down from their hills to celebrate (with alcohol), had taken a dislike to the Germans and killed them all. The police felt, therefore, that they must take special care of us. We thanked them again with deeper feelings, some of reproach, which we did not express.

We then drove for three days along the south (Mediterranean) shore of

Turkey, truly a scenic route with castles, theatres, sites of ancient battles, and something for every taste. Then we came to a delta. The map showed a road across, and we got most of the way, but then the road expired. Fortunately our branch of the river had a pebble bottom, not mud. We got out, reconnoitered, and decided to try it. The water was not deep, but there was a sharp bank at the far side. I was driving, and I thought I had crossed worse in Burma. The VW rose to the occasion and, after an anxious moment or two, delivered us onto the far side. After that it was easy driving to Marmaris. Here we left the VW on the quay (I presume we talked to someone first) and took a ship to Rhodes. There we visited the Palace and the Hospital of the Knights of Saint John, enjoyed the names of the streets: Herodotus, Homer, Socrates, Pythagoras, and others, and then took a bus to Lindos to see the beautiful, small Temple of Athena on the edge of the cliff, looking down on 'Saint Paul's landing place'. We enjoyed a swim from the sandy beach.

Back on the mainland we found the minibus where we had left it and as we had left it. We went up the West Coast of Turkey, ancient Ionia, visiting mostly Greek antiquities. We were impressed by the huge Temple of Apollo at Didyma (358 feet by 167 feet) but disappointed by the much more famous Temple of Artemis (Diana) at Ephesus, of which only a few column drums were to be seen then. This was the one day on the whole trip that I was feeling unwell, but even so I did enjoy walking along a marble street with a marble fence on either side. Saint Paul presumably walked along it too. We stood in the theatre and cried out, 'Great is Diana of the Ephesians' but not for three hours. I also enjoyed driving out to Meryemana to see the house, in a beautiful grove, where the Blessed Virgin Mary is said to have spent, in Saint John's care, her last years.

We were now in well-traveled areas, so detailed description is not needed. We made our way north via historically interesting Sardis and impressive Pergamum to Troy. There was a fine wall, and there were certainly windy plains, but the scholars then agreed about little else. We went on to identify to my satisfaction the place where Xerxes built over the Hellespont his three bridges (the first two were destroyed by storms). We failed to find the ferry advertised to be there, and so went back to the Bosporus and crossed over to Istanbul, and Europe.

We then drove back along the north shore of the Aegean through Kavalla, with its striking sixteenth century aqueduct high above the main street, and on to Thessaloniki, whose Archaeological Museum contains the magnificently embossed Derveni krater, three feet tall and looking golden but made of an alloy without any gold. The city buses had Thes/niki on the front. We passed through Lamia, where the storks nest on the housetops, and Larisa, where the anise-flavored aperitif, ouzo, is good, and so came to Thermopylae. The shoreline has changed since 480 BC when Leonidas and his 300 men defended the narrow pass against the Persian invaders. It is now much wider and less defensible. We took the beautiful road to Delphi over the mountains and came down to one the loveliest spots in Greece.

The oracle was the most famous, and had the reputation of being the most truthful, in Greece and in the world of its day. Visitors came from far and wide, often had to wait a long time, during which, presumably, the officials talked to them and extracted all the information they could. The priestess, a peasant over 50, drank the waters, inhaled the mephitic vapors, and uttered grunts, which were translated into verse by the well-informed officials, and given to the enquirer. There are the Treasury of the Athenians, the Temple of Apollo, a theatre, a stadium about 200 yards long, all on the hillside. There is the Castalian Spring, where pilgrims purified themselves, and a splendid museum. The stadium is at the top and is one of the best preserved in Greece. We duly ran the race. The museum has many treasures: the famous Charioteer is mesmerizing. There was also a mulberry tree whose mulberries were ripe. We reached up and the juice ran down our arms. The stain is hard to remove, and I was wearing a white shirt. From Delphi we drove, via the superb mosaics of Osios Loukas, named for Luke, a local hermit, and on through Thebes, and Eleusis to Athens.

Here we did all the usual things, and I add only that it was still possible to drive around Athens with comparative ease, and still possible to go right up to and onto the Parthenon. It was also the first time I visited the Benaki Museum. We left Athens to drive out to Sounion, where we camped, and so saw the dramatically situated Temple of Poseidon by sunset and sunrise. There was also some spectacular bougainvillea. In the morning we drove back through Athens on roads trimmed with oleander, over the Corinthian Canal, on to Mycenae and Tiryns, and then camped at Megalopolis. From there we ventured up a bad road to the remote Temple of Bassai. Being remote and tourist-free, it was also well preserved, but the west side was badly warped, its columns and architraves still standing but no longer in a straight line. The site is rocky and bleak and so somehow is the temple; and yet I was eager to go there again on a later trip. Modern pictures show it under cover for repair, but it was warped and uncovered in 1971, when we were there.

We were glad to get back onto a good road, and sped down to Kalamata, where there is a shop in the main square that sells fruit liqueurs of every sort. After trying a number, we settled on banana, with which we filled a two-gallon plastic container. We had brought this and another holding five gallons, which we filled with water or wine, until it sprang a leak. The wine did not always taste much better than the water, but it was safer. We crossed the mountains of Messenia to the west coast at Pylos, where, on the island of Sphakteria in Navarino Bay a large Athenian force took 292 Spartan prisoners in 425 BC, and in AD 1827 an allied fleet sailed in and defeated a much larger Turkish fleet. The surrender of the Spartans, despite the overwhelming odds against them, was a nine days wonder in Greece, since the Spartans were believed always to fight to the death and never to surrender.

We also visited Nestor's Palace, which gave us a surprisingly clear picture of what a Mycenaean palace might have looked like, partly because it was on a scale small enough to take in, and partly because of the main hall with its splendid circular hearth, thirteen feet across, and surrounded by pillars. Our next stop was at Olympia, the birthplace of the Olympic games, where we spent the night, and so saw it in the afternoon and evening sun and also at dawn. The light makes so much difference. Olympia has the Temples of Zeus and Hera, a fine museum, the stadium, a race-course for chariots, and the workshop of the great sculptor Pheidias: plenty to imagine. The 'Olympic Truce', when all Greeks stopped fighting, sadly has not survived effectively into our Olympic Games.

We continued via Patras to Rion, crossed the Gulf of Corinth on the ferry and headed North to Dodona, which should on no account be missed, but usually is. There was an ancient oracle here, which gave answers by the rustling of the leaves of the oak trees. In the Old Testament (2 Sam 5.24) the Lord communicated with David in a similar way. There are shrines, a council chamber and a well-preserved theatre, all in a lovely setting. It is also well off the tourist track. It would have been pleasant to camp there, but the ferry from Igoumenitsa to Brindisi left at 10 p.m., so we had to skip the camping, and Corfu too.

The crossing was uneventful until we reached the harbour at Brindisi, which our captain entered at full speed, threw out over the bow an anchor or two, on which the ship swung around, missing the quay at the far end by a few feet. It was then pointing in the right direction to go out again. We crossed Southern Italy to Villa San Giovanni and took the ferry to Messina, eluded both Scylla and Charybdis, and reached Palermo. We could have spent days there but we had time only to sip its beauties before leaving for Monreale and its mosaics (1182) and a mountainous road to Egesta with its temple, theatre, and panorama, an unexpected beauty. This was shortly before an election, and in one lovely, quiet village a jeep was shattering the quiet with a loud speaker mounted on its bonnet (hood). We rolled down the window, shouted 'Vota Coca-cola' and fled.

With the permission of the caretaker, we camped near Selinunte on the grounds of a magnate who lived in Palermo. On the way from there to Agrigento little urchins offered us 'genuine' fifth century BC Greek statuettes for a few hundred lire. At Agrigento I was disappointed, but Piazza Armerina made up for it with its acres of good mosaics, many depicting the wild beasts sent to Rome for the Games.

In Syracuse we enjoyed especially the Cathedral, with many columns from the old Temple of Athena built into its walls. We viewed the harbor and tried to imagine both the naval battle which doomed the Athenians' Sicilian Expedition of 415-13 BC., and the Romans' siege of Syracuse in 214-12 BC, in the course of which Archimedes was accidentally killed. We admired Taormina and its theatre with one of the world's most dramatic backdrops: Mt Etna and the sea. And so across the Straits of Messina again and back to Italy.

We stopped at Cosenza specially to see 'an extraordinary Byzantine reliquary', waited for them to awake from their siesta, only to be greeted with '*In restauro in Firenze*' (being repaired in Florence), which we heard almost as often as '*E chiusa la chiesa*' (the church is closed) both uttered with a hint of glee. Paestum, on the other hand, with its Doric temples and its paintings was magnificent, and we were able to camp in the woods and swim in the sea near the site. The temples are very different from the Parthenon, massive rather than elegant, bulldogs rather than greyhounds, but fully satisfying.

We then had three days for the Amalfi Drive, Pompeii and Herculaneum. I later saw the Amalfi Drive in a coach, praying that the driver would watch the bends and the climb and not be distracted by the breathtaking views. We tramped round the ruins of Pompeii and Herculaneum, climbed part of Mount Vesuvius, and came to rest in Naples itself. At Pompeii I enjoyed the Forum as much as anything; at Ercolano, after we had trudged round the amazing ruins on a very hot day, we found, half way up the high street on the left, the best ice-cream I have tasted. The owner and maker had half closed her stall, but we said we had come all the way from Missouri just for this, and she relented. At the Archaeological Museum, the Pompeii room held both treasures and everyday objects, and at the Capodimonte there was Titian's *Pope Paul III*, with very long fingers. And so much more. In Naples driving was difficult since many cars were triple parked.

We then made for Rome, but stopped at the monastery of Monte Cassino, where Saint Benedict in the 530s wrote his *Rule*, by which we still live. Being a national monument, whose rebuilding was financed mainly by the state, it was rebuilt to what it had been before the bombing, and, I suppose, would not otherwise have been rebuilt. But we all felt sad that it was not rebuilt more simply. I said Mass at the altar over Saint Benedict's grave, and I sat where he wrote his *Rule*. The monastery of Saint Benoît-sur-Loire in France also claims to have the bones of Saint Benedict, and I have said Mass at his tomb there too.

This was not my first visit to Rome, so I mention only some of the things that are in my memory from this visit: from the Vatican Galleries, the Laocoön, the Raphael Stanze (Rooms); from the unrestored Sistine Chapel, Michelangelo's ceiling and Last Judgment, of course, but also the large frescoes on the long side-walls; from Saint Peter's, the view from as high up the dome as one is allowed to go (to get there we had to walk bent slightly to the right to match the curve of the dome); the still undamaged Pietà, and Bernini's Ecstasy of Saint Teresa of Avila. I mention the Bernini because I was just learning to admire and enjoy, rather than despise, the baroque; – as I grew older, I became more catholic in my artistic tastes – from the Villa Borghese, Bernini's slightly bizarre Daphne and Apollo. We saw much more in Rome, and then we went outside Rome to Ostia, from which I still picture in my mind mosaics denoting shops, and the blocks of apartment buildings. On our way out of Rome, we had our only accident. I was accelerating away from one set of traffic lights when there was another one hardly a hundred yards farther on. We made a minute dent on the rear fender of a Mercedes in front of us, but considerably dented our own, more fragile, front panel. We found a police station, filled in forms for insurance, and left.

Next day we went, in the opposite direction, to Hadrian's Villa and the Villa d'Este at Tivoli, the former with its noble *Canopus* and bold use of water, the latter with its lovely gardens and fountains on the hillside. Farther up the mountains, we came to the monastery of Subiaco, where Saint Benedict started his monastic life in a cave. His fame for holiness spread, and he was persuaded to come out and found monasteries. But he was literally too good for the monks and they tried to poison him, so he fled to Monte Cassino. The monastery at Subiaco encloses his Sacro Speco (holy cave), and also has the only contemporary portrait of Saint Francis of Assisi, who visited in 1210. He was painted by a Benedictine lay-brother. There was always a good relationship between the Franciscans and the Benedictines, who gave Saint Francis the abandoned chapel in the plain below Assisi that became his Porziuncola. The excursion to Tivoli and Subiaco is a full day, easier by car, or even minibus, than by public transport, but not to be missed.

Father Giovanni O' Shaughnessy, OSB and I at Subiaco, near Rome, where Saint Benedict started monastic life as a hermit in a cave.

We drove to Tarquinia for its museum and Etruscan tombs. At one of them an Italian guide with a group of English women asked me to ask his group whether they really wanted to go in, as it was *poco pornografico*. They were undaunted. We went on to the striking thirteenth century Cathedral on its acropolis at Orvieto, stopped for lunch at Todi, one of the loveliest of the Italian hill-towns and lovelier, we thought, than the more famous San Gimignano, and reached Assisi in mid-afternoon. The buildings were still all intact, and so were the frescos by Giotto and others, and there was no denying their magnificence. Perhaps the magnificence was the trouble. At the back of our minds was, 'What would Saint Francis have thought of all this splendor?'

234

I did not feel this at the church of Saint Clare, and still less when we found our delightful campground, from which the view at sunset and in the twilight back over the town and over the plain, fully restored our peace. So it was too at Santa Maria degli Angeli, in the plain below Assisi, where, next day, we were able to linger and pray almost alone in the chapel of the Porziuncola, Francis' first headquarters, and where he died. We felt his spirit.

We visited lovely Perugia but we had all been there before and did not linger. At Lake Trasimene, we stood on the shore and imagined Hannibal pushing the Romans into the lake in 217 BC, paid a flying visit to Siena and to the Campo, where the crazy horse-race, the Palio, is run annually, and finally reached Florence, where we stayed for two days. Our only excuse for so short a time is that we had all been there before. We revisited the Baptistery, the Duomo and Campanile, the Convent of San Marco for its Fra Angelicos, Michelangelo's *David* at the Accademia, a wonderful contrast to the entrance corridor with his statues of prisoners struggling out of their marbled captivity. We could not miss Botticelli for *Primavera* at the Uffizi, nor Raphael's elegant and delicate brushwork at the Pitti Palace. Add the view at sunset from the Piazza Michelangelo, and you have two full days. We were told in Florence to beware of the tourists' disease: a surfeit of beauty. We laughed, but were told again quite sternly that it was real and debilitating. None of us succumbed, nor have I ever met anyone who did.

At Ravenna we visited Sant'Apollinare in Classe, Sant'Apollinare Nuovo, the Mausoleum of Theodoric, San Vitale, and also the museum. I know of no finer mosaics in the world. We each had our favorite: mine for buildings was San Vitale, but for the mosaics, the two churches of Sant'Apollinare.

In Venice we reached San Marco Square by *vaporetto* along the Grand Canal. In the Basilica we climbed to a gallery where we could be a few feet from the mosaics to study them in detail, but also in poor light. We admired the four, well-traveled horses, climbed the Campanile, (wherever there was a climbable campanile, we climbed it), and went on to the Doge's Palace. After that, we meandered around and looked at any number of masterly paintings, especially by the Venetians, and admired again the clarity of Bellini.

All too soon we headed west via Padua, a city we specially enjoyed even apart from the Giotto frescoes. Verona was another pleasant city, with the refreshingly straightforward church of San Zeno and the magnificent amphitheatre with seating for 22,000; and then came beautiful Sirmione on Lake Garda, so much loved by Catullus. We spent time at Milan, had a glimpse of La Scala, saw a little more of the Biblioteca Ambrosiana, and of Leonardo's *Last Supper*, in sad condition after World War II. Finally we climbed up to the roof of the Duomo, coming face to face en route with numerous saints and gargoyles, and reaching at the top 'a forest of pinnacles and flying buttresses', and a group of nuns selling ice-cream.

We were planning to go on via Monte Carlo, Aix-en Provence, and Avignon, but our time and stamina were running out, so we cut across to Lake Geneva and Dijon. We stayed at a beautifully neat campground near Geneva. The roads on which you could drive were marked with whitewashed cannonballs, and the walkways with smaller whitewashed stones. As we left, I thanked the owner warmly and commented on the typically Swiss neatness. He thanked me politely and added, 'but it so happens I am a Basque.' At Dijon we could smell mustard in the air, or was it our imagination?

Our next serious stop was at the Palace of Fontainebleau (fontaine belle eau, or clear water spring) with its lovely entrance stairway. In many ways it is more attractive, and certainly more digestible, than Versailles: charm versus splendor. In Paris, where we camped in the Bois de Boulogne, I do not remember that we did anything out of the way.

After two or three days we left for Calais. There we drove onto the hovercraft at 8.30 a.m,, 'sailed' at 9.00 a.m, disembarked, passed through customs and, just after 10.00 a.m, were driving through Kent. It was as close to hassle-free travel as one could hope for. The only drawbacks were that the spray all round the hovercraft made it very hard to get any view, and that hovercrafts' tolerance of poor weather is much less than that of a ship. We then drove by way of the Dartford Tunnel back to Norfolk.

The trip took us just over ten weeks, we covered about 10,000 miles, and it cost us about $300 each. We had a common purse out of which we paid all our communal expenses: food, petrol, camp fees, entrance fees, etc. It was certainly a bargain: everything would be far more expensive now, and most of our travels from Turkey eastwards would be either impossible or unacceptably dangerous. Finally Paul and Lila sold the VW for more than they paid for it.

I was especially interested then, and still am, in the Persian empire of sixth century and fifth century BC, so in general the farther east we went, the more I was interested, partly because I would never go there again. In Iran itself, I found Persepolis enthralling, but for sheer beauty I would choose Isfahan. Iraq fitted in with our biblical interests, especially the Old Testament. We thought of driving across the desert from Iraq to Israel, but were wisely dissuaded by my father, who had done it the 1920s. At the time of the trip and not counting World War II, I had never been farther east than Greece, so from Turkey on was quite new to me, and so was Yugoslavia. Even in the countries that I had visited I saw countless new places, people, and things. Traveling and camping as we were, and stopping to buy food, we saw much of the life and people and talked with them as best we could. Between us we could manage French, German, Greek, Italian, some Persian/Urdu, and a few words of Arabic. Our difficulty was to understand what they said in reply. All in all, apart from our means of transport and inelegance of lifestyle, it was a little like the Grand Tour so favored by the English and Continental aristocracy, but without the sowing of wild oats. Some fond goodbyes, and I returned to Saint Louis for our Retreat and the new school year.

Thirty-Two

I RETIRE FROM HEADMASTER

Fairly soon after my return I was asked to be Court Chaplain to the King of Biffeche. How bizarre! A parishioner of Saint Anselm Parish, Ed Schafer, had collected money to help the people of this tiny kingdom in West Africa, between Mauritania and Senegal. When their king died in 1963, they could not decide who should succeed, so they asked Ed Schafer, because he had helped them. He consulted the appropriate American authorities, who said he could, legally, accept. He then asked one of our monks, Father Leonard, to be his chaplain. Father Leonard returned to England in 1971. Shortly after, Ed, who was now King Edward I, asked me to be his Chaplain. I accepted. It was not an arduous job: the king held court once a year just before Christmas. I said prayers for the court and was available for consultation on spiritual matters at any time.

Later I became Secretary of State as well. That was not arduous either, but I did advise His Majesty to travel to his kingdom, taking his chaplain with him. I had learnt that by custom the king should enter his kingdom on camelback, so, when asked how he should pay for this, I suggested that he propose to Avis Car Rental, whose motto was 'We try harder', that they should provide two camels, pay our expenses, photograph the trip and use it for advertising. Avis dismissed their chance to try harder. Ed died, the kingdom passed into the hands of those 'who knew not Joseph'. I resigned and was pensioned off as Baron of Mells.[19]

I was headmaster for three more years. By now the school had been running long enough that there were no longer the continual, almost daily, challenges of the early days. Many problems could be met with 'What did we do last time?' But there was one event which would, had the decision been made, drastically have affected our future.

In 1963, Father (later Cardinal) Basil Hume succeeded Abbot Herbert Byrne as Abbot of Ampleforth. In about 1971 he came over from Ampleforth and

19. *Further information about Biffeche is on* **http://ChiefaCoins.com/Database/Micro-Nations/Biffeche.htm**

was worried that we were not growing in numbers. Unless we did grow, he said, he would have to withdraw the Ampleforth monks. On some occasion, for which there is no record of either time or place, Abbot Basil said to Prior Luke that he would do this, and Father Luke responded that in that case we would seek independence. That important dialogue must have been in 1971, and independence was granted us as an independent priory on July 25, 1973.

This meant that we could no longer look to Ampleforth for more monks; we would make all our own decisions, and be financially independent. At independence, the monks from Ampleforth had an absolutely free choice whether to stay or to return to the motherhouse. No one might tell them which to do. Some time fairly early in 1972 Prior Luke asked each monk to decide by the end of the year what he would do. Between Christmas and New Year's day I decided, not easily, to stay, and all the Ampleforth monks except one did the same. That meant that we transferred our stability to Saint Louis Priory and would presumably live there for the rest of our lives. We are now no longer monks of Ampleforth. It was a wrench, but by then most of our friends were in and around Saint Louis rather than in England. But nothing can alter the fact that the first thirty-five years of my life were spent either in England or, in the case of my birth and later my military service, abroad but under English auspices. I still, when I go back to England experience, often when I am least expecting it, the feeling that some of my roots are still there. When a plant or tree is transplanted, it takes its roots with it; it is not quite the same with people. And yet, by no means am I implying that I feel rootless in Saint Louis. The 'root' metaphor, used by Abbot Herbert when he said he was going to uproot me, and since then by many others and by me, is not quite apposite. A transplanted tree has no link with any roots it may have left behind, but people do.

While all this was seething in our minds, our regular life had to go on regardless. I was summoned to an entirely new experience: an alcoholic confrontation, now called intervention. We had a friend who was an alcoholic, had tried Alcoholics Anonymous (AA) and all the usual treatment centers without success. I was asked to be on the team that would confront him. We all had to be people on whose friendship and support he knew he could rely. First, the team had a three-hour training session with AA experts. At the end of the session we were told to pick a captain. I was the only cleric present, so I was chosen. We confronted our friend in his room, which was littered with bottles, full, empty, half-full, broken. There was also a dog, which had not been outside for some time. Our friend said there was nothing wrong; he was perfectly content in his alcoholic haze. We had been warned that the process would take some time and that we must not give up. Each of us told Tom (not his real name) how he came across to us. It was relentless and went on for about 75 minutes. I was almost ready to give up, when suddenly Tom burst into tears and agreed to come with us to a treatment center. It was a grueling experience for us, and I suppose more so for him, but it was successful. Tom's liver was shot, but he remained more or less clean and dry for the rest of his life.

Not too long after this, a friend invited me to attend an open meeting of AA. The leader gave his inspirational message and then they started round the room for the members to say 'I'm Joe, I'm an alcoholic' and then report on their status. It was evidently going to come to me, so I started 'I'm Timothy; I'm rather embarrassed, I'm not an alcoholic'. I went on to say, truly, how impressed I was with what I had heard. For the Twelve steps to be effective, the patient has to have great humility, and to be truthfully able to accept his state and his inability to escape from it by himself.

Another event, of a much happier kind, occurred in my last year as headmaster: we had a good year in football, qualified for the playoffs in class AA, and in due course became State Football Champions in that class. In the final game, against a school in Kansas City, played at the Kansas City Chiefs' stadium the total score, 60-26, was a record high.

Then at the end of June 1974 I retired as headmaster. I asked Prior Luke for this as, after nineteen years I was beginning to feel jaded; I also thought it was bad for a school to become, as far as the public were concerned, at all identified with an individual, especially if it were a founding individual; finally, by the end of any long tenure there tends to be some lack of tautness. I thought these were three quite adequate reasons, and if anyone wanted a fourth, there was Edwin O'Connor's *The Last Hurrah*, in which Mayor Skeffington retired after a long tenure, and immediately had a heart attack. Pat Rice from the Post-Dispatch came out to interview me. I told her my reasons for retiring, to which she listened patiently and then said, 'Now, what is the real story?' But that was the real story.

Father Paul Kidner took over, and I lived on happily. This may therefore be a good point at which to make some reflections on my years of tenure. I do not wish to repeat what I wrote in *In Good Soil*, pp. 108-111, but can perhaps add to that from a more personal point of view.

The most obvious reflection is that we monks were all convinced that God wanted this foundation, and therefore it would happen. There were some dark moments, but even in them I never thought we could fail. Secondly, the whole project would have been impossible without the amazing support and trust of INC and of all our friends and supporters, whom we called the Priory, now Abbey, Family.

As far as I know, there was never any legal document between INC and us. There were letters and statements, but fundamentally the partnership was based on trust. We said we would come to Saint Louis and found a monastery, which would run a school. They said they would support us; and we believed one another. As it turned out, INC did much more than just take care of us: they befriended and advised us. Without their friendship we could have been very lonely in a foreign country, and without their advice very much at sea in many areas. No less important, they also let us run our own show.

Initially INC was responsible for the fund-raising. That was an enormous burden off my back. My reputation as an educator never depended on my ability to raise money. We monks did, of course, at fund-raising meetings have to describe, as persuasively as we could, what we were doing, what we planned to do, and what progress we were making, but we were only occasionally asked to make fund-raising visits.

I never that I can remember had a written philosophy of the school, but it was, I thought, in my head. If I had written a mission statement, it would have been very brief, perhaps something like 'schools are about boys and their needs, which it is our mission to meet'. That would have needed many 'explications'.

By 1974, our policy for admissions had not changed. But we had found that despite all our efforts there were still those who thought that this was a ritzy school for the sons of affluent parents, or, at the other end of the spectrum, an elite school for Aristotles and Einsteins. Our counter attack was that while we welcomed and would try to challenge the most brilliant of boys, we also welcomed others who could, we thought, benefit from our program; and while we welcomed boys whose parents could pay the full tuition, we also welcomed those who could not, and would help them to the limit of our resources. Our criterion was still the good of the boy.

Corporal punishment had dropped out, but some form of punishment was inevitable. Most of us dislike both being punished and punishing. But one of our boys impressed me years later by coming back and saying 'Thank you for punishing me; you were the only person who cared enough to do so. My parents never did.'

It is hard, and perhaps impossible, to make good decisions unless one can keep one's own likes and dislikes, whether of people or of ideas and things, out of it. Yet it is often surprisingly hard to keep them out. For example, I would have liked to have cricket as our summer sport, but it is a technically difficult game; one probably needs to grow up with it; and anyway, we would have found no other schools to compete with. Or again, I did not like the idea of a Catholic school without daily Mass, but it seemed wise in our circumstances not to have daily Mass. In dealing with the boys themselves, of course, it is a matter of justice not to show favoritism and to be as impartial as one can, but that does not entail treating them all in the same way.

I learnt something from dealing with complaints. Hardly ever is there a complaint with no basis at all. Often enough the particular point made by the complainant is invalid, but almost always there is some real point close by. For example, someone complained that the main entrance to the school from Mason Road was not well lit. It was very well lit, but a smaller entrance was not. Maybe the complainer always used the smaller entrance, and thought of it as the main entrance. A sharp reply about the main entrance would have been true, but would have left the complainer aggrieved.

I have mentioned the primacy of the monastery. This is true not only for the schedule, but also for the teacher. If he is a monk, he is a monk first and a teacher or coach second. The formation of the boys in a Benedictine school does not deal only with their academic side. It also offers theological and moral and personal formation. The school usually has to offer most of the theology, but for practice of the faith we could, when we came, rely more than we could in later decades on the training given by the parents to reinforce the formation provided by our religion classes, Mass, and sacraments at school, and by the monastic example of the monks, picked up so well by the lay faculty; and so our approach then could be more low-key. The less one can count on from the home, the more the school has to provide, and the more overtly it has to supply it.

Since the primary educators of children are their parents, we needed good liaison and good communication with them, and if possible a margin of good will. The chief instrument of this became the Mothers' Club. Although I was hesitant, we did form one in April of our first year, and I thank God that we did.

Anyone involved in a school is very much influenced by his own schooling, and tends to teach and administer either in the way that it was done to him, or in any other way but not that way. I was influenced by a saying of the late Father Paul Nevill, headmaster of Ampleforth all the time I was in school, that there should be ordered liberty in the school, with more order in the early years and more liberty in the later. The teacher must of course be prepared both long term (knowledge of the subject) and short term (ready for this class). In England at that time almost all the teachers' preparation was in the subject matter and there were very few education courses. There was a certain amount of the apprentice system, with the apprentice teacher learning from the masters of the craft.

It seemed to me obvious that boys cannot learn from you unless they are paying attention to you, and therefore the teacher needed to be able to keep order in the classroom. The coach's cry of 'watch the ball' applies in the classroom, but the boys are the ball. I discovered also that when one is writing on the chalkboard, as was common then, and if one wears glasses, the glasses have some reflective ability and you can see some of what is going on behind you, and correct it, if necessary, without turning round. The boys may even think you have a pineal eye.

The curriculum was not revolutionary, but there were enough subjects to challenge the sharpest minds. Many subjects call for their basics to be memorized, and I saw no harm in that, provided that we also taught the boys to think. Young boys develop their memories before their speculative powers. This was why we started some subjects much earlier than was usual. Before high school I had had six years of Latin and French, some Greek, and at least two years of Algebra and Geometry.

I saw homework as the best way of finding out what had been absorbed, and consequently tried to impress on the faculty the value of its setting, correction, and prompt return. The same went for examinations, grades, and reports. To send the parents a written report from each of a boy's teachers, plus a summary by his form master and the headmaster, fostered the cooperation between school and home. I favored the greater accuracy of number grades over letter grades; there is also less of a descent from 80 to 79 than from A to B. There is, however, a real danger of over-competitiveness, especially as boys are instinctively competitive. I read that some psychiatrist experimented with giving a soccer ball each to a group of boys and to a group of girls. The boys instinctively formed teams and had a competitive game; with the girls, one kicked the ball and all the rest swarmed after it. I think competition is a natural thing and a good incentive, but it can easily get out of hand.

One great advantage of boarding schools is that there is much more time for personal contact between monks, lay faculty and boys in informal settings outside the classroom. All three groups have a chance to get to know one another, to like and to trust one another. At Ampleforth, the monk who ran the Carpentry Shop probably knew more about what was going on in the school than anyone else. Likewise there is more time for music, art, acting, photography, carpentry, debate, mechanical drawing, and similar activities that are not strictly academic. We provided what we could, and supplemented it, especially in the early days, with field trips to the Art Museum, the Symphony and such. Clubs came later; the most successful was the Science Club under Father Thomas Loughlin, whose friends enabled us to tour the Danforth

At home in the school library.

Company, Granite City Steel, McDonnell Aircraft, Monsanto, Tums, and others. Later still, Brother Symeon formed a stained glass guild with spectacular results.

Athletics are important for boys, and presumably for girls too, but the athletic tail must not wag the academic dog. As noted above, we became in due course members of the ABC League, and have been so ever since. Outside the regular sports, we have played rugby, ice hockey, and ultimate frisbee, and, much later, started lacrosse.

We also wanted to learn from, and contribute to, the local church and the local community. Much of this came through membership of various organizations, where much of the value came simply from meeting one's peers. Some of my organizations have already been mentioned. Others were:

Archdiocesan Priests' Council; (1978,79,80) I was secretary in 1980 and met with the Archbishop and executives before each meeting;

Archdiocesan Ecumenical Commission; for many years;

National Catholic Education Association (1956-74). They met often in Chicago, once at least in Saint Louis;

National Association of Secondary School Principals (1956-74). I addressed a small sectional meeting at Atlantic City, and found myself saying what I had resolved not to say, that sometimes it was best for the headmaster to stand back and let the Holy Spirit run the school;

Missouri Independent Schools Association (MISA, pronounced Meeza, 1970-74) At the inaugural planning meeting I narrowly escaped becoming president as I was going on a sabbatical later in 1970;

Society for the Promotion of Hellenic Studies, London (1964-88);

Saint Louis Classical Club (c.1960-90). I attended, gave occasional talks and one demonstration with our students;

Saint Louis Biblical Society;

The Institutional Review Board of Saint John's (now Mercy) Hospital. Our task was to review new procedures from the patient's point of view. If they were at all risky, was the risk proportionate to the gain? It was a useful experience; I learnt that in many areas doctors knew much, but there was also much that was still unknown. With cancers, for instance, they usually knew what family of cancer they were dealing with, but not necessarily with which member of that family. Various drugs might deal with various members of that family, but they could tell the correct one only by trial and error.

I had always taken a keen interest in the school library. Initially we had two libraries, monastic and school, then we amalgamated them for economy; now there are two again. When we arrived in Saint Louis, most college libraries were using the Dewey Decimal system of cataloguing books, and we followed suit. But before long colleges switched to the system of the Library of Congress, which is certainly more accurate for large collections. We held out for a while, mainly because we did not have the manpower to convert our catalogue, but eventually we bit the bullet, and with the invaluable help of Paul Falcey, a long-term guest in the monastery, we did it. We still believe that books have a future, but computers and the internet have certainly reduced boys' use of them.

In this connection, I was fortunate enough to enlist Julie Constantino as a library volunteer to help Father Miles. When Father Miles was appointed

Director of Development, he wisely asked Julie to come with him. She succeeded him and as Director was both devoted and successful in fund-raising and friend-raising.

We received various legacies of books, including a special collection from Bill Weld dealing mainly with recusant Catholics in England. Chris Peper and others made ongoing contributions. Countless individuals and some libraries gave us books, their duplicates in the case of the libraries. We also bought the residue of classical books from a Jesuit Seminary that was closing, and a curious collection, paid for by Henry Hughes, from a secondhand bookseller in the city. This collection was left by a man with three main interests: archaeology, the War between the States, and pornography. The first two groups were invaluable and the third made good landfill. Father Columba and I also wrote a number of book reviews and put the books in the library. Some of these reviews were for our two daily papers at that time: the *Globe-Democrat* and the *Post-Dispatch*; others I wrote for the *Saint Louis Classical Review*; one was an article for *Monastic Studies* on translating the Rule of Saint Benedict, and there were other reviews or articles, mainly on Catholic or classical subjects.

Both in the school and in the parish I relied much on my secretaries. I started with Christine Little, who stayed for three years. She organized our filing system. She also frightened one of our monks. He knocked on her door during her lunch break and was greeted with 'It's my lunch hour.' Another day he knocked and was greeted with 'The door's open', which it was not. The next secretary must have come from a very high-toned company. She did not expect to have to dirty her hands with copying machines, and when she discovered that I did expect that of her, she quit.

The next one, Nancy Dougherty, was seeking the job as therapy after her mother had died. I did not know this at the time. Her first day was a hectic one: we were sending out reports and grades. She drove home, let herself in, poured a stiff drink, left her keys on the kitchen table, and went out into the garden, slamming the door behind her. After the drink she tried to go back inside, but her keys were on the kitchen table and her husband was in Nebraska. She saw an open window and started to climb in. The next thing she knew was flashing lights and a policeman asking what on earth she was doing.

After some other frustration with me, she told me she waited till I had gone to class, then took her ruler and hurled it at the place where I had been sitting. She left, but we remained friends until she died. When her husband was back in town, they invited me over after dinner. While I was there, another friend stopped by. He had just been duck-hunting and asked if I would like some ducks for the monks. I said yes, and he gave me a frozen package. By the time I was back at the monastery, it had thawed a little but I did not notice. I took them down to the freezer in the basement, leaving a trail of blood down the stone stairs. In the morning Father Luke came down for Vigils, noticed the blood, and feared the worst.

I never had a first-class shorthand typist, but the next one, Virginia Mazy, was superbly accurate with figures. After spending hours with her on several occasions checking the tabulated mark sheets of every boy in every subject and finding no mistakes, I used to take them as read, and there were still no mistakes. Her husband was an Air Force colonel and had been posted to Alaska. She would not go with him, and came back to Saint Louis. I was sad when he came back from Alaska, reclaimed her, and was posted to Georgia.

They covered the exciting first six years, after which things settled down. My next was a Latter Day Saint, Joyce La Pointe, who taught me a bit about Mormonism, and was followed by a Jewish secretary, Jeannette Karp. Both were trustworthy, discreet, good on the telephone and at the files. Between them they lasted the rest of my time as headmaster.

In the summer of 1973, I was invited by Dr. Jerry Mudd, who had taught Biology for us for many years, to accompany his family on a ten-day trail ride in the Rocky Mountains in Montana. The high point, literally, was the Chinese Wall, a remarkable geological formation, 7620 feet above sea-level. The highest peaks in this part of the Rockies are nearly 9400 feet, so, as mountains go, they are not huge, but they are beautiful to ride among. I had a chestnut with a name I did not like, so we renamed him Caesar, which he seemed to like and by the end of the ride he was letting me put the saddle on his back and the bit in his mouth.

It was awe-inspiring because here I felt that we were in immediate contact with God's handiwork. I remembered Hopkins' poem, *The World is Charged with the Grandeur of God*, and his lines;

> *And all is seared with trade; bleared, smeared with toil;*
> *And wears man's smudge and shares man's smell.*

There was none of man's smudge or smell up there. I felt the same even more keenly when we went to Patagonia some years later.

Thirty-Three

MONASTIC ADJUSTMENTS

In the monastery, much of our time was spent on rearranging our monastic lives in line with Vatican II. This was a worldwide process, and proceeded at very different speeds in different places. Nearly ten years after the introduction of concelebration, I went to a parish in England and asked if I might say Mass there next morning at 8 am. The pastor said that was the time of the parish Mass. I asked if I might concelebrate. In surprise he replied, 'Concelebrate? My dear chap, you *are* up-to-date.'

In common with most Anglo-Saxons, and many others, we were allergic to sensitivity sessions, small group discussions, and such. We liked the joke, 'Come, blessed of my Father . . . and the rest of you go off into small groups'. Yet we needed some means for general discussion, so we looked for a facilitator.

After several false starts, we picked Father Conleth Overman, CP, a very likeable priest, who overcame most of our allergies. This entailed many meetings, often for several days in a row – these had to be during vacation – at which we labored with a mission statement, the establishment of priorities, the formulation of goals and objectives. Much of this was done in small groups, to which we gradually became accustomed, and at which we were sometimes even adept. Besides enabling us to find a direction, it did break down much of our reserve, improve our communication, and, since Father Conleth insisted that our objectives should be both attainable and verifiable, enabled us to judge how well we were progressing.

It was a turbulent time, and there was a wide range of opinion in the monastic community: some felt we were proceeding too cautiously, others that we were charging into change. Father Conleth told us we should be content to reach a solution with which we could all live, even if it was not all we desired. He called this, perhaps with some latitude, a win-win situation. Tie-tie might have been closer.

In all the discussions, when we set our priorities the most urgent was always

My first cousin, Dusty Springfield, OBE (1939-1999)
singer, musician, Top of the Pops.

vocations, because vocations, at least in the western world, dropped after Vatican II.

A man with a possible monastic vocation would usually stay with us for a while as a layman, but living our life. If there seemed to be a good fit between him and us, he would become a postulant, and then enter the novitiate for a year, at the end of which he would make simple vows for three years. At the end of that time he could make his solemn vows for life. Between 1966 and 1981 we had no Professions of Solemn Vows. There was a fairly steady flow of men entering the novitiate, but they then left at some time during their first four years. This was sad for us, but was not uncommon in the church at large.

At our meetings with Father Conleth, in about 1977 we undertook to attract and retain five men in the next five years. I was Director of Vocations at the time. In addition to what we had already been doing, which included much individual prayer, I thought it would be good if the whole community came together once a week for a communal hour of prayer for vocations. We did this for several weeks, but it was not popular, and Prior Luke transformed it into a night vigil once a month for each of us to watch for half an hour or an hour in front of the Blessed Sacrament, from after Compline, our night prayer, until Vigils early the following morning. Fairly soon our lay friends took over the watch before midnight and we did the rest. This vigil was much more popular than the holy hour, and was successful in that in the next five years we attracted and retained not five but seven men who made their solemn profession.

The English Benedictine tradition about seeking vocations was instinctively low-key. I can remember in high school being put off by sermons that openly emphasized religious vocations. Mine was not a good attitude, but was fairly typical among boys in England. We came to USA with the same instincts and

249

were slow to recognize that American boys might be different, and might think that if we did not speak openly about vocations, we were not much interested in them. We gradually became more direct, and God has blessed us with vocations. Only He knows why, but we all pray that it will continue.

Over the years we had a number of interesting visitors, some of whom stayed for quite a while. I have already mentioned Arnold Toynbee, who, as a friend of Father Columba, paid us several visits. Robert Speaight, a British writer and actor, was with us when we dedicated the church bells. Father Columba asked him to read the psalms of the dedication. He read them beautifully, but the church at the time had no windows in place, and was open to the elements. It was a bitterly cold and windy day, and hard to give one's whole attention. Bishop Butler was with us for several weeks after his labors at Vatican II, and told us all about it.

Rosalind Russell, the actress, visited the campus, but did not have time to talk to the boys, nor did Dusty Springfield. But as she was my first cousin, I went to meet her downtown after one of her TV appearances. Before she went to Hollywood she was a redhead, but red hair shows up black on a black and white screen, so she converted to ash blonde. But I did not know this and so was looking for red hair. I was quietly saying my prayers in the foyer of the hotel, when in walked this vision with an ash-blonde bouffant hairdo. I returned to my prayers, until she walked over and greeted me. Then I looked at her face and recognized her. We had a long visit that evening, and next morning I drove down to the hotel and took her to the airport. She, her father, and her brother were all most musically talented, but her mother was, if anything, 'musically challenged.' Dusty was at one time top of the charts in England. She died of cancer in her late 50s.

Much later Professor Elizabeth Anscombe, Abbot Thomas' tutor at Oxford, came over several times. She was a distinguished Catholic philosopher and a pupil of Wittgenstein. We had very interesting discussions with her. Later still, and in celebration of the golden jubilee of our presence in US, we had visits from Cardinal Dulles, a leading theologian, and George Weigel, biographer of Pope John Paul II. They both spoke to large audiences in our theatre about this Pope, with interesting complementarity.

Thirty-Four

OUTSIDE ACTIVITIES

In September, 1974, I was teaching full time, I continued to be head of the classics department until the following year, and Father Paul made me Dean of Studies, all of which, together with my teaching, kept me busy, but less hectically than when I was headmaster. I made a translation of the Rule of Saint Benedict and sent it to one or two monasteries for comments. Unknown to me, the American Benedictines of the two large Congregations, Swiss American and American Cassinese, were proposing to produce a translation and extensive commentaries on the Rule in honor of the approaching fifteenth centenary of Saint Benedict's birth in 480, and because of my translation they invited me to be part of the team. They also invited Father Mark Sheridan, of Saint Anselm Abbey in Washington, DC, one of the two other houses in US of the English Congregation. Our earliest meetings were at the Benedictine Sisters at Saint Joseph, Minnesota. They were a huge community, nearly 1300 at their largest, and when we three first arrived in Saint Louis, they had just made a foundation by sending two hundred sisters to the new house. They were most hospitable. Later meetings were held at Saint Joseph Abbey in Covington, Louisiana. It was just across the lake from New Orleans, and much warmer.

Various teams were formed, and I was one of the five translators. We divided the Rule into five sections, and each took a section. Our translations all matched well except for one, which was done in the style of the Knox translation of the Bible and was very good, but could not blend with the others. I was made head translator, and, with the heads of other sections, met at Atchison, Kansas in October, 1979 to finalize our text. We went through it sentence by sentence, reached an agreed final version, and handed it in for typing. A week later I received my copy and filed it.

Just after Christmas I had a call from Father Mark Sheridan, who was to write the notes, questioning the reading of a sentence in the Prologue of the Rule. When I checked it, I saw that it had indeed been changed from what we had agreed in October, and I told Father Mark. Next it occurred to me that there might be other changes, but by then our term had started and I did not have time for extensive checking, but I did spot some other changes. At the spring break I went off to a sequestered farm. I filled twenty-six legal folio pages, double column, with the changes and my comments on them. In May, 1980, we met in Saint Louis to settle once more the final text. I called it the Battle of Priory, but it was in fact very amicable. Again we worked hard and produced a complete text, but instead of the book coming out in March 1980, as we had hoped, it came out in March 1981, just within the year of celebration. Saint Benedict's feast day is March 21.

I was responsible for the translation, though I often did not get my way, and I contributed the name, *RB 1980*, a few of the notes, and a few paragraphs in the introduction. The book was designed by a committee and yet looked respectably like a horse. It all led to my being invited to give three workshops with Father Laurence Kriegshauser of our community, and some retreats on my own.

When I retired from being headmaster, the Mothers' Club wanted to mark the occasion, and I chose a trip to Ireland with my mother. They very kindly provided the funds and I flew over to England to pick her up. We flew to Dublin and rented a Baby Austin, into which we and our luggage fitted neatly. For this we went to a very grand office on Prince's Street, with a long counter and a battery of telephones. But the grandeur collapsed when a phone rang and the caller complained that they could not get out of their car because the door handles would not work.

Our Baby Austin served us very well and even took us over the very rough and rocky road of the Gap of Dunloe. We kissed the Blarney Stone, and did most of what tourists should do. We visited the Benedictines at Glenstal. We tried to stay at a government Rest House, but it was full. They said, 'If you go to the next village, and ask for Mrs. Kennelly the chemist, she'll make you very snug.' We went, and asked if she had any rooms. 'Oh, yes; I have a lovely double room'. I said my mother would prefer a single room. 'Oh 'tis your mother? I thought it was the Protestant clergyman and his wife.' My mother was delighted. I then said I had seen a church as we drove in. Did Mrs. Kennelly think I could say Mass there in the morning? 'Don't go there,' was her reply, 'the Canon is a great persecutor. Go to the Dominicans farther up the street.' I was so taken aback that I never asked her whom he persecuted. Perhaps it was the English.

At Limerick we coincided with the provincial finals of the game of hurling. We sat behind a little group of men who had come by way of the pub. When they heard our ignorant comments, they kindly undertook to explain the game to us. One man was carried off with blood streaming from the crown of his head. At the end of the game, which Munster won, they commented, 'Well, 'twas a fine, clean game you saw.' We thanked them and said truthfully that they had made it much more enjoyable.

In Dublin we saw the bullet holes in the Post office from the Easter Rising of 1916, and spent a day at the Dublin Horse Show watching riders from all over Europe. It was a very happy trip, and with the exception of one man –and he was very busy – all the Irish we met were helpful and delightful.

For some time before this I had been organizing trips to Chicago to visit exhibitions there, mostly at the Field Museum. These trips were for boys and their parents. The most successful was that to see the exhibition dealing with King Tutankhamun (King Tut). There were horror stories in the media of queues five hours long waiting to get in, so we were all a bit anxious. At the Conrad Hilton the night before, I said lights should be out by 11 p.m. At 11, I made the rounds and came to a room with both TV and lights on, flung open the door and started to say 'OK, let' s put out . . .' when I saw that this was a room with a father and son in it. I amended to 'Oh, sorry, Mr. Byrne.'

We got up early had Mass, and went to the Museum door for parties with advance booking. A young lady called Debbie met me. I said I had all the 93 tickets for our group here, and what should I do with them. She said follow me, and we walked straight in to the exhibit. After that, in the group's eyes, I could do no wrong. Building on this, I felt more disposed to think seriously about the urging from Mrs. Elizabeth Mudd to organize tours for the Priory family.

At that time we had with us Father Vincent Wace from Ampleforth. He had organized four trips to the Holy Land, and I had been to Greece two or three times, so we decided to offer a combined tour of The Holy Land and Greece. This was in 1976, the American Bicentennial, and was a success, except that we flew to Israel on the day of the Entebbe hi-jacking and flew from Israel to Greece on the day of the rescue, so security was at its height, and some of our party were strip-searched en route. We happened to be at Delphi on July 4, 1976, and the Mudd family organized fireworks and an entertainment, which delighted both us and the Greeks.

That was the birth of Timothy Tours. They continued, during my summer vacation, on alternate years well into this century. Initially we went to places like Greece and Italy which I thought I probably knew better than the agent, but I soon ran out of those, so I had to resort instead to intense study of the relevant *Blue Guide*. We toured Sicily, Italy (twice), France, England, Scotland, Spain, Central Europe, Greece again with a little of Turkey, Egypt, Thailand and Cambodia, and made a trip combining Brittany and South-West England. Our last trip was to Californian Missions and wineries: they went well together. I planned a trip to Turkey, but had to cancel it after terrorists bombed a group of tourists. On all these trips I arranged the itinerary and a travel agent made the bookings. I also took photographs, and put them together as slide shows or later, with technical help from Brother Alban, as power point presentations, and auctioned them and me at Xanadu, our annual fund-raising auction, so my labors paid for themselves, and considerably more.

On these tours the travelers were almost all people whom I knew and who knew one another. That and keeping the tours, with difficulty, to two weeks or a little less, and having Mass every day, helped to make them happy events. It would be tedious to describe them in any detail, but a few incidents might be of interest.

We always had a meeting or two before departure. Some of the group were seasoned travelers, but I was surprised how many, even of those, needed to be reminded to bring a sizeable plastic bag for laundry. Since many of them were bringing their spouse's camera, which, at least in the earlier tours, used rolls of film, I had to say, 'load a roll *yourself*, shoot all of it, unload it *yourself* and re-load a new roll *yourself* .' But I still received, a few days into a tour, pleas for help. My other two hints for beginners were: 'don't put the main point of interest in the middle of the photo, but try 2/3 of the way across, or up or down'; and, 'you will make fewer mistakes by being too close than by being too far away'.

On our very first tour, to Israel and Greece, security was super-strict. We arrived at Lydda and were waiting in the coach in the square in front of the airport, when a big truck back-fired. Everyone hit the deck, even those who were not physically suited for it. That broke the ice. Later at Bethlehem, after we had celebrated Mass at the Altar of the Crib, we emerged into the upper church effervescing loudly. The guardian yelled at us, 'Can't you keep silence. Don't you know this is a church?' shattering the silence much more effectively

The first Timothy Tourists visit Jerusalem.

than we had done. At first I was indignant, but then reflected that he probably had to do this countless times a day.

Jerusalem, despite tourism and indeed partly because of the pilgrims, is uniquely moving. I was most moved when walking down a newly unearthed stone stairway leading from the upper city down into the valley. This is almost certainly part of Jesus' route after the Last Supper to the Garden of Gethsemani, and because of its recent unearthing, I felt here most of all that we were treading exactly where he had trodden.

In 1987 I was on a tour to Israel as a guest of The Jewish Community Relations Committee; it might have been a different country. It started badly for me: We were met at the TWA terminal in New York and were asked to walk with our bags to the El Al terminal 'just a block away'. It was over half a mile and I had just had a hip replacement, and was carrying a bag without little wheels. When we reached the El Al terminal there was no seating, as the terminal was unfinished. When, after an hour of standing in line, it was my turn, security asked me for documentary evidence that I was part of the party. As our leader was standing by me, I suggested that they ask him. They repeated their request more severely. I produced a letter. They asked why I was chosen. I replied that they were unable to get the Archbishop. 'Don't be fresh with us, young man' they said. I explained that they had asked the Archbishop, the Chancellor, the editor of the *Review*, none of whom could come, so they had to be content with the secretary of the Priests' Council. I thought they would send me back to Saint Louis, and at that point I would have gone. But things looked up after that.

Only two of the Christians on the tour had been to Israel before. From our coach we saw a city in the distance. Someone asked its name. 'Nazareth'. But the bus kept straight on. Much the same happened on our walking tour of Jerusalem. We passed the Garden of Gethsemani. Again someone asked what it was, and was told; but we kept on walking.

In compensation we were taken to many places where tourists would not normally go, such as Kibbutz Hagoshrim, where we stayed the night, Martin Luther King Forest, where we could plant trees ($7 a tree), the Ethiopian immigrants at Zefat (their children had never seen an elevator, and spent their days riding up and down in them, as long as the elevators lasted), the Golan Heights border with Lebanon, plus meetings with Jewish dignitaries and warm hospitality in Jewish homes. On the shore of the Sea of Galilee, I celebrated an open-air Mass for the group. It was a well-arranged tour, showing us parts of Israel we would never otherwise see, and making clear the amazing progress since 1948.

One year when there was no tour, Father Luke and I were invited to a celebration at Sea Island, Georgia. Two events made it memorable: Father Luke played golf there and shot a hole in zero. He took two strokes, received a handicap stroke at that hole, and took his bisque. Then the two of us went 'deep sea fishing'. The name was a little grander than the event. We were never more than a few miles out into the Atlantic, but we did each catch a shark.

On a Timothy Tour to Italy some of us climbed to the top of Vesuvius. There were many small holes in the ground. Our guide invited us to sit over them. He went a little way off, lit a cigarette and puffed smoke into a hole. It came out under us, and he told to beware: the volcano might be acting up.

On our tour in France we had a very knowledgeable guide, a Parisienne, who not only explained what we were seeing but connected it to what we had already seen, or were to see. We were booked on the TGV (*Train à Grande Vitesse*, or high speed train) express to Beaune but flooding along the line reduced its speed to normal. Our hotel was in the middle of a vineyard, so we had wine for dinner. I asked the women in the party what they could taste in it. As most of them could list all the ingredients of a salad, I expected an interesting reply. At length one volunteered, 'It's a bit sweet, isn't it?'

At Arles, when we came down for breakfast, there were some apples with dirty, grey-green skin. They looked most unappetizing, but were delicious. The Sycamore trees in the streets came straight out of a painting. Our coach was burgled overnight and despite warnings to leave nothing on the coach, we lost a mackintosh, and our guide lost some guide books. Nonetheless I found Provence, with Avignon, the Pont du Gard, Nîmes, Carcassonne, and Arles itself, enchanting. At Lourdes we attended a windy, rainy candlelight procession in the evening, and Mass at the Grotto next morning. As a concelebrant, I was safely sheltered by the grotto itself, but our pilgrims were out in the heavy rain. Spirits were a little low at the end, so we stopped the coach at a liquor store, bought a bottle of brandy, passed it round, and lo! everyone was happy again.

We spent a wonderful night in the guest dormitory at Saint Benoît-sur-Loire, a Benedictine Abbey, founded in the seventh century, which, like Monte Cassino, claims to have the bones of Saint Benedict.[20] Two monks, they say, went to Monte Cassino some time after its sack in 580 by the Lombards, to rescue the bones of Saint Benedict and of his twin sister, Saint Scholastica, and brought them back. Monte Cassino is where Saint Benedict died. Each monastery has an altar with bones buried beneath it and I have celebrated Mass at each altar. No one knows which is right, but is it cynical to wonder whether, supposing the two monks of Saint Benoît-sur-Loire had not been able to find the true bones, they would, after so arduous a journey, have returned empty-handed? I back Monte Cassino.

On a tour of England, we visited Ampleforth Abbey, our motherhouse. They invited me to celebrate their school Mass that Sunday. The boys' singing was superb, but the microphones were not working. I said that in Saint Louis we could in no way match their singing, but I did not resist adding that our microphones usually worked. Their boys enjoyed that, but perhaps not all their monks.

I was a bit anxious about our Scottish tour because, compared with most of our other tours, there were few spectacular places. But the countryside was lovely, the people friendly, the highland cattle beautiful, and we even saw a distant highland stag. It turned out to be one of our best tours. Before going to John o' Groats at the northern tip of Scotland, I warned the tourists that it would be cold and windy with a chance of rain or even sleet. They all bundled up, and when we got there it was in the mid-eighties (F), a record for the day. We visited a distillery, where we were guided by a young man in full Scottish

20. See page 224.

dress and with an unbelievably Scottish accent, rolling his'r's and all. I suspected something, and at the end asked him where he was from. In broad Liverpuddlian tones he said 'I'm from Liverpool'.

Our trip to Spain was for me the least enjoyable of our trips. I still do not know why. I loved the Prado, Avila and Seville, and enjoyed much else, including a tourist dash across the Straits of Gibraltar to Algiers. The waves in the Straits were quite steep but no one was seasick except our guide. I was even disappointed with the Alhambra. Perhaps it was the terrain that felt oppressive. Anyway, I was relieved to move on to Portugal, where I took to Lisbon and admired the way that Fatima, in contrast to Lourdes, had kept the commercial area well away from the spiritual.

To Egypt, on the other hand, I could go back again and again, almost like Greece and Italy. The Tutankhamun Gallery still stuns me. We saw so many golden objects that by the end we were saying, 'What's that? Oh! Just another golden throne.' I sailed a felucca on the Nile. The breeze was so gentle that even with the very tall mast and a great expanse of sail, we did not heel at all – a little disappointing. At Aswan, our plane broke down and we were left for some hours in the waiting room. We started to sing, and soon all the Egyptians were singing too. We were petulant when at about 11 p.m. they stopped us and took us to a hotel; and still more petulant when they woke us at 2 a.m. to continue our flight. My only sorrow was that there was not time to visit Sinai.

We made other trips, but I will comment only on that to Thailand and Cambodia. Having been stationed in Thailand for six months at the end of World War II, I was keen to revisit it, but Bangkok had gone from a rather dilapidated city of some 300,000 to a modern metropolis of several millions. It was much cleaner, and many of the temples had been repainted. The airport, which had been miles outside the city, was now in the suburbs. Hua Hin, 125 miles south of Bangkok, which had been the royal summer palace and little else, had become a busy seaside resort and spa, with every kind of commercialization including even catamarans for hire, with a stern fine if you capsized.

Angkor Wat (twelfth century) in Cambodia was as grand as I had expected. They have also cleared other shrines in the area but we did not have time to see them. The building complex is surrounded by a wide moat, and has yards and yards of low reliefs. It is hauntingly serene and self-confident. In the end I may even have had the better of the deal with General Evans: the whole area had been better cleared and was far more accessible than when he was there, and I might have been, at the end of 1945.

The last Timothy Tour was to California, to visit Missions and wineries. We had a wonderful guide: I noticed that two of our very best guides were Croatian. The most interesting, though not the most beautiful, Mission was La Purisima Concepcion, near Lompoc. It was fully restored during the great depression by the Civilian Conservation Corps, using original materials and implements, as far as possible, and including the furnishings of the rooms. We also visited Hearst Castle, which includes much beautiful architecture, many fine objects rather higgledy-piggledy, a 'Roman' swimming pool and a roof tennis-court.

Our last three trips were more like small family parties and went to Northern California and Oregon, to Patagonia, and to Arizona. Our trip to Patagonia started with the Iguazu Falls, less known but more spectacular and much bigger than Niagara. They are the border between Argentina and Brazil. The walkway enables one to be within an arm's length of the falling water.

To get from Argentina to Chile we crossed the Andes by steamer on a series of lakes with bus trips between lakes, and then flew to Punta Arenas on the Strait of Magellan. Much of the land was as desolate as I have seen anywhere, (oddly, there is more pampas grass in Saint Louis than on the pampa of Patagonia), so it takes about 50 acres to pasture one sheep. It was incongruous in the midst of such desolation to find ourselves staying near the Torres del Paine at Explora Hotel in great luxury. Condors, flamingoes, penguins, vivid kingfishers, oyster-catchers, many other birds, and guanaco were common; we saw several rhea, a grey fox, but no pumas. But the mountains stole the show. They are the tail end of the Andes, and are cretaceous, sedimentary rocks with granite poking through. They have been carved by the incessant, high winds into weird shapes. There are also impressive glaciers that end in a tall wall of ice. Here again I felt very close to God's own handiwork. I needed a windbreaker, and I had one, with the label *Patagonia*, which I put in the car to go to the airport in Saint Louis, and which I found still in the car on my return. So I was cold.

We then flew back to Santiago, Chile, and there our small group left the tour to visit members of the Manquehue movement, a community of laity whose lives are guided by the Rule of Saint Benedict, but who are not monks or nuns. Their original connection was with Ampleforth Abbey. When Abbot Patrick Barry came to live with us for twelve years, he brought, as it were, a few links of the chain with him. So we were brought into connection too. The community has three schools in Santiago. I was most impressed by the one on the edge of the barrio and for children from the barrio. I talked briefly with one class of eight- or nine-year olds. They were convinced I had come all the way from Saint Louis specially to see them, and they sang a Marian hymn for me.

Our second small group tour was to Northern California and Oregon. We visited the myrtle capital of the world, which was of interest to me since myrtle wood has a most attractive grain and is highly lathe-worthy. So, incidentally, is mango wood. The Columbia River valley was scoured out by flood water from an ancient lake. The scouring lowered the river-bed, so that streams that had flowed straight into the river were now waterfalls of several hundred feet, some of them very beautiful.

Our third such tour was to Arizona in September, 2006. There the man-made highlight was the baroque Spanish Mission church of San Xavier del Bac, south of Tucson. Its style is Mudejar, a mixture of Spanish, Moorish, and Mexican Frontier Baroque. The church still serves the local Indians. Many experts have tried many styles of restoration with modest success. The present agreement is that what the Indians had been using before the experts, a mixture of lime, sand, and cactus juice, is the best. Nature's highlight was the Grand Canyon.

There was also a lowlight. We decided to reach the airport early, check in, go through security, and have a leisurely breakfast at the Admirals Club, but that had been closed since the destruction of the Trade Center in New York in 2001. Instead, we had a bagel at a delicatessen. The plane left the gate at noon, right on time. It then stood on the tarmac for three hours, because we were routed to Saint Louis via Chicago, where there was a mighty storm. When we reached Chicago the storm was still storming, and after a while in a holding pattern, our pilot flew on to Saint Louis. There we landed and stayed on the tarmac for four hours, as all American Airlines' gates were occupied by tomorrow's early morning flights. They then announced that we would fly back to Chicago, and a near riot ensued. When at last, for us to de-plane, they brought the old-fashioned stairs on wheels, they were too steep for some of the elderly. Two stalwart men were found to carry them down. We left the hotel in Phoenix at 9 am, and reached home in Saint Louis at about 2 a.m. next day. Our baggage went to Chicago, was mislaid, and reached us days later.

At the risk of making it sound as if our life were one long holiday, I will mention one or two of the countless other acts of hospitality by the Priory/Abbey Family to the monks.

I was taken to the Shakespeare Festival in Stratford, Ontario, where we saw Shakespearean plays, with one or two contemporary plays thrown in. The seats were arranged in U-shape, like bleachers, with a high rise, so that you could look easily over the person in front, and the stage was like a playing field in front of you. The plays were excellent, of course. We were taken on a tour of their enormous 'props' warehouse, which must have held millions of dollars' worth of dresses, furniture, and other items of remarkable variety. They asked for volunteers to don suits of chain-mail armor. They were heavy, hot, and uncomfortable. The two of us were eager to get out of them.

I also twice visited friends in Barbados. I was taken to the Metropolitan Opera in New York. I have been entertained in Florida and Oregon, San Diego and New Hampshire, and taken many trips to many places in between, and have enjoyed them all.

Thirty-Five

A WORKSHOP IN JAPAN

In the monastery, I was a member of the Prior's and then Abbot's Council on and off for many years between 1967 and 1995. That meant a monthly meeting to advise the Prior or Abbot on matters of his choice. I was Director of Vocations from 1975 until 1981, and Sub-Prior from 1976 to 1981, when I took over the parish. This was before we had an abbot, so the sub-prior was #2. I had to compose and post the routine notices and generally help the Prior with monastic routine. I was also chaplain to the Sacred Heart Sisters at Maryville University, close by us, and said their daily community Mass, heard Confessions and administered other sacraments as needed.

In 1975 I was asked to teach at the Archdiocesan Seminary, Kenrick. This was a mandatory course on Spirituality for third-year theologians. It was at short notice, and it was new material to me, at least in that form. The course met three times a week for seventy-five minutes each time. I spent five to ten hours, and sometimes much more, preparing for each class. As I was also teaching in the school, it was hard work. I learnt much from it, so did at least some of the seminarians, or so they told me. One spent a certain amount of class-time in the shower, and later became a bishop. In 1975 there were 25 men in the course, 16 to be priests for our Archdiocese. I taught the same mandatory course in 2000: there were seven in the course and only one for our Archdiocese.

In the summer of 1976 I received a quite unexpected invitation to attend a six-week workshop in Japan at the instance of the parents of our alumnus, Jimi Yui, whose uncle, Dr. Stanley Spector, was a professor at Washington University, and ran summer workshops in the Far East. This one was intended to reduce antipathy towards Japanese Americans. I had no such antipathy before the workshop, but as there were six Japanese-Americans with us, of whom two were rather difficult, by the end of the six weeks I had some potential for antipathy. There was an interview. They asked me what previous contact I had had with the Japanese. I said we had spent several years shooting at one another, and thought that probably ruined my chances, but they accepted me. I had to make my own way to the west coast, and then everything would be paid for.

This was my first visit to the Pacific Rim. The first four weeks we spent at Nanzan University, just outside Nagoya, on the Bullet railway about 200 miles (2 hours) south of Tokyo. The Bullet trains are run by computers. They stop for three minutes at each station, so you have to be at the door with your luggage or you will not get off in time. Their maximum speed was about 150 mph. For the last two weeks we were on our own and could go where we liked in Japan. This was economical as the exchange rate was 300 yen to the dollar; in 2011, it is about 80.

On our first weekend, we were taken, in formation, two by two, to visit Kyoto, the previous capital and a beautiful city, but not to be visited like that. The next weekend I went to the railroad station by myself and found myself confronted by 22 windows each listing the stations served from that window, but all in Japanese characters. I asked three Japanese in a row for the window for Kyoto, and they all walked straight on, although they all take several years of English in school. I nearly panicked, but then recovered and stood in line at one window. It was wrong, but the clerk directed me to the right one. I reached Kyoto, walked around there, caught a train to Nara, an ancient capital of Japan, which has beautiful buildings looking back to the eighth century, and in due course made my way back to Nanzan. The buildings do look back to the eighth century, because when they build a temple, they keep a lot vacant next to it. When the temple is decrepit, they build an exact duplicate on the vacant lot and then demolish the old one, leaving its lot vacant, and so on as needed.

The castles are memorable too, both for themselves and because from their upper floors you can see just how crowded Japanese cities are, even to the point of cutting part away from one roof to make room for the roof of the house next door. I attended a Sumo wrestling meet, where, as with bull-fighting, the pageantry, clothing, and ceremony are nearly as important and impressive as the fight. The wrestlers – 300 pounds is a small one – do various gymnastics to show they have no concealed weapons, and then get down like football linemen. They clinch and within a minute one forces the other either to the ground or to the edge of the ring. In one bout a strong novice was up against a wily old pro. At the last moment the old pro did a side step and the novice charged forward and out of the ring.

Much of Japanese etiquette arises from their need to maintain, in such close quarters, some kind of space between people. Over three quarters of the land is mountainous and uninhabitable, and they have over 127 million people; consequently land is very expensive. They cannot talk to you until they know whether you are senior, equal or junior to them, and so conversation starts with questions to find out, which often seems to us rude, but is not so intended. Until they know your rank, they do not know whether to offer you *chai* (tea) or *o-chai* (honorable tea).

In the buses some seats are facing one another. I was in a bus with two ladies on the workshop, one an African American and one a blonde with strikingly white hair. I had red hair. The Japanese facing us nudged one another, pointed at us and started to laugh. My two companions were so put out, that they never went out again. The next time I was in a bus and the Japanese facing me did that, I nudged my companion, pointed at them, and started to laugh. That was the start of a happy conversation for the four of us. It was a matter of different social conventions.

Our courses at Nanzan were an introduction to Japanese history, literature, language and culture, interesting and often fascinating, but inevitably superficial. There was nothing about religion, but I did manage to get an interview with the Abbot at a Zen monastery. We talked through an interpreter. The Abbot was a spiritual and contemplative man. When we talked about prayer it was evident that whereas our prayer is centered in God, his prayer was an emptying of all material thoughts in order to be in touch with the whole of creation. When my first question to him was about how they dealt with distractions, his immediate response was 'Ah, I see you understand about prayer'. Westerners would find the regime and discipline of that monastery strange. But they might feel that about Benedictine monasteries too.

Our last two weeks we spent traveling on our own as we saw fit. A brother of Mary and I visited Hiroshima and Nagasaki and their museums. Hiroshima's was the more impressive in both content and layout. It portrayed the whole nuclear drama without being melodramatic, and included the astonishing photo of the shadow of a capstan imprinted permanently on the wall behind it. We went to the shore of the Sea of Japan at Tottori to paddle in that sea and to see the mighty sand dunes, which are the setting for Kobo's novel, *The Woman in the Dunes*. Then we visited Kamakura to see the Daibutsu (Great Buddha). The statue was finished probably in 1252, is 44 feet high and weighs 93 tons. The Buddha is in the Lotus position with the hands in the Dhyani Mudra, the position of meditation. I admired the simple, soothing treatment of his clothing, and the whole impression was of great serenity, except for the mouth, which to European eyes looked ugly and grumpy. One can climb up, go inside, and read the graffiti, but we did not. We then rejoined the group in Tokyo.

I conclude with five cameos of life in Japan:

1. We visited a school and attended an English lesson. The teacher read the fable of the grasshopper and the ants, and then asked, 'Who visited the ants when winter came?' The boy sitting next to me whispered to me 'the grasshopper?' and I agreed. He put up his hand, said 'the grasshopper', and was told he was wrong. We looked at each other in dismay, while a girl said 'the grasshopper visited the ants when winter came'. That was correct. I remembered my introduction by Father Morris to the *Penny Catechism*.

2. On our travels I had to change trains at Kyoto, with a three-hour layover. I looked for a baggage locker (left luggage) in vain. I then went to the first class waiting room and left my bags there confident that I would find them there on my return. I did.

3. At the end of the workshop I wanted to have some friends to my room for a farewell drink of sakè. I went to a store and saw what I recognized as sakè bottles, arranged in ascending order of price and bought the right hand bottle. On the night, I opened it with great care and poured. We all raised our glasses and sipped. It was horrible. One of the group who could read Japanese looked at the bottle, laughed, and praised me for choosing the very best brand of cooking oil.

4. The fourth cameo also involved sakè. The grateful parents of Jimi Yui lived in Tokyo and took us out to dinner. We were having a convivial time. Luckily, I drank sparingly of the sakè, because late in the dinner there was an earthquake. I had had little enough sakè to be confident that it really was the earth shaking and not I, and I reassured the others.

5. The last cameo reflects Japanese honesty. I needed a zoom lens for my camera. Our friend, Henry Hughes, made an offer: either he would buy me the lens in USA for $600-700 or he would give me $500 to buy it in Japan. I took the $500, bought the lens for about $230 and spent the rest on books for the library. I wanted the books mailed to Saint Louis, which the bookseller arranged but, as I thought, overcharged me. When the parcel arrived at the Priory, the postage was indeed much less than I had been charged. Indignantly I tore open the parcel only to find, on top of the books, a letter apologizing for the overcharge, and enclosing a check for the balance.

The trip concluded safely, but when we got back to Los Angeles, we found that the travel agent had forgotten about the date line and had booked us on a plane for tomorrow, or was it yesterday? So we had an unscheduled day in Los Angeles.

It was an enthralling trip. The Yuis, born Chinese, reminded me of my grandfather's opinion that for the Chinese, their word was their bond and their gratitude boundless.

The Japanese are very obedient to due authority, and above all to the Emperor. They were capable of producing objects of exquisite beauty, and yet also of committing acts of exquisite cruelty. American residents told us that it was easy to make friends with Japanese, but difficult to get to the stage of being invited to their home.

It was hard to estimate the role of religion in Japanese life. Buddhism and Shinto are the predominant religions, with a majority of Japanese describing themselves as one or the other, or both, rather like Voodoo and Catholicism in Haiti. In the museums it was evident from the paintings and statues of their holy men that their tradition appreciated the ascetical value of voluntary poverty. Many western eyes found these paintings and statues of holy men in poverty repellent, but to a monk they were quite congenial. I greatly enjoyed those six weeks, and they have left a deep impression on me.

Thirty-Six

PASTOR OF SAINT ANSELM PARISH

I served from January 1978 through December 1980 on the Archdiocesan Council of Priests as a representative of the teaching orders in the Archdiocese. The Council met once a month with the Archbishop for about three hours. For 1980 I was its secretary and so met a week before the meetings for lunch with the Archbishop, Cardinal Carberry, and the executive committee to prepare the agenda. I was glad to make friends with a number of the Archdiocesan priests. Several told me that even if the meetings were not more lively, at least the Minutes were, and whenever I visited Cardinal Carberry in his later days, he reminded me of them. Each year the Council met for a day of prayer and deliberation. We were asked to write down our priorities for the next year. My first was ecumenism. When our priorities were prioritized, ecumenism ranked twenty-fifth out of twenty-five.

The next major event came quite unexpectedly: The Parish of Saint Anselm had been formed in 1966 when the Parish of Saint Monica was divided into two by the Archdiocese. We were in the half that became Saint Anselm Parish, and were flattered that the Archdiocese chose for it the name of the leading Benedictine philosopher and theologian. The first pastor was a diocesan priest, Father (later Monsignor) Robert P. Slattery. The parish started with about 150 families and had grown to about 450 when, in 1981, Father Slattery was made head of Catholic Charities in the archdiocese.

Out of the blue the Archbishop called Prior Luke and asked if we would like to take over the parish. We had discussed this possibility, and Prior Luke said yes. The Archbishop then asked who would be the pastor. This we had not discussed, but Prior Luke said he looked at the ceiling and seemed to see 'Timothy' there. So I became the first Benedictine pastor of Saint Anselm Parish, with little previous training for the job. I had similarly lacked experience for new positions in the army, and again when made headmaster.

I took over on March 31, 1981. Father Slattery told me to expect one or two

In my office.

funerals a month, but I had five in the first two weeks. The joke then went around that they had taken one look at the new pastor and said, 'I'm out of here'. But I did inherit Josephine Dielo and Peg Maguire as parish secretaries, Incarnate Word Sisters Helen Ann Collier and Annette Pezold as pastoral associates, and Dotty Sanning, poised to take over the School of Religion. Another great legacy to me was a very strong tradition of daily Mass and Holy Communion. The weekly parish bulletins always had a note about this. There was also a very active Society of Saint Vincent de Paul, one of the best in the Archdiocese. My lack of experience was also a stimulus to learn fast, so as to keep up.

What follows describes mostly the highlights, lowlights, and oddities of being a pastor, but the average day was a routine round of phone calls, letters, e-mails when we went digital, meetings, visits, and the preparation of liturgies and homilies. I was pastor until I submitted my resignation on reaching the age of 75. It was accepted for June 30, 1995.

The Parish Council is the primary official means of business communication between the parishioners and the pastor. At my first meeting, I said that I really wanted to hear what people thought. A friendly councilor took me aside afterwards and warned me that I might hear much that I did not like. I thanked him, but said I had been hearing that from the school faculty for many years, and before that from fellow-officers in the army.

Nearly as important is the Worship Committee, and as my first problems were liturgical, I quickly turned to them for advice. Music, a hot topic in almost every parish, was one of our first problems. I inherited an excellent musician and singer, but when she retired, the problems started. It is hard to find a choir director that most like, hymns that most will sing, and so on. Every pastor has heard both 'Why do we always sing hymns that no one knows?' and 'Why do we sing the same hymns week after week?'

I had, of course, been saying Mass for many years, but there were many special liturgies like Palm Sunday and the rest of Holy Week, Corpus Christi, and what, after the daily Mass at 7.30 a.m., became one of my favorites of the whole year, the Family Mass at 5 p.m. on Christmas Eve. Our Director of Religious Education, Dotty Sanning, arranged that Mass with bells, literally, and whistles, figuratively. There was a crib, occasionally with a live infant, Mary, Joseph and shepherds, all represented by children, and the Gospel read and acted with them. For the homily, the youngest children came and sat on little pads in the sanctuary. One year I asked them 'Where is Jesus?' A boy of six stood and pointed to the crib. 'Very good, and where else?' He pointed upwards to Heaven. 'Very good, and where else?' With a grand, sweeping gesture he raised his arm, placed his hand over his heart, and proclaimed 'HERE': one of the best homilies I have ever heard, and unrehearsed too. Out of the mouths of . . .

There were also the less familiar Sacraments, especially Baptisms, Weddings, and the Sacrament of the Sick, plus funerals. Monks are not regularly asked for these but pastors are. Many of them entail a homily, in addition to the regular weekend homilies. Every priest has been given many pieces of advice about homilies. The one I found most helpful was: ask and answer the question 'What am I really trying to do in this homily?' and then cut out everything else. This was like what I had learnt in the army when writing operation orders: the vital paragraph is *Intention*, what is the aim of this operation? If you express that accurately, other items tend to fall into place or to be discarded. The Information paragraph that precedes it is also important, and that applies to homilies too.

I thought that there should be some homily even at the weekday Masses, partly because they were so well attended. But the many doctors in the congregation pointed out that a five-minute homily would make them late at their hospitals, so we settled for one-liners. These became popular, being brief and easily remembered. They did, however, if they were to avoid being platitudinous, take nearly as long to prepare as a five-minute homily. The Sunday readings were by then arranged in three cycles and the weekday readings in two; on Sundays in the first year we read cycle A, in the second year B, in the third C, and in the fourth A, and so on. This meant that over the years we heard a fair selection of the word of God. Having to study the readings extended my knowledge of the Bible. I also decided to read the Bible and notes straight through, half an hour a day. It took two or three years, but was richly rewarding. When I finished, I started over.

We tried to visit all those in hospital, at least when we knew about them. Usually a priest feels that he is providing a real ministry to patients, but I soon discovered that there were some patients who by their faith and cheerfulness ministered to me. Once it was entirely reversed: I was in hospital myself and one visitor, undoubtedly wishing to be kind, stayed and stayed. Even when I dozed off, or pretended to, she stayed: 90 minutes in all. I learnt from that to keep my visits short.

Another time I was in hospital for a total hip replacement. The surgeon was an alumnus, and when he was in the school, he and several members of his class started to let their hair grow too long. I urged them to get their hair cut, or else I would cut it. Three, including my surgeon, ignored the warning and did receive a haircut from me. As I was being wheeled to the operating theatre, I remembered this. They had given me a happy pill to reduce worry, but I still mused whether he would really do my hip, or attack some other part of me instead, or even give me a haircut. He did in fact do an excellent job in the correct place. He later gave me another new hip and a new knee; and another alumnus gave me the other new knee. I am now having trouble with an Achilles tendon, and they could probably give me a new one. But enough is enough.

The administration of the parish was less of a problem as I had had some experience of administration both in the army and as headmaster. But I had to get used to the new routines and the presence of so many women on the staff. The school faculty had been almost all men.

Our first major project was operation RENEW, undertaken by the whole archdiocese. It involved setting up groups for this and committees for that, and numerous activities for all. This enabled me to get to know a large proportion of the parishioners very quickly.

Early on, I thought we should join the computer age, and that an IBM PC would be just the thing to start with. Then I recognized that I knew little about computers and ought to form a search committee. They met and recommended some brand, but the secretaries did not like the color; of the next one they were frightened of its mouse (I am not making that up); we went to a demonstration breakfast for the third one, but the demonstrator could not make it work. We felt sympathy for him but did not buy his product. After eighteen months, the committee recommended an IBM PC.

At the end of each year the parish had to produce its accounts and statistics: how much money, how many baptisms, funerals, marriages, Holy Communions, etc. At first these records were simple enough for me to understand and even to produce, but they gradually became more complex, and we hired a business manager. As it did everywhere else, complexification made its irresistible progress. This was not altogether a bad thing, but the more time one had to spend on administration, the less time there was to spend on people.

Later a system of Archdiocesan visitations arose, and one of the auxiliary bishops came round asking for our mission statement and its goals and objectives. We did much paperwork ahead of time, but I think we satisfied him. He was wearing a rather hot-pink soutane. He wanted to visit the classes of our parish school of religion. This was asking for trouble, and sure enough when he asked in one room for any comments or questions, a third grade boy, wishing, I'm sure, to compliment him said 'I like your soutane, Bishop: my mom has a nightgown just that color'. Whether *propter hoc* or only *post hoc*, there were no more visitations.

We never had a parochial school, but we did have a lively Parish School of Religion, headed after my first year by Miss Dotty Sanning. Classes were held on Sunday morning and Monday afternoon for boys and girls who attended public or non-Catholic schools. Besides the regular classes, we had, during Advent, *Tales for Tots*, to which young children came with their parents. Wearing slippers with a the face of a puppy on the toes, I was telling them about Saint Nicolas and how, by throwing a bag of gold through their window, he saved some young girls from a fate worse than death. Miss Dotty then threw out some gold-wrapped chocolates, and the kids went berserk. I do not remember myself at that age ever having any such reaction to chocolate.

There was also a Biblical Summer School, which was quite popular, with Miss Dotty dressed as a clown. On the feast of Saint Francis we blessed the children's animals: dogs, cats, gerbils, a snake and a pony among others. We had some good adult education programs too, but the difficulty was to get the busy adults to come to be educated.

Most parishes have a Saint Vincent de Paul Society, whose purpose is to help the poor. Ours was notably active, never gave out money or food stamps without visiting the recipients, and did untold good. It had been firmly established by my predecessor.

We were invited to support a parish in Haiti. The original plan was that each Haitian parish would be twinned with a parish in US. We wanted to visit the parish, and a parishioner had a friend who flew a twin-engine Cessna, so four of us flew down. We re-fueled in the Bahamas, noticed the constant patrols by anti-drug aircraft, and then set off across the sea to Haiti. The pilot looked down and asked me what those white things were. I said they were whitecaps on the waves. He said 'That's fantastic; I have never seen that before; in fact, I have never flown over the sea before.' When we reached land we were flying in cloud at 7000 feet. I had noticed from the map that some of the peaks in Haiti were nearly 9000 feet high, and suggested we might be wise to climb a bit. It took quite a while to raise the control tower but in due course we received permission to climb. When we reached Port-au-Prince the cloud base was low, and Control sent us out to sea to make a U-turn and come back under the cloud. My confidence had been ebbing for the past hour and was almost gone by the time we landed.

When we reached the parish, the pastor was out, but soon returned on a smart Harley-Davidson. He was well fed, and we soon decided that he had enough support already, and turned instead to Les Petites Soeurs de Sainte Thérèse, Haitian nuns who had several schools, one in the suburbs of Port-au-Prince and two out in the hills. We also had a delivery of money to make to a dentist who had established a medical clinic in Cité Soleil, the worst slum in the city, and one of the worst in the world. All four of us started off, but after about fifty yards, the smell was too much for two, who turned and fled. The remaining two of us delivered the money, some of which later helped to build in the slum *École Saint Anselme*, (*Saint Anselm School*) named in honor of our parish.

Several years later I went to Haiti again and visited one of the schools up in the hills in the North. The Sisters had just built a new auditorium. They had asked the parents to bring with them each day, when they brought their children, a large rock. With the help of a talented religious Brother, they then built a beautiful auditorium. We continue to support them as well as we can, but the chief difficulty is getting money there safely.

Closer to home, we supported an inner-city parish in Saint Louis, which then merged with another parish, and then merged again, ending as Holy Trinity. The original parish was African-American, but the last merger was with a white parish. Again, we not only contributed money, but when it was a matter of renovating their playground, our men went and did much of the manual labor. We attended some of their Masses and they some of ours. Until the last merger, the liturgical music was African-American, and the greeting of peace lasted ten minutes. It was a style quite different from ours, and I was invigorated by it, but it would not have suited me every day.

There were also people asking us for counseling and spiritual direction. One of the most interesting of these was a young Vietnamese woman, sent to us by a Rabbi in Rolla, Missouri. She went to him with some problems, and he told her to go and talk to those Benedictines on Mason Road in Saint Louis: 'They're smart boys.' She made an appointment with me. When she arrived, I was crossing our parking lot. She said she was looking for Father Timothy; I said I was he, so I became the smart boy.

For the next five hours she told her story. After the Communist invasion, she was sent to a re-education camp because she worked for Americans, and a neighbor reported that she was with the CIA. Every means, some most despicable, failed and she was released as incorrigible. She was able to raise money to buy a boat from friends who wanted their two daughters to escape. She and her party had to leave by night. They discovered too late that the boatyard had switched boats and given her a dud. Once at sea, the engine spluttered, but an Enclish merchant ship helped them to fix the it, gave them a compass, and a bearing to take them to the shipping lanes. The engine gave further trouble and her party said they wanted to limp back to Vietnam. She said 'Give me twenty-four hours, and if nothing happens, you can throw me into the sea. But I am not going back to Vietnam.' Fortunately, an American naval vessel came by, and took them to Singapore. Because she spoke Vietnamese, French, and English, she was employed as a translator for the US, French, Canadian and Dutch embassies. She then came to US, worked for Aetna Insurance in New England, got married, and moved to Michigan, where she had her own TV program on Vietnamese cooking. They then moved to Rolla.[21] She now has her Ph.D., and is a professor at the University of San Diego. I admired her courage and persistence. Later she re-married. Her parents had died and most of her senior

21. *As she is planning to write her own memoir, it would not be fair of me to say more. It was a fascinating five hours.*

relatives had either died or remained in Vietnam. I could not officiate at their marriage, but I served as the one to 'give her away'.

One of our most enjoyable projects in the parish was the athletic program. We decided to start small, in every sense, with boys and girls in kindergarten and first grade. The boys and girls enjoyed it, but to my mind the heroes were the coaches, the parents, and the referees. One coach was teaching a very small girl to catch a ball with her baseball glove. He stood a few feet from her, told her to watch the ball and to move her glove to where the ball would reach her. He lobbed the ball gently to her and it hit her on the shoulder. Then the heroism: he said to her 'Well done! now just move the glove over a little farther, and you will catch it.' In the end, she did. I also remember watching another very small girl trying to kick a small soccer ball. It was hard for her because even the small ball came almost up to her knee. But best of all, there was a final practice before our first ever game of soccer. At the end of the practice, the coach put the ball on the penalty spot and each player in turn was to have a kick at goal, then move over and let the next one try. They all did. In the game next day, our striker had the ball at his feet in front of their goal, their goalie was on his face in the mud, and everyone was yelling 'Shoot, shoot'. He must have kicked at the ball and missed it. More yells. Then he turned to the crowd and said 'I can't shoot; it's not my turn'. Coaches beware: small boys have a great sense of the force of rules, and are very literal-minded. We have since expanded to all the primary grades and to sports other than soccer.

Because of our large auditorium we were asked to host Clergy Days. These were days when the Archbishop and his Diocesan Clergy came together for prayer, talks on subjects of concern, lunch, and more talks. Ever since our arrival we had tried to get to know as many of the diocesan clergy as we could, and used to attend, with many other priests, the closing of the Forty Hours devotions at any parishes that invited us. But after Vatican II that form of Eucharistic devotion ceased. We were sad when the archbishop decided that these Clergy Days would be more appropriately held at the Archdiocesan Seminary.

From two other incidents among many I learnt much. The father of an alumnus was dying of cancer. I had been visiting him and then had to go out of town for a workshop. I said I would look in on the day I got back. It was a 300 mile drive on a hot and humid day and I was tired, but I kept my promise. When I reached their home, his wife told me I was too late: her husband had just died. We went out on the patio and talked for 30 or 40 minutes while her sons dealt with the undertakers. I left feeling very dissatisfied. I did not think I had said anything to comfort her. A month or so later, the phone rang, and the widow asked me if I remembered the day her husband had died, and went on to say that she had felt very angry with me. I said I was not surprised and that I had felt angry with myself. She then added that she had intended, in the grief of the moment, to take an overdose and go with him, and that I had just sat on the patio and would not go away. By the time I did go, the feeling had worn off. If one does what one can, God will do the rest.

The second incident occurred soon after we had published a parish pictorial directory. Several parishioners received envelopes bearing their name and address cut out from the directory, and containing anti-Catholic propaganda. My first inclination was to explode, or at least expostulate, but then I thought that a more irenic approach was preferable. So I wrote and suggested to the senders, an evangelical group in Texas, that if we sat down together we would probably find that we agreed far more often than we disagreed, and were they sure they were spending their effort and money more wisely in writing like this to fellow-Christians than if they gave witness to those who had rejected, or even had never heard, the good news of the Gospels. To my surprise they replied that they saw my point and would go into discernment over it. I thought that would be the end of the matter, but after a month or so, they wrote that their discernment led them to think they should indeed go in another direction. The happy ending was that my correspondent began to take an interest in things Catholic, eventually became a Catholic; and we still exchange Christmas cards. What did I learn from that? Saint James was right: 'God's righteousness is never served by man's anger'.

My mother was Catholic and my father Church of England. While they were in India and I was back in England, I was brought up entirely by the Church of England side of my family. I loved them, they were good people, and I could not believe that God did not love them too. So ecumenism came easily to me, and I was not ill at ease when I was taken by a friend to Lively Stones Pentecostal Church in the inner city, where some of her Junior College pupils worshipped. It was a very hot August day, and the church had no air-conditioning, only hand-fans. My friend and I were the only Caucasians present. I was invited to sit on the raised dais round the altar, with the elders.

The Bishop preached for forty minutes on the storm on the Sea of Galilee. At the end of his description he said 'And the Lord rose up, (pause) and stilled the waves'. As he said it, he must have sensed that this had a lilt to it. He repeated it, and this time the congregation was ready: He said 'The Lord rose up.' And they thundered back 'AMEN'. 'And stilled the waves'. 'AMEN'. I tingled all over. Later in the service the Bishop asked those on the dais to say a few words. I was unprepared for this, and when my turn came, I said who I was and noted how different I was: they were African-American and I was English, they were from the city, I was from the county, and so on, and I could sense them withdrawing, 'but' I said, 'I feel quite at home here, because after all there is one Lord', and they once more thundered 'AMEN', 'and one Faith,' 'AMEN', 'and one Baptism,' 'AMEN'. I added that I wished I could get a reaction like that in my own parish. It reminded me of the Psalm about leading the rejoicing crowd into the House of God, 'the throng wild with joy'. After nearly three hours we all tumbled out into the street, wringing wet and wonderfully happy. Tingling and joy are, I am told, signs of the Holy Spirit's presence.

In our parish centre, we had an ecumenical program for the week of Christian Unity in January each year. One year we had a dinner followed by a panel discussion on the topic *How does your Judicatory approach forgiveness*? The Episcopalian Archdeacon said half in jest 'Very gingerly', but the Rabbi startled us by saying 'We do not forgive'. No wonder Jesus made forgiveness so central to his teaching, and made it his only footnote to the *Our Father*.

I inherited a brand-new parish center, so there was not much maintenance to be done, except that one wall leaked. The contractor came to inspect and fix it several times with no success. After a while he stopped coming, and after another while the wall stopped leaking. The building itself has served the parish very well, but, even though Monsignor Slattery had planted some good trees round it, I still wanted to break up its austere outline. I bought one hundred ten-inch sticks of hybrid poplar for $37 and planted them in clumps around the building. They grew six to ten feet a year and soon dealt with the outline. Then we planted more elegant trees, and as they grew up we were able to cut down the weed-trees. The elegant trees gave us shade when we held Mass or a picnic outdoors. I planted six cedars during a thunderstorm, and pressed the wet clay firmly around their roots. They were well watered and grew almost as fast as the poplars. A parishioner planted impatiens along the wall outside my office, and we introduced red and white standard hibiscus along much of the rest of the walls.

A harder problem was the air-conditioning of the church. So long as only monks were using the church, we got along without it. But when the parish was established, and started to use our church, temporarily at first until they built their own, and then permanently, the parishioners wanted air-conditioning and the Priory did not. When the church was built, the donors did not want it, and for economy we did not during construction install ducts for air-conditioning. For several years in the summer the parish moved its weekend Masses out of the church and into the auditorium of the parish center. But the requests for air-conditioning continued and grew more emphatic. The monks had previously asked for estimates, which had come in around a half-million dollars. Now a parishioner gave us a bid of less than half that. He would use the existing heating ducts. The monks gave their approval, provided that it did not spoil the looks of the interior and that the parish paid for it. This was on the grounds that the monks would never use it. I never believed that, and have since been proven right. Now the Abbey makes an annual contribution to the air-conditioning.

On some special occasion in 1991, the parish very kindly paid me to go away, so I made my first trip to China, Hong Kong and Taiwan. It was a packaged tour visiting Beijing, Xian, Guilin, Canton and Hong Kong. Taiwan I arranged on my own. I knew no one on the tour and I was not in charge, so it was very different from Timothy Tours. I had no worry but less liberty. We saw all the usual sights: the Forbidden City, the Temple of Heaven, which had been freshly painted, the Summer Palace, the Ming Tombs, and the Great Wall. It was exciting to see what was to me a completely new style of architecture, of which I had seen only pictures. The streets were crowded with pedestrians, cyclists, and a fair number of buses, but very few cars. Housing was scarce, and very crowded with two or more families in a high-rise often sharing a kitchen.

At Xian they are still digging up more terracotta warriors, It is a unique sight. But I was almost more impressed with the city walls, forty or more feet high and forty or more feet wide at the top. A walk on those walls is strangely exhilarating.

At Guilin the real excitement is the Karst topography formed by the dissolution of layers of soluble bedrock such as limestone. The best way to see it is by the river cruise. There were some thirty steamboats in the flotilla, and our boat was towards the rear. Our captain, however, considered it his duty to pass the boats in front of him, so there were other excitements as well as the Karst. The similarity between the pillars of Karst and Chinese painted scrolls amazed me. I had always thought that those scrolls were highly abstract, but they are, in fact, almost photographic, especially on a misty day. Each boat bought shellfish from the fishermen on the river, and gave them to us for lunch. That evening they gave us a display of cormorant fishing. The cormorants have an elastic band round their throat so they cannot swallow the fish, but they get their reward at the end.

The most striking sight in Canton (Guangzhou) was the late nineteenth century Shen Clan Academy and Temple, a treasury of carving and sculpture in many media. We then went by train to Hong Kong. There I was both disappointed and relieved; disappointed because I had heard so much of its beauty, and relieved because I was no longer sorry that the British lease of Hong Kong was close to its end. And yet I enjoyed the harbor and Victoria Peak, was suitably impressed by I.M. Pei's building for the Bank of China, but the central area seemed to be devoted to money and sex. In an amusement park was the most garish and tasteless Buddha I have ever seen.

Our tour offered an excursion to Lantau Island for an excessive price, so I did it on my own, going first class on the boat and having a good lunch en route for one fifth of their price. I visited the Trappist monastery there, but the great Buddha of Po Lin, 112 feet tall and weighing 250 metric tons, was not yet open to the public; it was completed in 1993. Even from a distance and incomplete it was both mighty and serene.

I left the tour and flew to Taiwan. Unluckily, my travel agent had told me I needed no visa, but I did, and it took most of the day and many dollars to get one. My main object in Taiwan was to see the National Palace Museum, in which Chiang Kai-shek had deposited trainloads of treasures from mainland China. As England defends the presence in London of the Elgin Marbles, 'otherwise they would have been turned into lime', so Taiwan defends the presence in Taipei of so many treasures from the mainland, 'otherwise they would have been destroyed by the Cultural Revolution'. There were many beautiful, metal (especially bronze) and ceramic objects, but I remember best the paintings and calligraphy. I deeply regretted the day lost to the visa, and flew sadly back to USA.

Having visited Japan, I knew a little of what to expect in China, since China, many centuries ago, deeply influenced Japan. I knew that China is a huge country, similar in size to USA: I did not know that the western tip of China is West of most of India, nor that China is racially, linguistically, and geographically so diverse. Later, this was to be made even clearer by a trip along the old Silk Road. A much less pleasant surprise was the degree of pollution in the air. It was wise to wear a mask over nose and mouth, and to lay in a store of lozenges or hard candy for one's throat. I had also one small linguistic surprise: the character for mountain and its meaning are the same in Chinese and Japanese, but the Chinese read the character as *shan*, and the Japanese as *yama*.[22]

This trip was in 1991, and I was due to retire in 1995. During those four years I made a second visit to Haiti, this time by commercial airlines and in greater comfort. We grew in admiration for our Haitian nuns and their work, and also met a group of Haitian Religious brothers. I celebrated Mass for them one morning, and 'celebrated' is the right word: the entrance procession was with music and dancing, and there was a real feeling of fellowship and joy at the Mass.

I have not said much about the social life of the parish, having left that mostly to the laity. Operation RENEW, that I mentioned above, helped us to get to know one another, which was important in a rapidly growing parish. We had the usual round of celebrations: progressive dinners, golf and tennis tournaments, a bridge roundelay, and homegrown entertainment of great variety at Christmas, or whenever anyone felt like it. As with the Mothers' Club in the school, we found that most of the parishioners were not starved of social life and were also very busy, with the possible exception of the elderly. For them we did have a parish Guild that organized one event each month: an excursion to the Botanical Garden or to Sainte Genevieve, or to a lecture; a wide variety of events with one common feature: they all ended at Ted Drewes for frozen custard or ice-cream. This they ordered by cell phone ahead of time, so when they arrived, the trays were brought onto the coach and all received their own favorite flavor.

In 1993, two summers before retiring, I was able to repay much kindness of an English friend with a visit to Moscow and Saint Petersburg. Through the good offices of Greg Huger, an alumnus of the school, who was working in Moscow, we were able to get a guide, Olga, and a car with driver for $40 a day. With them we were able to see the Red Square, the Kremlin, Saint Basil's and other wonderful Cathedrals, the Russian Icons at the Tretyakov Gallery, and much else. The singing of the Orthodox monks was most impressive: so many basses and baritones worthy of Chaliapin.

22. To speak of Mount Fujiyama is therefore a pleonasm, (Mount Fujimountain), like Farmer George.

We then flew to Saint Petersburg, where we visited the Hermitage, and could have spent a year there. Quite apart from the collection, the building itself exacts admiration. There is a room with twenty-six Rembrandts on the walls, and another with a collection of Impressionist pictures that one seldom sees. One source of these treasures was the visits that the crowned heads of Europe paid to one another, bringing artefacts as their gifts. In almost every room there was also a resident gorgon, whose favorite word was 'nyet' (No). As we were for a while following a field trip of small children, the word was in the air all the time.

We also walked around Saint Petersburg, and then visited two of the Summer Palaces, Pushkin and Pavlovsk. Both were somewhat damaged during the 1917 revolution, but the main damage was done by the German troops in World War II. Much restoration has been completed, and Pushkin must have been repainted just before we saw it. It was palatial inside (not one of my favorite styles) but the outside was sparkling in its beauty, and so were the gardens. At Pavlovsk, the park was charming.

We liked the borshch, the caviar, and accepted the rest of the food. We liked also the Vodka and had several good wines from Georgia. We flew back to Moscow to visit Sergiy Posad, formerly Zagorsk. We met Olga again, and drove out there. We kissed the bones of Saint Sergius, and were struck by the atmosphere of prayer combined with light-heartedness, a little like the *Canterbury Tales*. At the end of our visit, Olga said she wanted us to meet her old friend, Father Stephan. He was entertaining his friend Andrew, a sculptor, who was to set off for Crete the next day to sell his sculptures. This alarmed us, as we had so far avoided getting into a vodka-slinging match. Here on our last day we were in danger. Sure enough, out came the bottle of Vodka and the glasses, and 'We must drink a toast to Olga' said Father Stephan. Then there was one to Andrew, and one to 'our English guests, whom God has sent to us'. That was three. I had sipped the first and was told firmly that it must all go down in one. I saw that we would have to reply, and so perhaps would the others. I said I would like to toast Father Stephan and Olga and Andrew all in one. 'You cannot do that' said Father Stephan. 'Oh yes I can' I replied. 'This is the monastery of the Most Holy Trinity, and the Trinity is three Persons in one Nature; so in this monastery we can have three toasts in one swig.' 'Oh, you're cunning', he replied, but we got away with it, and quickly said we had to leave to catch our plane.

We asked Olga about the fall of Communism. Her father was a card-carrying party member and her grandmother was a devout Russian Orthodox Catholic.

Olga said that the end of the Seventy Years – she never called it Communism – had left a vacuum. Communism had at least been an ideal and had called for sacrifice, and so had appealed especially to young idealists. I think she wished that the Orthodox Church would rush in to fill the vacuum, but it had been so reduced that it had neither the clergy, nor the means of training clergy, in anything like adequate numbers. We parted from Olga with tears all round. I asked her if she would rather have money or my *Blue Guide*. She chose the Guide. We reached London and were almost on the ground when Control told our pilot to accelerate, climb, and try again: there was something else on the runway. As we left the plane, he bade us farewell with 'Sorry about the rather sporty landing'. I wished later that I had replied 'Not quite cricket, old boy'.

My last two years as pastor passed quietly. Three small events may illustrate the unexpected in a pastor's life. I went to the reception after a wedding and was asked if I would like a drink. I asked what they had. 'Anything you like, Father.' I asked for a single malt scotch and they did not have any. I said any scotch would be fine, and thought no more of it. Two weeks later a package arrived, in which there was a wooden box, which we opened. It contained a twenty-five year old bottle of *The Macallan*, smooth and strong as it could be. What an *amende honorable*! The second event concerned Sicilian wine. A dealer had bought several cases of this wine, which was only just drinkable. I was polite about it and he asked me if I would like a case. When the case arrived, I put it in the trunk (boot) of my car and forgot about it. Winter came, all the bottles froze solid but did not burst. Later I found them and thawed them. They had vastly improved. The third small event was at one of our annual celebrations of the Sacrament of Confirmation. In the program one of the hymns was described as a Zimbabwean folksong. My interest was aroused, but when the hymn started I recognized the tune. It took me a little while to identify it as *The Song of the Lincolnshire Poacher*, relating his 'delight on a shiny night in the season of the year.' British colonists must have exported it to Southern Rhodesia, as Zimbabwe was then, where it evidently took root. The tune was the same, the words were not.

At the end of my tenure, there was a party, a fond *au revoir*, seven little books of letters from parishioners, a generous golden handshake but not, unfortunately for our endowment fund, on the Wall Street scale, and on June 30, 1995, I handed over to Father Benedict, who was to be Administrator of the Parish until Father Gerard took over.

Thirty-Seven

BACK TO THE MONASTERY

Just before this, I was made, by the Abbot President, titular Prior of Ely Cathedral, an honorary title that carries with it no duties. It is a long-standing papal privilege of the English Benedictine Congregation to confer on those judged suitable the titles of titular Abbot or titular Prior of English Cathedrals that before the Dissolution of the Monasteries were staffed by Benedictines. The Abbot in these Cathedrals was also the bishop of the diocese, and so in practice the Prior had to run the community. I visited the beautiful cathedral of Ely, near Cambridge, and was cordially entertained by the Dean, in the absence of the Bishop, but it is hard, at this distance, to maintain any close relationship. I keep by my desk a painting by the English artist, John Piper, of the carving of Our Lady over the Prior's door from the cloister into the cathedral.

We have a good custom that when a man has been doing a job for some time, he does not breathe down his successor's neck. The best way of ensuring this is to let the man go away. This did not happen when I stopped being headmaster, but did when I stopped being pastor. I went to England, visited such family and friends as were still alive, visited Ampleforth, drove around the country a bit, made a reconnaissance for a future Timothy Tour to Budapest, Vienna and Prague, and returned refreshed and reinvigorated to Saint Louis.

In 1989 we were elevated from being a priory to being an abbey, and elected Prior Luke Rigby as our first abbot. After twenty-eight years as Superior (prior of the Priory and abbot of the Abbey) he resigned in 1995. This year was a watershed in our history. In it we elected as our first American abbot, Abbot Thomas Frerking. He had been headmaster, and appointed as his successor Father Gregory Mohrman, an alumnus of our school. The administrator of the parish was American and was to be succeeded in the following year as pastor, by another American, Father Gerard Garrigan. The only English monk left in a significant position was Father Paul Kidner as Prior.

I was in an anomalous and rather uncomfortable position. I was no longer, as I had been for forty years, fully involved in our activities, but neither was I fully detached from them. I was only partially retired, because one never retires from being a monk. Further, although I no longer held any official office, and was not teaching in the school, I had been headmaster for nineteen years and pastor for over fourteen. I was bound, therefore, to have connections with those who still wanted me for Baptisms, Weddings, Funerals, or simply wanted to visit or be visited, or to come out for counseling. A surprising number also wanted translations into or out of Latin, and sometimes Greek. These included requests for mottoes, an inscription on a chalice, and on a crozier, or abbot's staff, and on a funeral pall, and on the Mothers' Club quilt. One alumnus wanted a translation of four folio sheets of the Nuremberg Chronicle. I also had a running skirmish, lasting several years, with the Yearbook of the English Benedictines about the lettering on the Benedictine medal. Both the transcription and its translation were faulty, but it took many letters across the Atlantic to get them corrected.

At some time after 1995 I was added to the team of priests to celebrate Mass for the Visitation Sisters nearby, and still do so on Fridays. They offer us breakfast afterwards, the best of the week.

My telephone and e-mail were and are about as busy as before I retired. I no longer had a secretary, so even when there were fewer letters to write and phone calls to make, they took longer because I had to find telephone numbers, addresses, etc. and then file my copy. I also did all this less quickly than before. There was one good change: there were fewer tasks that had to be done at a particular time, and so my schedule was more flexible. I also experienced the truth of Parkinson's Law, that the work to be done expands to fill the time available for doing it. For example, I used previously to collect all my items for laundry, tumble them into the washing machine, transfer them to the drier, take them out, and tumble them into a drawer. Now I separate whites and colors, wash and dry them separately, fold them carefully, and put them away. It takes much longer.

I had hoped that I would have more time for writing and for woodworking. I had even dreamed of writing in the morning, woodworking in the afternoon, and office work in the evening. The only task that turned out at all like my dream was writing, and even that had to wait for five years.

Here are some items from one page of 'things to be done': Marriage counseling for an alumnus; Invocation for a fortieth wedding anniversary;

Enquiry about the cost of air-conditioning in the church; Problems with the adoption of a child from Vladivostok; Consoling parents of a suicide; Get permission to attend Cardinals' baseball game; Thank Sister Y for shoes with Velcro instead of laces; Answer a request for details about dead members of our monastery; Discuss the plight of migrant farm-workers in New England; Have the pastor from United Church of Christ to lunch; Entertain for the week-end the Vietnamese family of the brother of a friend.

These, chosen at random, are diverse and interesting, but not quite as I had dreamt.

My biggest single project was that Abbot Luke asked me to write a history of Priory. This was daunting. Although in the course of the years I had written many articles, reviews, homilies and speeches, I had never written a book; and I had very little space. I worked in a small office with a bookcase along one side. This reduced the available space for desk, computer, printer, and left almost no room for spreading out resources.

Through 1974, I kept a file with a copy of every important document or notice for all the time that I was headmaster. This was invaluable, and there were many other sources too. Our independence was granted in 1973, so this seemed an appropriate terminus. I started on the outline of the book in 1995, but it had to be fitted in between other activities. For one period of about six months, I did no work on it at all. It emerged in 2001.

There were all sorts of difficulty. One that I had not expected was with people's memories. I had a very clear memory that when we arrived in New York we stayed with the Hoguets on 92nd Street. Another monk said he had a very clear memory that it was 94th Street. 92nd was right; should I therefore always trust my own memory? Several times I had to rely on other monks' memory, and mostly that came out all right. It was a rush at the end, and there was not as much time for review as I would have liked. We sent a copy and a disk off to the printers, thinking that they would do the final editing, but to my surprise they simply photographed what we sent them. It was called *In Good Soil*. It sold well; understandably, the people who enjoyed it most were those who knew the characters involved, sometimes even themselves. It led to a review/interview in our local *Post-Dispatch*, a review in the *New Oxford Review*, and had a brief review in the *Times Literary Supplement* (London). It was a particular satisfaction to me that the last payment of $7000 of the debt on the new monastery was paid from profits of the book.

On two occasions in Saint Louis my past in Burma has come back to visit but not to haunt me. I was invited to give the invocation at a reunion dinner of US Air Force Thunderbolt pilots. The Thunderbolt was a short and tubby; so, by that time, were many of the pilots. Then in 2002 there was a joint convention of the American CBI (China, Burma, India) Veterans' Association and the British Burma Star Association. Someone heard that I had been in Burma, and so I was asked to say Mass for any Catholics attending. The local committee invited me to lunch to vet me, and then asked me to reminisce to a section of the meeting. I agreed and had the pleasure of making some new friends and of meeting the President of the Council of the Burma Star Association, who had come over from England for the convention. Until then, I had not wanted to think much about my years in Burma in World War II, but I found that, nearly sixty years later, I could think and reminisce quite peacefully about them. I had two chances to return to Burma, but did not take either, mostly because we would not have been allowed to go to most of the places where I had been, and partly because of the government there.

In 1999 I was again invited by friends to stay in Barbados. One special attraction was that there would be during my stay a Test Match (cricket) between West Indies and Australia, in which the incomparable Brian Lara, whom I specially wanted to watch, would be playing for the West Indies. We watched one day of the match at the Kensington Oval in Bridgetown and then I had to fly back to the Abbey in time for Palm Sunday. I missed by one or two days Lara's greatest innings, which, against all the odds, won the match. I have since watched some of it on video with amazement, but without the tense excitement of the real thing. Wisden called it the second greatest Test match innings, after one of Bradman's. Bradman was immaculate but Lara was scintillating.

My hosts later moved from Barbados and took to spending the Saint Louis winters in Florida. I have stayed with them there too. They took me once to the Everglades Park, where we were told of an Italian family, whose young son was riding a bicycle, lost control and ended up in a small pond with an alligator. The alligator's jaws closed on the boy until his mother jumped into the pond and started beating the alligator on the nose with her umbrella. Amazingly, the alligator released the boy and dived to the bottom. The boy was rushed to a hospital and survived.

I was also invited by Elizabeth Mudd to accompany her family on a trip to Rome for Archbishop Rigali's reception from Pope John Paul II of the *Pallium*,

Archibishop, later Cardinal, Justin Rigali and I at the North American College in Rome after the Papal Mass of the Pallium.

signifying that he was a Metropolitan, or head of several dioceses. This took place at a Mass at the main altar in Saint Peter's. I luckily took my monastic habit to wear in Rome and so was chosen to stand with a few others at the foot of the altar. This Bernini altar has seven steps, so I was that close to the Pope during the Mass. The others and I distributed Holy Communion to the strangely unorganized congregation. This was in 1994, and already the Pope's hands were a little shaky as he raised the chalice.

Thirty-Eight

THE OLD SILK ROAD

In 2000, I was taken, again by Elizabeth Mudd and family, on a tour to end all tours. It took us from Beijing to Moscow along the 'Old Silk Road', which was really neither old, nor silk, nor a road. The name originated in the nineteenth century; many other people and things traveled on it besides silk; and it was many tracks rather than a single road. We left Beijing in Mao's special train, which had basins, but no showers; so every two or three nights we had to stop at a hotel to clean up. At the border with Kazakhstan we switched to the Nostalgic Istanbul Orient Express, which did have showers but was neither so comfortable nor so decorative. Some of the carriages were from the original Orient Express.

It was a fantastic (almost literally) experience, and was the other great trip of my life. We were a party of ninety-four, and the oldest member was in his nineties. We started in Beijing with the mandatory sights, including a visit to a lesser-known part of the Great Wall, and then, with a great send-off of fireworks, song and dance, boarded Mao's special train. We made for Xian, where we visited the terracotta warriors – they are still uncovering warriors and had many more on view than on my first visit – climbed the magnificent city walls, and toured two splendid museums, one of which had a book printed before 1000 AD, but not by movable type, although the Chinese did have movable type long before Gutenberg.[23] They also took us to a very old Mosque, fourteenth century as we see it, but originating probably in the seventh century. The minaret is like a pagoda. It was due for destruction in the Cultural Revolution. Its parishioners prepared to defend it by force, but the Imam welcomed the Red Guard in, let them destroy a building no one liked, and then told them a story, The Chinese love stories, and asked for another. After several stories, he said he would tell them one more story, but first they must go away and come back after several hours. They went away, and never came back. Thus he saved his mosque.

We climbed the western end of the Great Wall. Next day, we visited the

23. *The Chinese type was ceramic, Gutenberg's was of a specially durable metal.*

Mogao caves at Dunhuang. This is where Sir Aurel Stein bought 5000 ancient and largely Buddhist manuscripts for a modest sum and brought them to the British Museum. There are 492 caves[24] with 45,000 square meters of frescos, over 2400 painted sculptures, and a nine-storey Buddha carved into the rock. In the late afternoon we had a very comfortable ride on two-humped, Bactrian camels past the 'singing sand dunes', but they sing only in certain kinds of weather. We now had the Gobi Desert behind us and to our North, and the Takla Makan Desert in front of us to our West, a barren landscape.

From the train at the next stop we took coaches to Turfan, on the fringe of the Takla Makan. This fertile area is over 400 feet below sea level, and the record temperature is 121° F. It has a fascinating system of irrigation whereby melted snow is brought underground through sand tunnels from the mountains north of Turfan. The total length of the tunnels and their branches is about 5000 Km. The population is Uighur (pronounced weegore). They were most friendly to us, fed us, and sang and danced for us, and the little boys were fascinated by some pictures of our church that I had with me. We passed by the Emin Minaret, at 144 feet the tallest in China. It was of interest to me as having entasis, or a slight bulge in the middle, similar to what Greek columns normally have. Standing next to a severely rectangular mosque, it was strangely beautiful. We came back to the train by dusk and a violent wind had risen. Our big coaches had to keep at the road's centre line for fear of being blown off the road. When we got back to the station, there was a wide flight of shallow steps down to the train. I was nearly blown off my feet on it; the wiser ones saw this and clung to the wall at one side.

We reached the border of China and Kazakhstan and had to change trains because the gauge was different, China using standard and Kazakhstan broad gauge. This was no problem but took ages because of security. As we hobnobbed with passengers from our new train, they warned us, correctly, of the strong possibility of stomach upset. We welcomed the showers and, equally, the waiter who came round before dinner each evening pouring vodka from his pitcher into a glass two or three feet away, as can be done with wineskins. The scenery was mountainous and spectacular, but we passed through much of it by night.

We stopped at Tashkent, the capital of Uzbekistan, and visited a church with a fine façade and a statue which might politely be called sturdy, and then went on to Samarkand. My imagination, like that of so many others, had been caught by Flecker's poem about the Golden Road to Samarkand, so I had high

24. *More have now been discovered.*

expectations and was not disappointed. Tamburlaine or Timor (1336-1405) made it his capital. The old city center, Registan (place of sand) has three old Madrasahs of glittering ceramic tile, and is in the middle of the modern city. Traffic swirls around you as you walk towards it. The place is vibrantly alive. It reminded me of Isfahan. This was not surprising, as its architect was Persian. He kissed Timor's wife, was threatened with death, jumped from the top of a minaret, sprouted wings and flew back to Persia. The architecture and the brilliant colors are well set off by the bright sunlight and sandy soil. Nearby is a market-place selling everything, including brightly embroidered cloth. We bought two tablecloths, which did not look garish back in Saint Louis. There is also Ulugh Beg's observatory, a fifteenth century center for the study of astronomy. They calculated the length of a year correctly to within a minute. It was a reminder that not only had this area produced distinctive architecture of exquisite beauty, but had also been far ahead of the West in mathematics, science and astronomy, and, earlier, in theology and philosophy.

Either here or at Khiva, a young wife was condemned to be thrown off the top of a minaret. When they were about to do so, she complained that she did not like the dress she was in, and asked if she could send for another. Her maid, not knowing which she would like, brought her forty. She put them all on, and when they threw her off the minaret, she bounced. The judge was so amused that he released her. Or so we were told. It was news, sad news, to me that minarets were ever used for this purpose.

And so we went on our way to Moscow, along the shores of a diminishing Caspian Sea, across the Russian steppes and over the mighty Volga. In Moscow we visited again the Tretyakov Gallery, with its superb icons, but which also has an interesting and impressive collection of more modern Russian paintings. Tretyakov was Jewish, and his collection was confiscated by the Bolsheviks in 1917. He went into exile in Paris. When asked whether he resented the loss of his icons, he replied most magnanimously that at least he was glad that the Russian people should have a good opportunity to see them.

The traffic in Moscow is an almost continuous jam. The tour coach took over an hour to travel a few blocks. Mrs. Mudd and I were not on it; she hired a car, with a Russian 'guide', to take us to Sergiy Posad, formerly Zagorsk. In the fourteenth century Saint Sergius of Radonezh, a patron saint of Russia, blessed the Russian army that went out and defeated the invading Tatars. He founded a monastery, which survived even the Communist rule, and is a major spiritual center. The Saint's bones, which we venerated, are there, and there is a prayerful atmosphere within the high walls that enclose five cathedrals and a seminary on two or three square miles of grounds. When besieged, the people joined the monks within the walls, and the monks joined the people on the walls to pelt the enemy. There was no vodka this time, so we returned to Moscow and flew back to Saint Louis.

After all that, it was an anti-climax to learn from the internet that I had died. I was verifying some facts about my grandfather, when I caught sight of my own name, and learnt that the Oxford University Gazette had noted my recent death. Almost my first reaction was the fear that some eagle-eyed civil servant would see this and cancel my pension. I wrote to the Gazette, quoting Mark Twain, and asking not for a notice of resurrection but for adequate correction, which they did. It seems that I replied to a fund-raising request explaining that as a monk I had no income, and had been crossed off the list, from which it was inferred, very unoxonially, that I had died.

Thirty-Nine

QUIETLY ACTIVE

In 2000 and 2001 for just over eighteen months, we lived in trailers on the lawn while the old monastery was torn down and the new one built. The transfer of our belongings in large cartons from the old monastery to the trailers and later from the trailers to the new monastery was carried out with remarkable skill. My only complaint was that by some fault in the ducts the heating system blew cold air into my room, so I grew a beard to help me stay warm at night. The only other time I have done that was when I was on my sabbatical trip, and that was largely to save shaving. I was not in on the planning of the new monastery. The first thought was to renovate the existing monastery and to add a small irregular quadrangle at one end on the side away from the church. At an inconveniently late stage it struck me that this would have been the first time we had planned a building without having regard to the church, which was always seen as the centerpiece of the campus. I said so, and some agreed. Our architects then told us that to build a new building would cost one dollar more per square foot than to renovate the old, so planning started afresh and the planners came up with our present ample and airy quadrangular building south of the church and linked to it by a slype, or corridor.

In 2001 and for several years afterwards, I was taken with the Mudd family to the Metropolitan Opera in New York. Everything was of the highest quality; the leading men and women were youngish, as befitted their roles; Pavarotti made a brief appearance in one opera, but stumbled on his entrance and had to start over. On the back of the seat in front of you is an electronic strip with an English translation of what is being sung. You can read it only from directly in front, and so are not distracted by your neighbor's. You can also turn yours off. My only sadness was that they turned the grand march in *Aida* into a Light Infantry scamper across the stage. I had seen *Aida* in Rome's Baths of Caracalla with an elephant in the procession. I was also taken for many years to the Saint Louis Opera Theater's operas, which, too, were wonderfully well staged and sung.

Portrait by Mr. Thomas O. Mulvihill, Priory parent.

292

Soon after this I was made moderator of the Alumni Mothers' Club. It was unique at the time of its formation, a good indication of the strength of the 'Abbey Family'. It went well, and a surprising number of mothers of alumni came to the meetings, which were, deliberately, comparatively few each year. But as I had left the school staff soon after 1981, when I became pastor, it seemed after a while that someone who knew the younger mothers should take over, and I handed on to Father Laurence Kriegshauser.

Then in 2003, I started to take over the strangely named group of Ostriches. This group had existed almost from our beginning under name of the Friends of the Priory. One day, the cards went out addressed to the Fiends of the Priory. Perhaps that caused the change to Ostriches. Father Columba was their original moderator, with other monks, including me, addressing them when he could not. In the early 1960s, I took them on a brisk canter through the Old Testament, which was quite new to many of them. The topics were spiritual and mostly Benedictine, looking at the Rule of Saint Benedict. After Father Columba, Father Luke took them over for many years. As this became more of a strain for him, I substituted on occasion. The occasions became more numerous, and eventually I took over. By that time *lectio divina* (divine reading), or prayerful reflection on a short passage of the Bible, was widespread, and we followed suit, studying one of the readings for the next Sunday. Later I suggested that they might like to change the name, but there was no enthusiasm at all.

In this year I was struck by a line from a poem by Solon of ancient Athens: γηράσκω δ' αἰεὶ πολλὰ διδασκόμενος (I grow old, learning much all the time). In this year, too, I first saw Yosemite, and wished I had seen it before.

I was asked to celebrate Mass and witness a wedding in Yucatan. We arrived a day or two ahead of time and visited not only Chichen Itza but also Uxmal, which we thought more beautiful. Both featured the macabre ball court, but no one knows for sure how the ritual game was played, nor who was sacrificed at the end of the game, winners or losers, but somebody was, or maybe more than one. We were housed in extensive haciendas. On the night of the wedding there was an eclipse of the moon. I was flown back to Saint Louis in a private jet, and so there was no waiting in line, and we were through customs in a minute or two. When the next couple asked me to marry them, I gladly agreed, on condition that the wedding would take place in Yucatan.

2004 was for me the year of the knife. I had a total hip replacement and then five months later a total knee replacement. Both went well.

When we came to our twin Golden Jubilees, of the monastery in 2005 and of the school in 2006, Abbot Thomas Frerking, whom we elected in 1995 on Abbot Luke's retirement, and re-elected in 2003, wanted us to produce a book to commemorate these events. Each professed monk was to write an essay on whatever topic he chose. My task, apart from my essay, was purely editorial. The heaviest part of the job was collecting the twenty articles. The busiest monks were the easiest. For the last one to come in, I had to threaten to write an article about him myself and publish it under his name, unless I received his copy by the following morning. The threat was successful. I also wrote an introduction, and short paragraphs leading into each essay. The second part of the book was an album of photographs arranged by decades of our existence. Some enjoyed that part more. The book was called *A School for The Lord's Service*.

As a corollary, we produced a transcript of all the fifty-eight homilies, lectures, addresses, speeches and some less serious pieces that were delivered during and about the Jubilees. It was called *Words of Thanksgiving*, and again my heaviest task was collecting the pieces. The authors were generous, but the proof-reading was more arduous, as some pieces were wholly or partly hand-written.

With these jubilees we combined a celebration of the fortieth anniversary of the founding of Saint Anselm Parish. This meant a fine dinner and, for me, my too-lengthy reminiscences about the parish.

I mentioned above that, when pastor, I thought there should be some comment on the readings even at weekday Masses. This led to what became known as the one-liners. I made a collection of them, one for each weekday of the year of both cycles. They need some polishing, but one day they may see the light.

The book and the transcripts were serious, mainstream work, and I was glad to do them, but there was one side-show that gave me special pleasure: I had a short article published in *The American Woodturner*, a magazine devoted to lathe-work. The piece described how to turn the loose change that most travelers bring back from abroad, and which banks will not exchange, into the center-piece of a small medallion worn on a chain round the neck. It was the first time I had ever been published in a crafts magazine. I was impressed by the care they took over even a short piece.

Working on a wood lathe is an excellent hobby. The circular motion is soothing; the lathe does the laborious work; wood is a beautiful material; the results are tangible. I was given a gilded, metal bowl, and made a series of chalices to hold the bowl. This could have gone on indefinitely, but a sacristan dropped the bowl, and it was never again a perfect circle, and so would not fit the chalices. The range of products from a lathe is limited by having to be circular in at least one plane, but it includes bowls, plates, lamp-stands, boxes, medallions, balls, egg-cups, balloons, mobiles, wind chimes, parts of chairs, and more, all of which I have made. I have been able to continue past my ninetieth birthday, and am limited now mainly by how long I can remain standing.

Just before Christmas, 2006, I took a World War II friend who was staying with us to visit Westminster College in Fulton, Missouri, where, in 1946, Mr. Churchill delivered his *Iron Curtain* speech. In 1969, The College founded the Churchill Museum, one of the best memorials to him that there is. It is in the basement of the Wren church of St. Mary's Aldermanbury, which was brought over, stone by stone, from London. While walking round the exhibits, I was, for a moment, scared by hearing the unmistakable whistle of a bomb dropping. It was on the sound track of a presentation, in the next room, of an air raid on London in World War II. It brought back to me the lugubrious sirens, the black-out of all windows, no street lighting, air-raid wardens' bells, and the discovery that we have a built-in sonar, which sometimes warns us when we are about to run into a hard object. The president of Westminster College at the time of the speech, Dr. Franc McCluer, was a member of the Higher Education Council with me. He was short in stature. When we were discussing the role of small colleges, he caused a welcome break in the serious discussion by pleading that instead of referring to small college presidents we said 'presidents of small colleges'.

Not long after this I renewed my resident alien card and learnt that I no longer have recognizable fingerprints, so now could commit crimes without being detected, at least in that way. Then I had cataract surgery. I was told it would be a breeze and last twenty minutes. Instead it took two hours because the suction machine, which removes the remains of the old lens, broke down. There was a back-up machine in the operating theater, but that would not work either. The surgeon had to remove the debris by hand, which took much longer, but he did it very well. The year ended happily, however, as Jim Switzer, one of our alumni, arranged for a large and very elegant roundel with beautiful lettering by the Cardozo-Kindersley workshop in Cambridge, England, to be set up in the high school in my honor, I have always been interested in the arts and crafts, especially lettering, but apart from lathe-work and photography have never practiced them. The inscription, from Luke 12.48, read;

EVERYONE

to whom much is given

of him much will be required

One day I was standing with a student of Saint Louis University outside their Pius XII library and beside a large seated statue of Pope Pius XII by Mestrovic. I asked him if he liked the Mestrovic. He looked puzzled. I explained and asked him if he knew who was portrayed in the statue. More puzzlement. I asked him the name of the building, which he knew, and then the penny dropped. This led to a slide show.

There are in Saint Louis many remarkable statues, sculptures and other such objects out in the open, quite apart from those in museums and galleries. I photographed a number and produced the slide show, with a questionnaire. Few scored well, and I felt embarrassed, not wanting to look like a know-all foreigner teaching Saint Louisans about their city. I later reduced the show to pieces standing out in the open and by internationally known sculptors: Mestrovic, Lipchitz, Henry Moore, Alexander Calder, Carl Milles, and some Chapungu artists from Zimbabwe. An abstract sculpture by Henry Moore was originally at the airport. When its area was remodeled, it was put into storage, and then replaced upside down. The donor removed it to the Botanical Garden, whence it returned to the Saint Louis Art Museum, so it was no longer 'out in the open'.

I conducted two tours of these sculptures, This led to a request for a tour of some of the *objets d'art* in the Abbey itself. This tour I have also conducted twice, both times with great help from Brother Symeon, who is himself the *artiste* of several of the *objets*, notably the two superb stained glass windows in the high school. For one window, Brother Symeon drew the cartoons, arranged the layout, and supervised, and the boys of his Guild, which was modeled on the medieval guilds, did most of the cutting, grinding, painting (where necessary), and assembling. For the other window he did all the work. My main qualification for conducting these tours is that I am not an art major, nor an art historian, and so may talk the same kind of language as most of my hearers.

In 2010 we had the fiftieth reunion of our first graduating class. Almost all who could come, did come. At their fortieth reunion, there was one I could not recognize, until he spoke. The same was true this time., but a different one. We started with the dedication of our renovated baseball field to Marty McCabe, our athletic director for many a year, and continued with a dinner on Friday night without speeches, and on Saturday night with speeches. There were also informal gatherings for re-connection and reminiscence. After I celebrated Mass for them at the Abbey on Sunday morning, they had brunch in the Stannard/Switzer House. The three living monks and some of the lay faculty who taught the class attended various events. It was a unique occasion: there cannot be another fiftieth reunion of our first class; they have a special place in our hearts. It is a fitting place at which to stop.

EPILOGUE

The son of Sirach writes, 'Speak, you who are older, for it is your right, but with accurate knowledge.' (Ecclus 32.3) I have tried to do so. In the *Preface* I referred to 'events'. I have described many, and this reunion was one of the most heart-warming. But far the larger part of my life has been regular, uneventful routine. Comparatively little of that shows up in my account. It would be of little interest to write: "I went across to the school to teach Latin; Joe translated *Catullus cvi*." or "I got up to Vigils, and we sang Psalm 88 a little flat." Or "this morning I spent half an hour in meditation, and another half hour reading the Bible." And yet I have spent far more time on activities like those – and they have been the more important – than on traveling along the Silk Road, or learning to hit a playing card with a Colt 45 at thirty yards, an ability I have never tested since. This regularity is especially true of religious life, and in the most literal sense. Our life is called 'regular' because we follow a *regula* (rule), in our case *The Rule of Saint Benedict*, a document written soon after AD 530, whose principles are still applicable today. So again I ask readers to remember that most of my life has been spent in the routine called for by my status at the time.

As I look back, what strikes me first is that so much has turned out so differently from anything I had expected. The first twenty years were quite normal, but although I knew that war was statistically probable in my lifetime, and although I was member of the Oxford ROTC, I never imagined myself as a soldier. So that was a shock. When it came, I spent very little time imagining what active service would be like, beyond hoping that mine would not be spent in trenches in Northern Europe. Nor, when we were in India and knew we were going to be in the jungle, did I spend time wondering about that; nor, when we were surrounded by Japanese, did I try to imagine what it might be like as a prisoner of war. It was partly because we were so immersed in our daily activities that there was not much time to spare for speculation, and partly that such was not my cast of mind. It spared me much anxiety.

I have wondered whether life can be called better in 2010 than in 1920. I leave aside spiritual progress: all-important as it is, only God can judge that. Clearly there has been enormous material progress: cars and highways, aeroplanes, wireless, movies, cameras, telephones, fabrics, plastics, medicine, agriculture, nuclear science, armaments, and much else have developed enormously. Aeroplanes have changed their spelling to airplanes, and wireless has changed its name to radio. There have been many inventions: TV, jet propulsion, computers and all things digital, washing machines, microwaves, cell phones, GPS, Skype, Kindle, etc.

But has life become more pleasant? There were two world wars in the first half of the twentieth century, but none since, despite some scares. But there have been countless smaller wars, and the nuclear threat has at times hung heavily over us, and is still a threat. Air travel is in almost every way less pleasant than it was in, say, the 1960s and 1970s, and security becomes more and more intrusive and even humiliating. Organized Terrorism was unknown in 1920. I find the question, 1920 versus 2010, fascinating and ultimately unanswerable. How can one weigh the potential of nuclear disaster, etc. against the actual convenience of computers, etc.? And I have not even mentioned politics and economics.

I have mentioned travel often. My first long journey was from India to England when I was eighteen months old. What effect that had on my subconscious or unconscious I cannot say. As an undergraduate I bicycled around Northern France. In the army I traveled continually and extensively. As a monk at Ampleforth I traveled very little, but when we came to Saint Louis I traveled extensively within the country, mostly visiting schools and colleges, and then outside the country mainly with Timothy Tours. Why?

Parts of my answer may seem abstruse. Many politicians, probably the majority in the United States, have a background in the law; but many who are statesmen as well as politicians, Lincoln, Churchill, Roosevelt, Truman, and others, read voraciously in History and Biography. Travel is visual history. It seems that the study of history, whether written or visual, deepens both one's knowledge and one's appreciation of human nature, how it lives and thinks, what it does, and what it makes, how it expresses itself. In my youth I loved classical architecture and dismissed baroque. As I read more and saw more, I came first to tolerate baroque and then to love it too. What was true in that field is true in many others: the more I find out about other people's languages, their ways of living, traveling, thinking, and making things, the more I appreciate and enjoy them, and also, by contrast, the more I appreciate and enjoy our own ways. How often we hear 'It's good to get away, and it's good to get back'. I also came to appreciate the people more. Very seldom indeed in my travels, if I presented a friendly face to them, did they present an unfriendly face to me. If in addition you can speak even a few words to people in their language, that is a great help. Good international relationships are, in a small way, part of a traveler's function, so is spending money in poorer countries.

There is another aspect of travel, more fitting, perhaps, for a monk: The children's hymn, *All things bright and beautiful . . . . .the Lord God made them all*[25] expresses for us a great truth. All things reflect God's artistry. That, you will say, is true at home, and so it is. But it is easy to take the familiar for granted, and anyway the things abroad are different, except perhaps nowadays in the big cities. There is nothing like Athens, Gibraltar, or Hong Kong in Saint Louis. So there is a sense in which any travel abroad is a kind of pilgrimage to God's creation and a pilgrimage to God's people. Saint Augustine was right when he said, 'the world is a book; those who do not travel read only one page'.

I am now often asked three big questions: Has the school changed? Am I glad to have come to the United States? If I had my life over again, would I become a monk again?

The first is the easiest: of course the school has changed. The boys, their parents, the life-style surrounding them, have all changed – think only of computers and cell phones – and so has the best way of responding. Not only that, but the rate of change has itself changed for the faster. Our basic Benedictine principles, monastic and scholastic, have, as far as I can judge, changed very little. The change has been in how we adapt our principles to the new circumstances. I have also been asked whether the changes in the school have been for the better or not. It is not for me to answer that, but I can say that life in Saint Louis was much more exciting in our early days, when every decision was new, and had to be thought out. Now we can often say, 'What did we do last time?' The school now is much larger, and so has more flexibility, more variety, less immediacy.

The second question, 'Am I glad to have come to the United States?' goes deeper. There have been rough spots, of course, but overall I have been very happy here, and much of that happiness has come from the trust that INC

25. *James Herriot, who used phrases from that hymn for titles of some of his books, did for a while care for Ampleforth's cattle.*

placed in us and vice versa, and from the generosity of our friends, especially the parents of our boys, of our alumni, and of the parishioners of Saint Anselm Parish. Sometimes the questioner goes deeper and asks whether I have been happier here than I would have been at Ampleforth. That is unanswerable. I can only say that, had I been left at Ampleforth, I would have been very happy there, with also some rough spots; and I would be different from what I now am. Here again arises the question of size. Even though at Ampleforth many of the monks lived in parishes at a distance from the abbey, the resident community was much larger than ours. This largeness made for a more stately liturgy at Ampleforth, but ours in Saint Louis was more personal, and I have found more scope for priestly activity here. There are more resources of all kinds in a larger monastery, there is more support in a smaller, even though differences of temperament and outlook are more obvious. There has also been a difference of geography: Ampleforth is remote; we are on the outskirts of a large city. The school families and our other friends are close to us in a way that was unthinkable at Ampleforth. Even American generosity and hospitality would have had far less scope at Ampleforth. The two monastic life-styles are different: I have enjoyed both.

It is curious that though I am a British subject, I have been outside Britain for over two thirds of my life. And yet, when I go back to England, I feel at some point, and always when I am not expecting it, that, as I said above, some of my roots are still in England. I do not believe, however, that I have ever quoted to myself Browning's poem, 'O to be in England.' I have missed family and friends in England, of course, but there have been so many new and generous friends here. Those early roots are partly why I have remained a British subject. Another reason was that when I was taken to a naturalization ceremony, I discovered that I would have to forswear any former national loyalties; I could not do that. So we have two monks who are not US citizens, one Irish and one English. There is also a third who is rumored to have become a US citizen because of the high cost of renewing his 'green card' as a resident alien.

To the third question, whether I would again become a monk, my answer is without doubt, yes. But it has seldom been a topic of my thoughts. The prayer and work have been congenial and natural. I have seen no other life that would have given me the same happiness, fulfillment, meaning, and feeling of support both from the community and from God. A monk feels very surely that if he is living his monastic life well, he is serving God well. Any worries come from whether he is living it well. I hope it is not contradictory to add that if *per impossibile* I could have three lives, I would hope one of them would be as a married man.

A man is not any more a monk nor any less a monk for being a priest, but in my case, I do not think that I would have survived without first the prospect, and then the reality, of the priesthood. For historical reasons, Ampleforth's tradition when I joined the monastery was strongly priestly, and that was partly why I chose Ampleforth. There are monks who are strictly enclosed and contemplative. I admire them and value them, but it is not the life for me. We have been blessed here in that our 'active' works, the school, the parish, and scholarly work, are all on the same campus as the monastery, and I have been blessed to have had a part in all our works.

In the nursery, in school, in college, I was learning. I was doing many other things too, but learning was the dominant activity. In the army as a cadet I learnt about guns, vehicles, wireless sets, and trigonometry. In my regiment I added man-management and later, as a staff officer, planning and administration. Much of this was 'in service' training, learning the job and doing it at the same time. That continued in the monastery: as a monk I had not only to learn how to be a monk but also to try to be a good one. I learnt more about scripture, philosophy, theology, music, and teaching. When I was made headmaster I had had little experience of educational administration, and when I became pastor, hardly any more of parochial administration, so I had to learn those; and when I was asked to write a book I had to learn how to do that, and am still learning. I imagine that those who are blessed enough to get there will learn all the rest of what they need to know in heaven.

So Solon the Wise was wise indeed when he wrote

γηράσκω δ' αἰεὶ πολλὰ διδασκόμενος
(I grow old, learning much all the time).

Portrait by Mr. Thomas O. Mulvihill, Priory parent.

Solon the Wise was wise indeed when he wrote:

γηράσκω δ' αἰεὶ πολλὰ διδασκόμενος
(I grow old, learning much all the time).